Local Government Board

Local Government Board for Ireland : Eighteenth Report

Local Government Board

Local Government Board for Ireland : Eighteenth Report

ISBN/EAN: 9783741105722

Manufactured in Europe, USA, Canada, Australia, Japa

Cover: Foto ©ninafisch / pixelio.de

Manufactured and distributed by brebook publishing software (www.brebook.com)

Local Government Board

Local Government Board for Ireland : Eighteenth Report

ANNUAL REPORT

OF

THE LOCAL GOVERNMENT BOARD

FOR IRELAND,

BEING

THE EIGHTEENTH REPORT UNDER "THE LOCAL GOVERNMENT BOARD (IRELAND) ACT," 35 & 36 VIC., c. 69.

Presented to both Houses of Parliament by Command of Her Majesty.

DUBLIN:
PRINTED FOR HER MAJESTY'S STATIONERY OFFICE
BY
ALEXANDER THOM & CO. (LIMITED),
And to be purchased, either directly or through any Bookseller, from
EYRE and SPOTTISWOODE, East Harding-street, Fetter-lane, E.C., or 32, Abingdon-street, Westminster, S.W.; or ADAM and CHARLES BLACK, 6, North Bridge, Edinburgh; or HODGES, FIGGIS, and Co., 104, Grafton-street, Dublin.

1890.

[C.—6094.] *Price* 1s. 7d.

TABLE OF CONTENTS.

Medical Charities Act and Vaccination Acts.

Dispensary Houses Act.

Sanitary Acts.

APPENDIX.

APPENDIX A.—Orders, circulars, and correspondence, under the Poor Law Acts and other Acts not included in Appendix B or C.

I.—Orders

II. Circulars.

III.—Correspondence, &c.

Dissolution of Boards of Guardians.

Probate Duties Grant.

APPENDIX B.—Medical Charities Act and Vaccination Acts.

Circulars.

APPENDIX C.—Orders, Circulars, &c., under Sanitary Acts.

I.—Orders.

II.—Circulars.

III.—Correspondence, &c.

APPENDIX D.—Tables connected with Poor Relief and Expenditure.

APPENDIX E.—Tabular returns in connection with relief under the Medical Charities Act.

ANNUAL REPORT

OF THE

LOCAL GOVERNMENT BOARD FOR IRELAND,

BEING THE

EIGHTEENTH REPORT UNDER "THE LOCAL GOVERNMENT BOARD (IRELAND) ACT," 35 & 36 VIC., CAP. 69.

TO HIS EXCELLENCY LAWRENCE DUNDAS, EARL OF ZETLAND, &c., &c., &c.,

Lord Lieutenant General and General Governor of Ireland.

Local Government Board,
Dublin, 12th May, 1890.

MAY IT PLEASE YOUR EXCELLENCY,

WE, the Local Government Board for Ireland, submit to your Excellency this our eighteenth annual Report under the Statute 35 & 36 Vic., cap. 69, entitled "The Local Government Board (Ireland) Act, 1872," relating to our proceedings up to the 31st of March, 1890.

POOR RELIEF.

1. We submit, in the first place, in continuation of similar returns in previous annual Reports, summaries of weekly returns showing the number of persons in receipt of relief, in the workhouses and out of the workhouses, at the close of each week from the week ended the 9th of February, 1889, to the week ended the 8th of February, 1890, both included; and we annex two diagrams,* in illustration of these and previous returns, showing the fluctuations which have occurred in the number of workhouse inmates and the number of persons in receipt of out-door relief, respectively, during the weeks embraced in the following statement and those included in each of the six preceding years.

* Facing page 46.

Summaries of weekly returns of

STATEMENT, compiled from weekly returns, showing the number of persons ended the 9th of February, 1889, to the week

Week ended Saturday.	Relief in Workhouses. Able-bodied. Males.	Able-bodied. Females.	Able-bodied. Total.	Healthy Children under 15 years of age.	Sick in Workhouse Hospitals. Fever patients.	Sick in Workhouse Hospitals. Other cases.	Sick in Workhouse Hospitals. Total.	All other classes. Males aged 15 and upwards.	All other classes. Females aged 15 and upwards.	All other classes. Total.	Total number in Workhouses.	Average weekly cost per head for Maintenance (exclusive of clothing).	Deaths. No. in the week.	Deaths. Weekly rate of mortality per 1,000.	No. of persons labouring under fever removed to Workhouses under 14th sec. of 6 & 7 Vic., &c. — No. of patients under the 14th sec. of 6 & 7 Vic., c. 92, and the 3rd sec. of 25 and 26 Vic., c. 83. Fever cases.	Other cases.	Total.
1889.												s. d.					
Feb. 9,	2,908	4,888	7,191	8,223	449	17,912	18,361	6,881	7,056	13,906	47,074	2 8½	196	4·2	19	241	260
16,	2,355	4,840	7,[illegible]	8,270	470	18,116	18,[illegible]	6,860	7,020	13,[illegible]	48,340	2 8½	200	5·5	17	257	274
23,	3,118	4,[illegible]	7,118	8,[illegible]	441	17,707	18,148	6,910	6,[illegible]	13,[illegible]	18,011	2 8½	212	4·4	16	257	273
Mar. 2,	3,129	4,251	7,200	8,102	404	17,[illegible]	18,[illegible]	6,[illegible]	6,979	13,[illegible]	47,797	2 8½	228	5·0	21	261	282
9,	3,077	4,257	7,331	8,[illegible]	431	18,[illegible]	18,[illegible]	6,[illegible]	6,[illegible]	13,[illegible]	47,[illegible]	2 8½	274	5·7	22	264	283
16,	3,014	4,157	7,[illegible]	7,[illegible]	451	17,[illegible]	18,[illegible]	6,[illegible]	6,[illegible]	13,451	44,[illegible]	2 8½	244	5·2	20	254	274
23,	2,854	4,187	7,[illegible]	7,[illegible]	417	17,[illegible]	18,[illegible]	6,[illegible]	6,677	13,[illegible]	46,[illegible]	2 8½	241	4·7	10	255	244
30,	2,[illegible]	4,100	6,[illegible]	7,[illegible]	410	17,[illegible]	18,[illegible]	6,459	6,[illegible]	13,[illegible]	46,[illegible]	2 8½	221	5·4	20	206	226
April 6,	2,636	4,008	6,702	7,[illegible]	387	17,411	17,[illegible]	6,[illegible]	6,[illegible]	13,199	46,731	2 8½	220	4·8	11	220	231
13,	2,618	4,[illegible]	6,707	7,[illegible]	341	17,473	17,[illegible]	6,[illegible]	6,[illegible]	13,101	45,277	2 8½	204	4·4	18	200	218
20,	2,[illegible]	3,[illegible]	6,[illegible]	7,[illegible]	370	17,[illegible]	17,[illegible]	6,[illegible]	6,[illegible]	13,[illegible]	45,[illegible]	2 8½	247	5·6	3	282	231
27,	2,540	4,012	6,[illegible]	7,[illegible]	342	17,148	17,[illegible]	6,[illegible]	6,713	13,[illegible]	44,[illegible]	2 11½	237	5·3	5	240	253
May 4,	2,405	4,023	6,618	7,081	394	17,174	17,[illegible]	6,[illegible]	6,510	13,071	44,706	2 8	213	5·4	5	244	260
11,	2,[illegible]	4,[illegible]	6,[illegible]	7,650	374	16,[illegible]	17,[illegible]	6,[illegible]	6,[illegible]	12,917	41,931	2 8	190	4·3	6	243	248
18,	2,[illegible]	3,[illegible]	6,[illegible]	7,430	391	16,[illegible]	17,207	6,[illegible]	6,[illegible]	12,[illegible]	44,778	2 8	170	5·6	6	251	257
25,	2,232	3,[illegible]	6,[illegible]	7,251	374	16,[illegible]	17,[illegible]	6,108	6,[illegible]	12,[illegible]	43,[illegible]	2 7½	172	4·1	6	210	216
June 1,	2,255	3,[illegible]	6,[illegible]	7,021	396	16,471	16,[illegible]	6,[illegible]	6,[illegible]	12,881	42,[illegible]	2 8	181	4·3	16	233	249
8,	2,[illegible]	3,[illegible]	5,[illegible]	7,225	410	16,278	16,[illegible]	6,[illegible]	6,[illegible]	12,578	42,[illegible]	2 7½	173	4·1	14	192	216
15,	2,010	3,[illegible]	5,[illegible]	7,277	411	16,170	16,[illegible]	6,110	6,442	12,[illegible]	42,148	2 7½	162	3·8	8	220	205
22,	1,940	3,641	5,581	7,140	401	16,[illegible]	16,[illegible]	6,[illegible]	6,[illegible]	12,127	41,[illegible]	2 7½	152	3·7	8	170	183
29,	1,[illegible]	3,[illegible]	5,[illegible]	7,027	398	15,[illegible]	16,217	6,[illegible]	6,[illegible]	12,616	40,[illegible]	2 7½	164	4·0	9	197	209
July 6,	1,872	3,600	5,[illegible]	7,108	372	15,[illegible]	16,[illegible]	5,[illegible]	6,[illegible]	12,680	40,[illegible]	2 7½	182	4·5	23	161	189
13,	1,936	3,[illegible]	5,[illegible]	7,[illegible]	367	15,[illegible]	16,[illegible]	5,[illegible]	6,[illegible]	12,[illegible]	40,106	2 7½	153	3·9	7	184	191
20,	1,[illegible]	3,[illegible]	5,[illegible]	6,[illegible]	325	15,[illegible]	16,[illegible]	5,[illegible]	6,[illegible]	12,[illegible]	40,[illegible]	2 7½	174	4·3	6	180	186
27,	1,905	3,[illegible]	5,[illegible]	6,[illegible]	310	15,[illegible]	15,[illegible]	5,[illegible]	6,[illegible]	12,[illegible]	40,431	2 7½	182	4·6	7	186	193
Aug. 3,	1,936	3,480	5,466	6,[illegible]	288	15,[illegible]	16,[illegible]	5,[illegible]	6,[illegible]	11,[illegible]	40,249	2 7½	175	4·3	8	179	187
10,	2,[illegible]	3,[illegible]	5,[illegible]	6,[illegible]	291	15,[illegible]	15,[illegible]	5,[illegible]	6,[illegible]	11,914	40,201	2 7½	160	3·6	7	179	186
17,	2,[illegible]	3,[illegible]	5,[illegible]	6,727	280	15,[illegible]	15,[illegible]	5,[illegible]	6,[illegible]	11,[illegible]	40,[illegible]	2 7½	157	3·9	6	184	192
24,	2,100	3,[illegible]	5,[illegible]	6,[illegible]	288	15,[illegible]	15,[illegible]	5,[illegible]	6,[illegible]	11,[illegible]	40,[illegible]	2 7½	214	3·9	17	179	185
31,	2,[illegible]	3,[illegible]	5,[illegible]	6,[illegible]	284	15,671	15,[illegible]	5,718	6,103	11,011	40,[illegible]	2 7½	160	3·7	25	172	196
Sept. 7,	2,070	3,[illegible]	5,[illegible]	6,616	288	15,714	16,[illegible]	5,[illegible]	6,[illegible]	11,870	40,446	2 7½	107	3·0	23	170	204
14,	2,[illegible]	3,[illegible]	5,075	6,[illegible]	281	15,[illegible]	16,[illegible]	5,[illegible]	6,[illegible]	11,[illegible]	40,[illegible]	2 7½	140	3·8	21	164	186
21,	2,[illegible]	3,[illegible]	5,[illegible]	6,[illegible]	285	15,[illegible]	16,[illegible]	5,[illegible]	6,[illegible]	12,[illegible]	41,[illegible]	2 7½	161	4·4	23	172	202
28,	2,110	3,[illegible]	5,[illegible]	7,008	288	15,900	16,[illegible]	5,[illegible]	6,[illegible]	12,[illegible]	41,[illegible]	2 8	160	3·9	23	186	208
Oct. 5,	2,346	3,[illegible]	5,[illegible]	6,[illegible]	284	15,[illegible]	16,[illegible]	5,[illegible]	6,274	12,026	41,108	2 8½	165	3·8	25	181	206
12,	2,[illegible]	3,713	6,[illegible]	7,[illegible]	300	16,[illegible]	16,[illegible]	5,[illegible]	6,[illegible]	12,[illegible]	41,419	2 8½	185	4·4	25	171	196
19,	2,[illegible]	3,[illegible]	6,[illegible]	7,130	271	16,[illegible]	16,118	5,[illegible]	6,[illegible]	12,[illegible]	41,717	2 8½	165	4·0	15	174	190
26,	2,[illegible]	3,[illegible]	6,[illegible]	7,[illegible]	280	16,170	16,[illegible]	5,[illegible]	6,[illegible]	12,[illegible]	41,[illegible]	2 9	160	3·4	16	167	183
Nov. 2,	2,[illegible]	3,771	6,[illegible]	7,063	274	16,[illegible]	16,[illegible]	5,[illegible]	6,[illegible]	12,[illegible]	42,[illegible]	2 9½	170	4·0	16	189	205
9,	2,[illegible]	3,[illegible]	6,[illegible]	7,121	283	16,451	16,[illegible]	6,[illegible]	6,[illegible]	12,[illegible]	42,[illegible]	2 9½	140	4·4	23	190	215
16,	2,100	3,[illegible]	6,214	7,[illegible]	279	16,[illegible]	16,[illegible]	6,[illegible]	6,173	12,[illegible]	42,[illegible]	2 9½	148	3·8	24	196	238
23,	2,[illegible]	3,[illegible]	6,[illegible]	7,[illegible]	404	16,[illegible]	17,[illegible]	6,[illegible]	6,[illegible]	12,[illegible]	42,[illegible]	2 9½	164	3·0	28	207	233
30,	2,[illegible]	3,977	6,[illegible]	7,[illegible]	480	16,[illegible]	17,[illegible]	6,[illegible]	6,616	12,757	43,[illegible]	2 9½	181	4·0	23	220	241
Dec. 7,	2,[illegible]	3,[illegible]	6,[illegible]	7,[illegible]	480	16,[illegible]	17,[illegible]	6,[illegible]	6,[illegible]	12,[illegible]	44,065	2 9½	211	4·8	21	209	230
14,	2,[illegible]	3,[illegible]	6,[illegible]	7,367	480	17,[illegible]	17,467	6,[illegible]	6,650	12,[illegible]	44,294	2 9½	207	4·7	23	203	226
21,	2,[illegible]	3,[illegible]	6,[illegible]	7,[illegible]	498	16,[illegible]	17,[illegible]	6,[illegible]	6,616	12,[illegible]	44,013	2 9½	227	5·3	19	203	221
28,	2,[illegible]	4,029	6,[illegible]	7,310	419	16,[illegible]	17,[illegible]	6,[illegible]	6,[illegible]	12,[illegible]	44,135	2 9½	232	5·4	15	201	230
1890.																	
Jan. 4,	2,741	4,076	6,817	7,[illegible]	418	17,[illegible]	17,[illegible]	6,407	6,[illegible]	12,[illegible]	44,[illegible]	2 11½	202	4·3	14	218	234
11,	2,[illegible]	4,[illegible]	6,924	7,[illegible]	450	17,[illegible]	17,[illegible]	6,[illegible]	6,[illegible]	13,117	45,467	2 10	285	5·3	19	270	289
18,	2,719	4,161	6,[illegible]	7,[illegible]	490	17,[illegible]	18,[illegible]	6,[illegible]	6,961	13,[illegible]	46,900	2 9½	252	5·1	11	226	237
25,	2,[illegible]	4,[illegible]	7,081	7,[illegible]	546	18,[illegible]	18,[illegible]	6,619	6,725	13,344	60,[illegible]	2 0½	269	6·3	15	232	245
Feb. 1,	2,[illegible]	4,[illegible]	6,973	7,212	721	18,[illegible]	19,467	6,[illegible]	6,[illegible]	13,[illegible]	47,[illegible]	2 0½	218	5·0	19	261	280
8,	2,770	4,[illegible]	6,908	7,[illegible]	648	18,[illegible]	19,[illegible]	6,[illegible]	6,[illegible]	13,145	46,[illegible]	2 9½	218	6·5	24	241	265

in receipt of relief in unions in Ireland, at the close of each week, from the week ended the 8th of February, 1890, both included.

included in the ... who were admit... houses under the 7 Vic., c. 92, and ... of 41 and 42 ...			No. of persons sent for treatment to Hospitals not connected with Workhouses, under sec. 16 of 6 & 7 Vic., c. 92, or sec. 7 of 25 & 26 Vic., c. 83.		No. of Blind and Deaf and Dumb persons maintained in Institutions under sec. 14 of 6 & 7 Vic., c. 92, and Sec. 8 of 41 & 42 Vic., c. 66, and number of Idiots and Imbeciles maintained in Asylums under Sec. 4 of last-mentioned Act.			Out-door Relief. Under section 1 of 10 Vic., Cap. 31.		Under 18 Vic., cap. 83, section 1, and under 11 & 12 Vic., c. 17, s. 4.		Under 25 & 26 Vic., c. 83. Number of Orphans and Deserted Children out at Nurse.			Total number of persons in receipt of out-door Relief.	Total number of persons in receipt of Relief.
No. of Constabulary patients, under the 5th sec. of 25 & 26 Vic., c. 83. Fever Cases.	Other Cases.	Total.	Fever Hospitals.	Other Hospitals.	Blind.	Deaf and Dumb.	Idiots and Imbeciles.	No. of Cases.	No. of Persons.	No. of Cases.	No. of Persons.	Males.	Females.	Total.		
1	10	11	69	70	451	398	14	56,078	63,183	461	847	1,272	1,409	2,681	64,[illegible]	118,[illegible]
1	11	12	71	72	453	397	14	56,412	61,155	460	848	1,301	1,418	2,704	57,087	114,704
1	10	11	69	60	452	398	14	56,[illegible]	61,671	410	811	1,290	1,418	2,706	64,187	114,[illegible]
3	11	13	75	65	455	398	14	56,[illegible]	61,[illegible]	485	878	1,301	1,412	2,703	64,449	114,147
3	13	16	54	65	450	406	11	55,[illegible]	61,329	487	868	1,326	1,400	2,711	65,481	114,143
1	13	14	72	66	454	448	14	54,[illegible]	62,147	423	881	1,[illegible]	1,416	2,721	64,[illegible]	110,449
1	11	12	78	611	451	458	14	55,[illegible]	58,[illegible]	801	784	1,108	1,118	2,520	65,[illegible]	110,[illegible]
–	13	13	63	64	810	440	14	53,[illegible]	61,741	876	785	1,103	1,[illegible]	2,700	63,[illegible]	110,[illegible]
–	15	19	103	09	847	460	14	53,087	60,471	408	708	1,398	1,307	2,705	64,[illegible]	111,083
1	13	15	108	73	817	403	14	55,[illegible]	60,791	841	752	1,416	1,300	2,716	61,156	110,717
1	14	16	59	74	814	447	15	56,[illegible]	60,714	874	812	1,148	1,[illegible]	2,716	64,108	110,[illegible]
3	10	15	58	77	850	418	14	54,[illegible]	60,730	813	607	1,434	1,294	2,708	64,[illegible]	108,717
3	9	13	64	63	830	411	14	55,[illegible]	64,[illegible]	378	861	1,414	1,[illegible]	2,709	68,[illegible]	109,[illegible]
3	7	10	61	61	844	410	14	56,[illegible]	61,[illegible]	370	690	1,416	1,[illegible]	2,707	64,019	109,140
3	4	7	78	67	851	418	11	55,[illegible]	61,[illegible]	361	696	1,407	1,301	[illegible]	64,[illegible]	108,704
4	3	6	69	60	856	408	14	55,[illegible]	61,[illegible]	384	701	1,400	1,[illegible]	2,703	63,[illegible]	104,[illegible]
6	6	12	78	71	865	465	14	56,114	61,[illegible]	846	784	1,411	1,[illegible]	2,708	63,740	107,467
3	8	11	78	73	868	462	14	54,010	60,[illegible]	[illegible]	713	1,407	1,[illegible]	2,[illegible]	63,[illegible]	108,[illegible]
4	8	9	78	04	834	462	11	51,[illegible]	58,[illegible]	376	690	1,103	1,390	2,414	62,[illegible]	100,[illegible]
5	4	9	70	71	861	467	11	55,[illegible]	[illegible]	880	690	1,410	1,350	2,705	62,[illegible]	103,[illegible]
3	5	9	73	70	856	467	14	51,010	54,[illegible]	646	694	1,407	1,304	2,711	63,097	104,700
3	7	16	46	69	852	465	14	54,646	60,807	383	680	1,408	1,380	2,708	63,083	104,088
3	8	12	37	74	856	403	13	51,811	59,110	347	695	1,316	1,164	2,707	63,813	101,145
3	6	10	48	60	858	407	13	51,[illegible]	50,[illegible]	851	631	1,417	1,[illegible]	2,705	62,728	104,[illegible]
1	7	6	61	68	862	367	14	54,721	54,107	347	663	1,415	1,886	2,701	63,[illegible]	106,400
3	10	13	41	71	864	407	15	54,811	69,020	391	791	1,407	1,302	2,[illegible]	61,848	102,780
3	13	14	30	72	867	411	15	54,140	57,010	413	778	1,180	1,[illegible]	2,104	62,113	102,[illegible]
3	9	11	85	79	851	406	16	53,[illegible]	57,[illegible]	431	768	1,[illegible]	1,397	2,[illegible]	61,[illegible]	101,014
3	13	14	35	65	881	411	16	56,[illegible]	58,[illegible]	471	748	1,[illegible]	1,[illegible]	2,[illegible]	58,[illegible]	100,[illegible]
3	13	16	23	71	864	408	16	55,[illegible]	56,077	879	657	1,303	1,386	2,[illegible]	59,014	104,[illegible]
–	10	13	33	73	861	416	14	53,890	65,990	308	687	1,310	1,[illegible]	2,[illegible]	63,167	108,448
1	8	17	36	74	858	413	14	53,[illegible]	57,[illegible]	472	431	1,403	1,301	2,[illegible]	60,[illegible]	109,[illegible]
1	0	7	55	79	859	411	14	53,861	55,[illegible]	814	672	1,403	1,347	2,[illegible]	58,[illegible]	100,773
1	6	6	35	74	852	412	14	53,868	61,[illegible]	508	447	1,180	1,794	2,[illegible]	56,[illegible]	100,770
3	5	7	80	70	861	413	14	53,891	55,170	390	644	1,409	1,271	2,671	59,[illegible]	100,449
1	7	9	80	75	862	413	14	53,100	65,[illegible]	448	496	1,400	1,310	2,670	60,408	101,186
3	6	8	48	62	858	414	14	51,927	55,870	857	450	1,441	1,270	2,674	60,077	101,416
1	9	10	47	77	846	420	14	58,610	60,[illegible]	516	480	1,400	1,278	2,[illegible]	60,647	104,087
1	8	7	51	73	861	418	14	55,[illegible]	58,294	336	690	1,401	1,378	2,[illegible]	63,443	109,890
1	7	8	45	74	861	471	14	53,777	60,890	400	[illegible]	1,418	1,370	2,[illegible]	60,[illegible]	108,007
1	7	8	46	78	841	430	14	58,836	56,507	381	809	1,418	1,[illegible]	2,[illegible]	60,730	107,[illegible]
3	9	10	50	77	861	421	14	53,[illegible]	60,736	[illegible]	670	1,471	1,[illegible]	2,701	60,[illegible]	101,[illegible]
3	9	18	41	76	860	424	14	54,147	57,100	[illegible]	612	1,410	1,473	2,[illegible]	64,[illegible]	108,361
8	0	11	46	77	862	423	14	54,800	57,147	303	637	1,417	1,372	2,[illegible]	60,778	105,718
3	6	10	46	81	861	424	16	51,840	57,936	871	817	1,410	1,271	2,801	61,878	100,878
3	4	7	39	73	861	424	16	54,714	60,412	559	767	1,417	1,370	2,[illegible]	61,809	106,718
4	6	8	38	65	863	424	17	54,796	60,803	412	767	1,416	1,380	2,[illegible]	63,184	107,138
3	6	4	47	65	866	424	17	54,818	58,710	460	795	1,410	1,375	2,858	60,218	107,774
1	6	9	48	66	853	446	17	54,858	58,900	381	980	1,418	1,376	2,847	62,470	105,844
1	13	14	48	68	863	424	18	54,097	58,956	507	886	1,414	1,378	2,801	61,880	107,647
8	65	87	45	70	868	428	18	53,800	58,963	500	827	1,414	1,365	2,840	60,000	111,943
3	86	94	33	73	854	426	19	53,696	60,873	68	874	1,417	1,264	2,681	64,313	118,838
–	80	90	31	66	854	485	10	53,687	61,111	68	1090	1,418	1,240	2,678	64,061	112,889

2. The following tables show the maximum, minimum, and average daily number of persons in the workhouses and on out-door relief, respectively, during each of the seven years included in the diagrams :—

RELIEF IN WORKHOUSES.

—	Maximum Number.	Date.	Minimum Number.	Date.	Average Daily Number.
1883–84, .	56,843	17 February, 1883	44,216	15 September, 1883	49,236
1884–85, .	52,184	16 February, 1884	43,522	23 August, 1884	47,327
1885–86, .	50,420	7 February, 1885	42,206	20 August, 1885	46,188
1886–87, .	50,327	6 February, 1886	42,328	4 September, 1886	45,899
1887–88, .	49,402	5 February, 1887	43,225	6 August, 1887	45,558
1888–89, .	49,820	25 February, 1888	41,207	22 September, 1888	44,729
1889–90, .	46,340	10 February, 1889	40,248	3 August, 1889	43,536

OUT-DOOR RELIEF.

—	Maximum Number.	Date.	Minimum Number.	Date.	Average Daily Number.
1883–84, .	63,909	24 February, 1883	53,629	6 October, 1883	60,304
1884–85, .	61,589	22 March, 1884	53,427	11 October, 1884	57,829
1885–86, .	64,458	30 January, 1886	51,316	3 October, 1885	58,965
1886–87, .	102,428	22 May, 1886	59,845	2 October, 1886	78,241
1887–88, .	69,473	28 May, 1887	50,681	8 October, 1887	65,506
1888–89, .	67,219	17 March, 1888	58,199	6 October, 1888	63,080
1889–90, .	65,690	16 March, 1889	58,397	5 October, 1889	62,286

3. In our last annual Report we drew attention to the fact that there had been a decrease in the average daily number of persons relieved both in and out of the workhouses from February, 1888, to February, 1889, as compared with the number so relieved in the preceding year.

We have now to report that the returns for the weeks included in the statement on page 2 show a further decline in the average daily number of persons relieved in the workhouses, whilst there is also a decrease in the average daily number of persons who received out-door relief.

The average daily number in the workhouses in the weeks included in the statement was 43,536, and on out-door relief 62,286, making a total of 105,822, which is less than the average daily number relieved in and out of the workhouses in the year 1888–89 by 2,587.

The following table shows the number of persons in receipt of in-door and out-door relief, respectively, in the last week of each month of the year ended the 25th of January, 1890, as compared with the preceding year:—

4. NUMBER of PERSONS in WORKHOUSES and on OUT-DOOR RELIEF in the last week of each of the twelve months ended the 25th of January, 1890, and in the corresponding weeks of the preceding year (ended the 26th of January, 1889).

YEAR 1889-90.				YEAR 1888-9.				Increase in the year 1889-90.		Decrease in the year 1889-90.	
WEEK ENDED	Number of persons			WEEK ENDED	Number of persons						
	In Workhouses.	On Out-door Relief	Total.		In Workhouses.	On Out-door Relief.	Total.	In Workhouses	On Out-door Relief	In Workhouses	On Out-door Relief.
1889.				1888.							
February 23,	48,011	65,187	113,198	February 25,	49,828	66,916	116,742	—	—	1,818	1,729
March 30,	46,183	65,208	111,340	March 31,	47,911	65,859	113,770	—	—	1,779	651
April 27,	44,728	64,085	108,813	April 28,	46,416	65,731	112,147	—	—	1,688	1,646
May 25,	43,180	63,963	107,143	May 26,	44,320	66,156	110,476	—	—	1,140	2,193
June 29,	40,876	63,007	103,883	June 30,	42,176	66,140	108,316	—	—	1,300	3,133
July 27,	40,411	62,260	102,671	July 28,	41,756	64,994	106,750	—	—	1,345	2,734
August 31,	40,330	59,014	99,340	August 25,	41,418	62,217	103,635	—	—	1,088	3,203
September 28,	41,083	58,815	99,898	September 29,	41,333	59,678	101,011	—	—	250	863
October 26,	41,873	59,447	101,320	October 27,	42,489	58,902	101,391	—	545	616	—
November 30,	43,920	60,408	104,337	November 24,	44,017	60,260	104,277	—	148	098	—
December 28,	44,135	62,104	106,239	December 29,	45,669	62,685	108,354	—	—	1,534	581
1890.				1889.							
January 25,	46,735	63,696	110,431	January 26,	47,348	64,008	111,356	—	—	613	312

The returns summarized in the foregoing table show a decrease in the number of persons relieved in workhouses in each of the weeks of the year 1889–90 included in the table as compared with the corresponding weeks of the preceding year. They also show a decrease in the number of persons who received out-door relief excepting in the two weeks ended on the 26th of October and 30th of November, 1889, respectively.

5. The following is a tabulated account of admissions to the workhouses during the year ended the 29th of September last, in comparison with those of the thirty preceding years:—

Year ended 29th September.	Number of paupers in Workhouses at the commencement of the year.	Number of Persons admitted during the Year.						Number of births in the Workhouses during the year.	Total number of persons relieved in the Workhouses during the year.	Number of deaths in the Workhouses during the year
		Number admitted in Sickness.				Number admitted who were not sick.	Total number admitted during the year.			
		Suffering from Fever or other contagious disease.	Suffering under other diseases.	Suffering from accidental injury.	Total number admitted in sickness.					
1859,	38,834	9,553	32,555	2,157	44,260	70,334	114,594	2,276	153,706	8,022
1860,	38,296	9,157	35,480	2,925	47,562	85,312	132,806	2,448	170,549	9,677
1861,	34,294	9,255	38,878	2,217	49,803	114,880	164,683	2,455	205,422	10,866
1862,	41,205	11,183	44,858	2,225	58,264	165,403	223,667	2,815	267,807	12,740
1863,	45,131	14,400	44,987	2,431	61,857	178,276	240,127	2,977	285,288	13,394
1864,	50,087	13,757	46,027	2,280	62,064	151,157	213,221	2,869	261,147	12,765
1865,	49,693	13,410	41,408	2,383	57,201	130,099	201,380	2,751	252,170	12,362
1866,	44,957	10,559	38,537	2,803	54,448	130,144	184,587	2,365	232,154	11,341
1867,	44,278	11,703	43,178	2,433	57,312	153,955	211,267	2,334	253,189	12,162
1868,	45,818	11,206	41,334	2,564	55,007	185,289	245,849	2,307	288,953	11,870
1869,	47,775	8,876	41,682	2,441	52,810	131,868	185,677	2,410	236,862	11,247
1870,	43,012	8,158	39,086	2,510	49,749	133,384	183,133	2,292	230,429	10,697
1871,	42,375	8,718	38,212	2,610	49,540	131,402	181,037	2,103	225,510	10,054
1872,	40,691	10,249	39,835	2,546	52,569	137,289	190,748	1,963	232,230	11,848
1873,	40,884	8,236	40,747	2,422	51,404	152,078	200,482	1,882	240,296	12,354
1874,	41,440	8,469	39,983	2,078	50,459	159,506	209,003	1,844	250,395	10,794
1875,	42,880	8,515	37,554	2,888	47,957	121,182	169,148	1,789	218,794	11,470
1876,	40,555	6,570	36,878	2,385	45,831	95,070	140,601	1,919	182,749	15,673
1877,	39,773	6,049	31,460	2,520	40,120	108,235	157,835	1,709	198,831	10,798
1878,	40,711	8,110	43,150	2,781	54,041	151,094	205,005	1,796	245,162	11,838
1879,	43,868	8,283	47,592	2,708	58,583	190,705	249,288	1,928	294,503	13,127
1880,	48,150	8,553	50,717	2,829	62,500	254,626	317,238	1,959	367,883	13,475
1881,	47,977	7,222	40,154	2,701	50,027	267,044	312,971	1,901	363,844	11,850
1882,	47,011	7,073	44,891	2,672	54,436	230,161	284,508	1,906	338,813	10,645
1883,	46,185	6,873	45,812	2,891	56,076	201,856	255,042	1,942	305,398	13,161
1884,	44,773	5,691	44,015	3,300	53,105	200,237	250,342	1,843	290,865	16,966
1885,	44,010	4,840	44,837	3,171	52,298	222,455	274,589	1,858	316,550	11,445
1886,	42,966	3,869	41,300	2,897	47,930	268,160	316,135	1,871	334,972	10,663
1887,	42,534	4,050	44,279	2,896	51,244	291,685	342,929	1,782	337,575	10,130
1888,	43,255	4,451	45,747	2,840	53,974	298,560	351,601	1,868	396,997	10,294
1889,	41,588	3,432	45,369	3,263	52,162	274,383	326,484	1,760	309,870	9,721

It will be observed from the above that there has been a decrease of 972 in the total number admitted in sickness, and a decrease of 24,148 in the number admitted who were not sick, thus showing a decrease of 25,120 in the total number admitted during the year as compared with the previous year. The number suffering from fever or other contagious disease was less by 1,020 than in the previous year, and the total number of persons relieved in workhouses shows a decrease of 27,127.

6. The following statement shows the average daily number of the several classes of persons relieved in workhouses during each of the last thirty-three years ended on the 29th of September:—

Average daily number in workhouses during the year, average number of deaths per week, and rate of mortality.

Year ended 29th Sept.	Estimated population.	Able-bodied.			Healthy children under 15.	Sick in Workhouse Hospitals.			All other classes.			Total No. in Workhouses.	Deaths per week.		Per-centage of In-door Paupers to Population.
		Males.	Females.	Total.		Fever.	Other cases.	Total.	Males.	Females.	Total.		Average number during week.	Average weekly rate of mortality per 1,000 inmates.	
1857,	6,047,492	2,607	7,765	10,372	17,292	1,264	15,176	16,440	2,224	4,137	6,361	50,665	170	3·3	0·84
1858,	6,012,103	2,312	7,121	9,433	14,266	1,108	14,939	16,047	2,129	4,015	6,144	45,790	180	3·9	0·76
1859,	6,069,112	1,803	5,890	7,704	11,811	974	13,802	14,776	2,211	4,088	6,299	40,380	184	4·6	0·67
1860,	5,888,620	1,867	6,060	7,927	11,216	904	13,694	14,598	2,778	4,752	7,530	41,371	184	4·5	0·70
1861,	5,798,564	2,702	6,300	9,002	13,307	1,032	14,345	15,377	3,139	3,321	6,460	45,136	202	4·5	0·78
1862,	5,794,674	3,039	8,310	11,349	14,917	1,262	16,133	17,395	3,976	6,031	10,007	53,668	244	4·6	0·93
1863,	5,762,711	3,237	8,589	11,826	16,368	1,575	16,901	18,476	4,649	6,601	11,250	57,919	257	4·4	1·01
1864,	5,723,810	2,849	7,670	10,519	16,178	1,054	16,746	17,800	4,706	6,722	11,428	55,925	244	4·4	0·98
1865,	5,673,808	2,540	6,657	9,197	15,260	1,824	16,362	18,186	4,620	6,590	11,210	53,917	237	4·3	0·95
1866,	5,582,625	2,213	5,873	8,086	14,278	1,317	15,703	17,020	4,411	6,477	10,888	50,272	221	4·4	0·90
1867,	5,557,196	2,307	6,133	8,440	15,300	1,237	15,504	16,741	4,819	6,954	11,773	52,254	252	4·8	0·94
1868,	5,543,285	2,406	6,133	8,539	16,024	1,106	15,503	16,609	5,334	7,094	12,428	53,600	221	4·1	0·97
1869,	5,536,217	3,172	5,892	9,064	15,344	1,020	15,568	16,588	6,282	6,069	12,351	53,347	219	4·1	0·96
1870,	5,515,674	2,037	5,270	7,307	13,057	916	13,344	14,260	5,354	6,608	11,962	46,586	198	4·1	0·85
1871,	5,402,759	1,852	4,591	6,443	12,060	922	15,632	16,554	5,001	6,479	11,480	46,537	193	4·2	0·86
1872,	5,358,165	1,709	4,628	6,337	11,462	1,036	15,107	16,143	5,140	6,600	11,740	45,682	229	5·0	0·85
1873,	5,344,131	1,831	4,827	6,658	11,681	930	15,448	16,378	5,260	6,734	11,994	46,711	237	5·1	0·87
1874,	5,314,844	1,875	4,700	6,575	11,072	893	16,010	16,903	5,454	6,777	12,231	46,781	207	4·4	0·88
1875,	5,307,404	1,773	4,305	6,078	11,187	601	15,721	16,322	6,534	6,524	13,058	46,645	221	4·8	0·87
1876,	5,321,618	1,679	4,130	5,809	10,124	667	15,666	16,333	5,281	6,097	11,378	43,644	204	4·7	0·82
1877,	5,338,906	1,749	3,995	5,744	9,885	706	15,900	16,606	5,320	6,142	11,462	43,697	207	4·7	0·82
1878,	5,351,060	2,047	4,449	6,496	10,346	835	16,928	17,763	5,736	6,512	12,248	47,022	227	4·8	0·88
1879,	5,362,337	2,109	4,780	7,106	11,128	812	17,798	18,610	6,255	6,811	13,066	49,910	254	5·1	0·93
1880,	5,327,100	2,816	5,164	7,980	12,230	1,007	18,936	19,943	6,843	7,250	14,093	54,246	259	4·8	1·02
1881,	5,129,336	2,793	4,973	7,766	11,616	632	19,147	19,779	6,494	7,180	13,674	52,835	228	4·3	1·03
1882,	5,098,009	2,603	4,737	7,340	10,566	856	18,392	19,248	6,179	6,928	13,107	50,261	204	4·0	0·99
1883,	5,015,326	2,609	4,720	7,329	10,308	782	18,227	19,009	6,456	7,155	13,611	50,257	253	5·0	1·00
1884,	4,962,870	2,322	4,424	6,746	9,299	671	17,409	18,080	6,360	7,140	13,500	47,625	210	4·4	0·96
1885,	4,924,342	2,336	4,300	6,636	8,836	602	17,157	17,759	6,329	6,911	13,240	46,471	219	4·7	0·94
1886,	4,890,420	2,477	4,274	6,751	8,709	486	16,758	17,244	6,407	7,083	13,490	46,194	204	4·4	0·94
1887,	4,837,383	2,471	4,167	6,638	8,332	470	16,729	17,199	5,345	6,967	12,312	44,481	194	4·4	0·92
1888,	4,777,545	2,637	4,101	6,738	8,006	564	16,836	17,400	6,306	6,770	13,076	45,220	190	4·2	0·94
1889,	4,730,532	2,507	3,876	6,383	7,662	398	16,669	17,067	5,820	6,614	12,434	43,546	187	4·3	0·92

7. We here continue from last Report a table showing for the last thirty-five years the per-centage in each successive year of the several classes of workhouse inmates as compared with the whole number—

CLASSIFIED RETURN of the number of inmates of workhouses in Ireland, on the first Saturday of January; and the per-centage of the several classes on the total number of inmates.

First Saturday of January.	Inmates not in Hospital.				Number in Hospital.	Total number in Workhouses.	Per-centage on total number.				
	Ablebodied.		Children under 15 years of age.	Other classes.			Ablebodied.		Children under 15 years of age not in Hospital.	Other classes not in Hospital.	In Hospital.
	Males.	Females.					Males.	Females.			
5 Jan., 1856	4,040	13,702	27,263	7,717	18,920	72,247	5·4	19·0	37·7	10·7	26·2
6 ,, 1857	3,513	8,383	19,177	6,041	18,071	55,183	6·4	15·8	34·8	12·0	32·6
2 ,, 1858	2,801	8,331	15,626	6,367	16,003	48,308	5·8	16·9	31·7	13·0	32·3
1 ,, 1859	2,317	6,920	12,732	3,447	15,233	42,609	5·1	15·9	30·2	14·3	36·0
7 ,, 1860	2,151	5,701	11,707	7,527	16,000	43,319	5·0	13·7	27·1	17·4	36·7
5 ,, 1861	3,022	7,799	12,706	8,473	15,780	47,332	6·5	16·5	26·8	17·9	33·3
4 ,, 1862	3,494	8,181	15,212	9,811	17,455	55,168	6·3	14·7	27·6	17·8	31·5
3 ,, 1863	4,030	8,044	16,730	11,103	18,421	60,888	6·7	13·1	27·0	18·3	30·7
2 ,, 1864	3,628	8,921	17,170	11,833	18,283	59,837	6·1	14·9	28·7	19·8	30·8
7 ,, 1865	3,303	8,084	16,661	12,104	16,340	56,498	5·7	13·5	28·8	20·3	32·0
6 ,, 1866	2,901	6,204	15,404	11,501	17,645	54,438	5·3	11·7	28·3	21·1	32·4
5 ,, 1867	3,015	7,228	15,701	11,691	17,205	54,930	5·5	13·2	28·7	21·3	31·3
4 ,, 1868	2,908	7,089	16,006	12,961	18,736	56,068	5·1	12·5	30·0	23·0	32·2
2 ,, 1869	3,032	7,069	16,944	12,136	16,870	56,934	5·1	13·4	29·8	22·1	29·6
1 ,, 1870	3,050	6,339	13,069	12,725	16,800	52,087	5·9	11·8	25·1	24·7	31·4
7 ,, 1871	2,603	5,570	16,024	12,380	16,859	53,816	4·9	11·6	30·6	24·2	33·3
6 ,, 1872	2,353	5,197	13,421	12,303	16,852	48,735	4·6	10·7	28·8	25·2	34·9
4 ,, 1873	2,231	5,447	12,340	12,683	17,023	49,880	4·7	10·9	24·8	25·8	34·1
3 ,, 1874	2,285	5,230	13,136	12,777	16,893	50,193	4·6	10·7	26·7	23·9	33·8
2 ,, 1875	2,332	5,100	13,187	12,853	17,313	50,866	4·7	10·4	24·5	25·9	34·5
1 ,, 1876	2,083	4,490	10,971	11,080	16,397	45,214	4·6	9·9	23·7	25·6	36·3
6 ,, 1877	2,187	4,309	10,528	11,947	16,784	45,702	4·7	9·6	23·0	26·1	36·7
5 ,, 1878	2,510	4,671	11,170	12,808	18,002	49,363	5·1	9·5	22·6	25·9	36·5
4 ,, 1879	2,913	5,119	11,386	13,306	19,083	51,784	5·6	9·9	22·0	25·8	36·8
3 ,, 1880	3,509	5,769	13,123	14,733	20,310	57,456	6·1	10·0	22·8	25·7	35·4
1 ,, 1881	3,306	5,415	12,303	14,430	19,833	55,304	6·0	10·0	22·0	26·1	35·8
7 ,, 1882	3,378	5,294	11,432	13,793	19,854	53,731	6·3	9·9	21·2	25·7	36·9
6 ,, 1883	3,218	5,142	11,063	13,982	20,334	53,749	6·1	9·6	20·6	25·9	37·8
5 ,, 1884	2,613	4,874	9,907	13,869	18,621	49,884	5·6	9·8	19·9	28·0	37·7
3 ,, 1885	2,778	4,641	9,330	13,676	18,287	48,909	5·7	9·5	19·1	28·4	37·4
2 ,, 1886	2,588	4,532	9,086	13,829	17,489	47,774	5·4	9·5	19·0	29·0	36·6
1 ,, 1887	2,906	4,474	8,656	13,842	17,482	47,360	6·1	9·5	18·3	29·2	36·9
7 ,, 1888	3,321	4,334	8,403	13,316	16,861	46,236	7·2	9·4	17·4	28·8	36·1
5 ,, 1889	3,044	4,156	8,123	13,464	17,673	46,864	6·5	9·0	17·3	28·8	37·6
4 ,, 1890	2,741	4,073	7,885	12,966	17,518	44,263	6·2	9·1	18·0	29·0	39·2

8. Subjoined is a tabular statement showing the number of "night lodgers" (a term corresponding to "casuals" in England), relieved during the first week of each of the past twelve months, in continuation of a similar table in last Report.

RETURN of NIGHT-LODGERS, OR CASUALS, relieved.

Week ended	Number relieved during the week.				Number in Workhouses at close of the week.				Number relieved in corresponding week of previous year.
	Males.	Females.	Children under 15.	Total.	Males.	Females.	Children under 15.	Total.	
6th April, 1889,	3,309	670	646	4,633	488	100	97	685	4,823
4th May, "	3,585	737	573	4,895	531	109	89	729	5,116
1st June, "	2,754	684	535	3,973	437	98	94	629	4,909
6th July, "	1,839	563	526	2,928	296	95	110	501	4,304
3rd August, "	2,744	655	589	3,988	415	102	71	588	4,438
7th September, "	2,554	662	580	3,796	344	98	86	528	4,097
5th October, "	2,213	610	545	3,410	321	93	89	503	4,082
2nd November, "	2,295	499	450	3,244	316	85	56	457	4,272
7th December, "	2,524	697	526	3,747	341	120	86	547	4,033
4th January, 1890,	2,770	529	439	3,738	381	84	57	525	3,048
1st February, "	2,579	503	411	3,493	377	81	60	518	4,074
1st March, "	3,050	606	498	4,154	408	112	93	613	4,759

It will be seen that the number of night lodgers relieved in each of the weeks included in the foregoing table was less than in the corresponding week of the previous year.

9. As part of the statistics which are brought up very nearly to the date of this Report, the following table exhibits in the accustomed form:—

A CLASSIFICATION of the causes of death in workhouses during the period from the 12th of January, 1889, to the 8th of February, 1890.

CAUSES OF DEATH.	In the four weeks ended															Previous corresponding period.
	9th Feb.	9th March.	6th April.	4th May.	1st June.	29th June.	27th July.	24th Aug.	21st Sept.	19th Oct.	16th Nov.	14th Dec.	11th Jan.	8th Feb.	Total.	
Age, . .	300	248	243	182	196	132	180	136	130	140	182	172	205	206	2,825	2,606
Apoplexy, .	4	9	8	8	8	5	3	3	4	7	5	9	7	2	81	90
Asthma, . .	8	6	18	10	9	6	2	8	6	4	8	11	7	10	109	122
Atrophy, . .	76	60	77	82	61	81	59	51	59	70	75	77	78	89	995	897
Brain Disease, .	36	31	46	30	35	37	29	34	37	34	37	38	37	33	479	444
Cancer, . .	21	13	23	24	12	8	23	27	25	20	18	24	12	16	263	253
Childbirth, .	1	1	2	2	1	2	–	1	3	–	–	1	1	1	15	13
Cholera, . .	–	–	–	–	–	–	–	–	–	–	–	–	–	–	–	–
Consumption, .	93	92	81	110	80	70	78	65	61	61	55	88	64	125	1,124	1,086
Convulsions, .	10	19	12	20	13	9	10	11	8	10	9	17	7	18	175	184
Croup, . .	–	–	1	1	2	–	–	–	1	–	–	–	4	1	10	12
Diarrhoea, .	13	19	14	20	7	18	15	18	12	16	8	12	20	20	209	219
Dropsy, . .	7	12	11	15	7	11	16	12	10	14	7	10	10	10	143	188
Dysentery, .	–	1	–	2	1	1	1	1	6	–	–	2	1	–	16	5
Dyspepsia, .	3	–	1	4	2	3	3	4	1	1	1	1	3	8	29	33
Epilepsy, . .	8	13	13	8	8	9	7	10	6	7	5	8	13	7	118	89
Fever, . .	32	27	28	31	23	21	34	21	18	28	26	21	27	31	372	388
Gangrene, .	2	7	3	–	4	2	3	3	5	3	–	3	1	4	38	43
Heart Disease, .	64	60	42	64	43	88	42	90	91	48	37	44	30	69	808	831
Hooping-Cough,	5	3	8	4	3	2	3	2	3	–	1	4	4	3	44	66
Inflammation or other disease of																
Bowels, .	10	13	7	7	4	10	11	7	10	6	0	11	10	10	122	148
Kidneys, .	15	10	12	9	0	10	4	13	12	15	12	7	16	12	164	183
Liver, . .	8	11	7	6	4	8	7	8	7	4	6	9	7	5	91	91
Lungs, .	160	188	104	170	117	102	62	78	98	107	107	135	183	209	2,010	1,880
Measles, . .	2	–	9	1	2	–	1	1	–	–	–	–	25	6	46	80
Paralysis, .	25	33	33	28	19	24	14	21	18	20	22	26	23	37	340	325
Pleurisy, . .	1	2	1	3	–	1	1	–	–	–	–	–	–	1	11	18
Rheumatism, .	7	8	4	6	8	5	3	2	4	5	3	3	2	8	64	101
Scarlatina, .	1	2	1	1	2	3	4	1	2	1	1	2	3	4	28	18
Scrofula, . .	–	14	6	15	7	10	0	0	10	4	1	4	9	18	104	88
Small-pox, .	–	–	–	–	–	–	–	–	–	–	–	–	–	–	–	1
Ulcer, . .	8	0	6	8	3	0	7	8	2	6	2	4	4	7	73	89
Other Disease,	36	37	28	30	21	38	36	30	23	51	33	34	35	41	464	429
Total, . .	813	986	995	909	717	652	673	593	583	651	647	772	859	1,126	10,973	–
Previous corresponding period,	960	1,126	1,053	808	737	670	678	684	843	615	826	651	918	645	–	10,737

The total number of deaths in the workhouses in the period comprised in the above table was 10,973. In the previous corresponding period the total number of deaths was 10,737; there has, therefore, been an increase of 236 deaths as compared with the number in the previous period.

Deaths by fever were 372, as against 388; by lung disease 2,010, as against 1,880; and there was no death from small-pox.

Orphans and Deserted Children.

10. The number of orphans and deserted children out at nurse from the workhouses in Ireland under the provisions of the Act 39 and 40 Vic., c. 38, on the 8th of February last was 2,676, being a decrease of 5 on the number at the corresponding date in the year 1889.

Emigration.

11. We mentioned in our last Report that steps were being taken to assist the emigration of poor families in the Belmullet union by means of a grant under the Arrears of Rent (Ireland) Act, 1882, and the Tramways and Public Companies (Ireland) Act, 1883. Twenty families in all emigrated consisting of 109 persons, the total grant made for the purpose being £800 12*s.* 8*d.*

The Ardfert emigration committee who conducted emigration proceedings in the Tralee union in previous years were reconstituted last year, and they effected the emigration of 23 families consisting of 143 persons. The grant made for this purpose was £831 9*s.*

12. We now continue the series of recent statistics by repeating, with one additional year, the table showing the number of persons assisted by Boards of Guardians to emigrate under the provisions of the Irish Poor Relief Acts and the cost incurred for that purpose in each year, that is to say, for forty years ended on the 25th of March.

Emigration under sec. 26 of the Act 12 & 13 Vic., c. 104, dated the 1st of August, 1849.

Period.	Amount authorised to be expended by Sealed Consents.			Number of Persons assisted to Emigrate.			
				Men.	Women.	Children under 15 years of age.	Total.
	£	s.	d.				
Aug., 1849, to 25 Mar., 1851,	11,151	14	11	561	1,244	787	2,592
Year ended 25 March, 1852,	21,010	5	4½	790	2,644	953	4,886
" " 1853,	14,517	0	11½	492	2,218	1,115	3,825
" " 1854,	12,446	17	6	403	1,202	996	2,601
" " 1855,	24,868	5	2½	159	2,847	788	3,794
" " 1856,	3,618	6	9	64	383	403	850
" " 1857,	2,719	15	1	76	363	363	802
" " 1858,	4,177	10	1½	58	469	302	829
" " 1859,	2,555	16	6	37	270	180	487
" " 1860,	1,729	19	2	45	178	141	364

EMIGRATION under sec. 26 of the Act 12 & 13 Vic., c. 104, dated the 1st of August, 1849—*continued.*

PERIOD.	Amount authorized to be expended by Sealed Consents.			Number of Persons assisted to Emigrate.			
	£	s.	d.	Men.	Women.	Children under 15 years of age.	Total.
Year ended 25 March, 1861,	1,465	19	11	44	178	125	347
" " 1862,	528	17	4	12	72	38	122
" " 1863,	2,439	10	8	41	317	139	497
" " 1864,	4,770	4	5	123	501	345	969
" " 1865,	2,316	17	11	93	315	430	840
" " 1866,	3,425	9	11	100	360	660	1,120
" " 1867,	2,023	10	0	56	238	469	763
" " 1868,	1,983	9	6	71	263	485	819
" " 1869,	1,838	18	9	71	205	439	715
" " 1870,	1,659	12	5	49	219	449	717
" " 1871,	2,268	9	11	53	226	422	701
" " 1872,	2,093	3	10	34	223	339	596
" " 1873,	1,504	14	8	44	173	364	581
" " 1874,	2,246	3	3	67	323	474	864
" " 1875,	1,247	15	1	36	192	380	608
" " 1876,	891	0	0	38	97	223	358
" " 1877,	556	17	4	13	71	116	200
" " 1878,	338	4	7	13	49	84	146
" " 1879,	651	1	3	32	89	120	241
" " 1880,	721	5	1	55	91	146	292
" " 1881,	3,452	16	0	210	558	546	1,314
" " 1882,	4,211	2	2	298	564	603	1,465
" " 1883,	4,292	16	8½	312	654	690	1,656
" " 1884,	4,346	5	2	417	840	904	2,161
" " 1885,	1,589	5	3	105	309	499	913
" " 1886,	1,153	13	1	64	283	334	681
" " 1887,	1,493	13	0	103	249	386	738
" " 1888,	1,371	0	0	116	282	332	730
" " 1889,	1,319	12	6	122	261	410	793
" " 1890,	879	12	1	85	190	258	533
Total, . . £	157,906	9	1½	5,571	20,114	17,253	42,938

AMALGAMATION OF UNIONS.

13. In our last annual Report we referred to the fact that we had under consideration the question of dissolving the unions of Bawnboy, Dunfanaghy, Glin, Killadysert, and Tulla. From the report received by us from our Inspector, Mr. W. L. Micks, of the inquiry held by him respecting the proposed dissolution of the Bawnboy union it did not appear that sufficient reason or argument was advanced in favour of the proposal. We have also received and considered a report made by the same Inspector of an inquiry held by him respecting the suggested amalgamation of the Dunfanaghy union with those adjoining it, and we do not at present propose to make any alteration in regard to that union either. The necessary proceedings have not as yet been completed to enable us to arrive at a decision in the case of Glin union, and we do not propose to take any further action at present in regard to the other two unions mentioned above.

Dissolution of Boards of Guardians.

14. During the past year we deemed it necessary, in pursuance of the powers vested in us by the 18th section of the Irish Poor Relief Extension Act, to dissolve the Boards of Guardians of the Portumna and Cork unions, and to place the management of these unions in the hands of paid officers. The letters assigning our reasons for dissolving these Boards will be found in the appendix.*

School District.

15. Our Report for the year ended March, 1888, contained an Order which we made on the 24th of February, 1888, combining the unions of Trim, Drogheda, Dunshaughlin, Navan, and Kells for the maintenance and education of children who are inmates of the workhouses of such unions, in pursuance of the 2nd section of the Act, 11 and 12 Vic., cap. 25.

Since that time the proceedings for establishing the school have been in progress. The school Board has been formed, and, having obtained the county gaol at Trim, which is no longer required as a prison, they have caused the necessary structural alterations to be made for the purpose of converting the building into a school.

The officers required for the school have been elected, and, all other arrangements being now nearly completed, it is expected that the school will be opened in about a month.

Financial statistics.

16. We now proceed to the statistics arising out of the accounts of the unions for the year ended the 29th of September, 1889.

We deal in the first place with poor relief expenditure.

Year ended 29th September	Net Annual Value	Poor Rate lodged.	Poor Relief Expenditure during the Year.						Numbers relieved.			
			In-Maintenance and Clothing.	Out-door Relief.	Cost of Relief in Blind and Deaf and Dumb Institutions, and of patients in Extern Hospitals.	Salaries and Rations of Officers.	All other Expenses.	Total.	In Workhouses.	Out-door.	In Blind and Deaf and Dumb Institutions.	Total.
	£	£	£	£	£	£	£	£				
[illegible]	[illegible]	[illegible]	[illegible]	[illegible]	[illegible]	[illegible]	[illegible]	[illegible]	[illegible]	[illegible]	677	[illegible]
[illegible]	[illegible]	[illegible]	[illegible]	[illegible]	[illegible]	[illegible]	[illegible]	[illegible]	[illegible]	[illegible]	[illegible]	[illegible]
Increase,	[illegible]	[illegible]	148	—	312	190	[illegible]	[illegible]	—	—	—	—
Decrease,	—	—	—	[illegible]	—	—	—	—	[illegible]	[illegible]	11	[illegible]

From the preceding table it will be seen that there was an increase of £148 in "in-maintenance and clothing," of £312 in "cost of relief in blind and deaf and dumb institutions, and of patients in extern hospitals," of £190 in "salaries and rations of officers," and of £8,092 in "all other expenses," while there was a decrease of £5,082 in "out-door relief," making a net increase of £3,660 in the expenditure on the relief of the poor during the year.

* See pages 57–60.

TREASURY SUBSIDIES.

17. The following is a statement of the expenditure from the parliamentary grant for medical and educational purposes and for salaries under the "Public Health (Ireland) Act," during the year ended 31st of March, 1889:—

—	Amount expended during the Year.		
	£	s.	d.
Medical purposes,	71,807	8	8
Educational purposes,	9,634	16	2
Total for medical and educational purposes,	81,442	4	10
For salaries under Public Health Act,	14,458	18	1
Total,	95,901	2	11

The total amount expended under the parliamentary grant for medical and educational purposes during the year ended 31st of March, 1889, namely, £81,442 4s. 10d., is less by £1,154 6s. than the amount during the previous year.

The amount for salaries under the Public Health (Ireland) Act, namely, £14,458 18s. 1d., is more by £28 19s. 4d. than the amount during the previous year.

PROBATE DUTIES (SCOTLAND AND IRELAND) ACT, 1888.

18. The above-mentioned Act, which received the Royal Assent on the 24th of December, 1888, assigns to Scotland and Ireland certain shares of the probate duties in each year, and provides for their application.

The amount payable to Ireland under the Act in respect of the year ended the 31st of March, 1889, was £126,000, and was distributed as follows:—

	£
Royal Dublin Society,	5,000
Boards of Guardians of poor law unions,	60,500
Road Authorities,	60 500
	£126,000

Copies of the Regulations made under the Act, with the schedules of sums paid to the Guardians of poor law unions and to Road Authorities in respect of the grant for the year referred to, are printed in the appendix.*

* See pages 61-67.

[TABLE.

EXPENDITURE FOR ALL PURPOSES FOR TWENTY-ONE YEARS PAST.

19. STATEMENT of the collection and expenditure of poor rates, showing the net annual value of property rated, the amount of poor rate collected, and the expenditure under the Poor Relief and Medical Charities Acts, &c., for each year ended on the 29th of September, from 1869 to 1889, inclusive.

Year ended 29th September	Net annual value of property rated	Amount of Poor Rate collected	Expenditure in Relief of the Poor						Expenses under Medical Charities and Vaccination Acts	Expenditure for Burial Grounds paid out of the Poor Rates	Expenditure for Sanitary purposes	Payments under Contagious Diseases (Animals) Act	Expenses on the Registration Acts	Payments under National School Teachers Act	Expenditure not included in preceding columns	Total Expenditure	Poundage of the Expenditure on Valuation	
			In-Maintenance	Out-door Relief	[illegible]	Salaries and Rations of Officers	Other Expenses	Total Poor Relief Expenditure									Poor Relief	Total
1	2	3	4	5	6	7	8	9	10	11	12	13	14	15	16	17	18	19
	£	£	£	£	£	£	£	£	£	£	£	£	£	£	£	£	s. d.	s. d.
[illegible]	[illegible]	[illegible]	[illegible]	[illegible]	[illegible]	[illegible]	[illegible]	[illegible]	[illegible]	[illegible]	[illegible]	—	—	—	[illegible]	[illegible]	[illegible]	[illegible]
[illegible]	[illegible]	[illegible]	[illegible]	[illegible]	[illegible]	[illegible]	[illegible]	[illegible]	[illegible]	[illegible]	[illegible]	—	—	—	[illegible]	[illegible]	[illegible]	[illegible]
[illegible]	[illegible]	[illegible]	[illegible]	[illegible]	[illegible]	[illegible]	[illegible]	[illegible]	[illegible]	[illegible]	[illegible]	—	—	—	[illegible]	[illegible]	[illegible]	[illegible]
[illegible]	[illegible]	[illegible]	[illegible]	[illegible]	[illegible]	[illegible]	[illegible]	[illegible]	[illegible]	[illegible]	[illegible]	—	—	—	[illegible]	[illegible]	[illegible]	[illegible]
[illegible]	[illegible]	[illegible]	[illegible]	[illegible]	[illegible]	[illegible]	[illegible]	[illegible]	[illegible]	[illegible]	[illegible]	—	[illegible]	—	[illegible]	[illegible]	[illegible]	[illegible]
[illegible]	[illegible]	[illegible]	[illegible]	[illegible]	[illegible]	[illegible]	[illegible]	[illegible]	[illegible]	[illegible]	[illegible]	[illegible]	[illegible]	—	[illegible]	[illegible]	[illegible]	[illegible]
[illegible]	[illegible]	[illegible]	[illegible]	[illegible]	[illegible]	[illegible]	[illegible]	[illegible]	[illegible]	[illegible]	[illegible]	[illegible]	[illegible]	—	[illegible]	[illegible]	[illegible]	[illegible]
[illegible]	[illegible]	[illegible]	[illegible]	[illegible]	[illegible]	[illegible]	[illegible]	[illegible]	[illegible]	[illegible]	[illegible]	[illegible]	[illegible]	[illegible]	[illegible]	[illegible]	[illegible]	[illegible]
[illegible]	[illegible]	[illegible]	[illegible]	[illegible]	[illegible]	[illegible]	[illegible]	[illegible]	[illegible]	[illegible]	[illegible]	[illegible]	[illegible]	[illegible]	[illegible]	[illegible]	[illegible]	[illegible]
[illegible]	[illegible]	[illegible]	[illegible]	[illegible]	[illegible]	[illegible]	[illegible]	[illegible]	[illegible]	[illegible]	[illegible]	[illegible]	[illegible]	[illegible]	[illegible]	[illegible]	[illegible]	[illegible]
[illegible]	[illegible]	[illegible]	[illegible]	[illegible]	[illegible]	[illegible]	[illegible]	[illegible]	[illegible]	[illegible]	[illegible]	[illegible]	[illegible]	[illegible]	[illegible]	[illegible]	[illegible]	[illegible]
[illegible]	[illegible]	[illegible]	[illegible]	[illegible]	[illegible]	[illegible]	[illegible]	[illegible]	[illegible]	[illegible]	[illegible]	[illegible]	[illegible]	[illegible]	[illegible]	[illegible]	[illegible]	[illegible]
[illegible]	[illegible]	[illegible]	[illegible]	[illegible]	[illegible]	[illegible]	[illegible]	[illegible]	[illegible]	[illegible]	[illegible]	[illegible]	[illegible]	[illegible]	[illegible]	[illegible]	[illegible]	[illegible]
[illegible]	[illegible]	[illegible]	[illegible]	[illegible]	[illegible]	[illegible]	[illegible]	[illegible]	[illegible]	[illegible]	[illegible]	[illegible]	[illegible]	[illegible]	[illegible]	[illegible]	[illegible]	[illegible]
[illegible]	[illegible]	[illegible]	[illegible]	[illegible]	[illegible]	[illegible]	[illegible]	[illegible]	[illegible]	[illegible]	[illegible]	[illegible]	[illegible]	[illegible]	[illegible]	[illegible]	[illegible]	[illegible]
[illegible]	[illegible]	[illegible]	[illegible]	[illegible]	[illegible]	[illegible]	[illegible]	[illegible]	[illegible]	[illegible]	[illegible]	[illegible]	[illegible]	[illegible]	[illegible]	[illegible]	[illegible]	[illegible]
[illegible]	[illegible]	[illegible]	[illegible]	[illegible]	[illegible]	[illegible]	[illegible]	[illegible]	[illegible]	[illegible]	[illegible]	[illegible]	[illegible]	[illegible]	[illegible]	[illegible]	[illegible]	[illegible]
[illegible]	[illegible]	[illegible]	[illegible]	[illegible]	[illegible]	[illegible]	[illegible]	[illegible]	[illegible]	[illegible]	[illegible]	[illegible]	[illegible]	[illegible]	[illegible]	[illegible]	[illegible]	[illegible]
[illegible]	[illegible]	[illegible]	[illegible]	[illegible]	[illegible]	[illegible]	[illegible]	[illegible]	[illegible]	[illegible]	[illegible]	[illegible]	[illegible]	[illegible]	[illegible]	[illegible]	[illegible]	[illegible]
[illegible]	[illegible]	[illegible]	[illegible]	[illegible]	[illegible]	[illegible]	[illegible]	[illegible]	[illegible]	[illegible]	[illegible]	[illegible]	[illegible]	[illegible]	[illegible]	[illegible]	[illegible]	[illegible]
[illegible]	[illegible]	[illegible]	[illegible]	[illegible]	[illegible]	[illegible]	[illegible]	[illegible]	[illegible]	[illegible]	[illegible]	[illegible]	[illegible]	[illegible]	[illegible]	[illegible]	[illegible]	[illegible]

* These poundages are calculated upon the expenditure exclusive of the amount thereof defrayed from loans. The sums so excluded from the poor relief expenditure and the total expenditure will be found in the appendix to the Report (appendix B, Part I, No. 1).

It will thus be seen that while the total expenditure for poor relief, medical relief, burial-grounds, sanitary measures, superannuation, payments under the Contagious Diseases (Animals) Act, payments under the National School Teachers Act and all other purposes was, in 1888, 1,458,383, the expenditure in 1889 was 1,420,866.

SEED SUPPLY ACT.

20. It will be observed from paragraph 18 of our last Report that on the 30th of March, 1880, twenty-seven unions remained indebted under the Seed Supply Act to the extent of £22,885 13*s.* 11*d.* During the year following that date ten unions completed the repayment of the loans obtained by them under the Act, and the total amount repaid to the Commissioners of Public Works during the year was £5,383 8*s.* 9*d.*, which left a balance of £17,502 5*s.* 2*d.* due on the 31st of March last by the Guardians of seventeen unions.

The amount advanced to Boards of Guardians under the Seed Supply Act in the year 1880, after crediting the unions with certain sums refunded, was £598,306 10*s.* 9*d.*, of which £580,804 3*s.* 7*d.* had been paid on the date mentioned, viz.—the 31st of March last.

MARKETS AND FAIRS (WEIGHING OF CATTLE) ACT, 1887.

21. Since the 31st of March, 1889, we have made Orders exempting eight more fairs from the provisions of the Act for periods not in any case exceeding one year.

In 22 cases where Orders of exemption had been made for a limited time the market authorities have applied to us for renewal of the Orders for a further term, and in 11 instances we have renewed the Orders exempting the fairs for a further period of two years, and in the remaining 11 for one year.

MEDICAL CHARITIES ACT AND VACCINATION ACTS.

22. We next submit to your Excellency a report of the proceedings under these Acts for the year ended the 30th of September, 1889.

The annexed table exhibits, in the usual form, the fluctuations in the number of cases in which medical relief was afforded under the Medical Charities Act, during each of the last twelve years ended on the 30th of September, for each province and for the whole of Ireland.

In Ulster there was an increase of 307 in the number of cases prescribed for at the dispensaries, and a decrease of 4,275 in the number of those attended at their own houses.

In Munster there was a decrease of 4,054 in the number of cases prescribed for at the dispensaries, and a decrease of 7,302 in the number of those attended at their own houses.

In Leinster there was an increase of 807 in the number of cases prescribed for at the dispensaries, and a decrease of 8,356 in the number of those attended at their own houses.

In Connaught there was an increase of 226 in the number of cases prescribed for at the dispensaries, and a decrease of 1,687 in the number of those attended at their own houses.

The last three columns in the table show a decrease of 24,424 cases for all Ireland, including both classes, as compared with the previous year.

Summary of cases of medical relief.

SUMMARY of the NUMBER of CASES of MEDICAL RELIEF under the Medical Charities Act.

Year ended 30th September.	Province of Ulster.			Province of Munster.			Province of Leinster.			Province of Connaught.			Total for Ireland.		
	Dispensary Tickets.	Visiting Tickets.	Total.	Dispensary Tickets.	Visiting Tickets.	Total.	Dispensary Tickets.	Visiting Tickets.	Total.	Dispensary Tickets.	Visiting Tickets.	Total.	Dispensary Tickets.	Visiting Tickets.	Total.
	1.	2.	3.	4.	5.	6.	7.	8.	9.	10.	11.	12.	13.	14.	15.
1878, . . .	[illegible]	[illegible]	172,616	144,9[illegible]	67,0[illegible]	[illegible]	166,2[illegible]	62,[illegible]	220,616	53,630	17,4[illegible]	70,816	663,4[illegible]	183,[illegible]	670,214
1879, . . .	118,[illegible]	[illegible]	178,[illegible]	137,041	56,[illegible]	[illegible]	158,971	66,263	225,214	58,[illegible]	16,[illegible]	74,948	471,377	200,979	673,[illegible]
1880, . . .	[illegible]	41,446	199,679	144,[illegible]	62,[illegible]	208,[illegible]	161,212	63,670	226,0[illegible]	60,[illegible]	22,[illegible]	83,[illegible]	480,180	218,221	708,[illegible]
1881, . . .	118,[illegible]	[illegible]	174,[illegible]	128,[illegible]	34,[illegible]	[illegible]	148,[illegible]	68,876	197,[illegible]	67,[illegible]	19,710	76,[illegible]	444,[illegible]	187,[illegible]	[illegible]
1882, . . .	113,[illegible]	54,[illegible]	166,118	121,780	61,779	178,811	190,170	90,[illegible]	200,[illegible]	54,[illegible]	18,010	73,978	430,[illegible]	184,[illegible]	615,180
1883, . . .	111,182	58,421	169,[illegible]	112,[illegible]	50,105	162,[illegible]	143,[illegible]	60,[illegible]	203,129	61,[illegible]	18,[illegible]	70,183	410,927	106,938	693,[illegible]
1884, . . .	[illegible]	[illegible]	[illegible]	114,618	47,[illegible]	[illegible]	164,790	[illegible]	[illegible]	[illegible]	[illegible]	[illegible]	437,[illegible]	171,[illegible]	[illegible]
1885, . . .	104,[illegible]	54,[illegible]	160,[illegible]	111,[illegible]	51,[illegible]	[illegible]	146,[illegible]	[illegible]	204,[illegible]	61,700	16,[illegible]	67,[illegible]	414,678	180,016	[illegible]
1886, . . .	[illegible]	56,[illegible]	159,[illegible]	104,[illegible]	47,615	152,[illegible]	137,677	55,538	193,215	53,[illegible]	17,012	71,712	400,101	177,[illegible]	577,[illegible]
1887, . . .	107,[illegible]	55,617	[illegible]	104,910	44,[illegible]	149,[illegible]	143,[illegible]	58,107	201,[illegible]	61,[illegible]	18,671	[illegible]	[illegible]	173,787	[illegible]
1888, . . .	107,[illegible]	[illegible]	147,314	100,[illegible]	49,124	[illegible]	140,[illegible]	[illegible]	205,[illegible]	52,181	14,[illegible]	[illegible]	[illegible]	[illegible]	594,[illegible]
1889, . . .	102,[illegible]	[illegible]	[illegible]	99,[illegible]	61,748	161,[illegible]	148,[illegible]	32,571	180,210	52,[illegible]	14,[illegible]	67,[illegible]	485,[illegible]	164,[illegible]	670,[illegible]

Vaccination.

23. In the following table is shown the number of cases of vaccination by medical officers of dispensary districts in each year since 1863, when the Compulsory Vaccination Act was passed:—

Table.

—	Number of Cases of Vaccination.	—	Number of Cases of Vaccination.
Year ended Sept. 30th, 1864,	191,810	Year ended Sept. 30th, 1877,	117,679
" " 1865,	169,142	" " 1878,	133,045
" " 1866,	137,124	" " 1879,	126,911
" " 1867,	125,741	" " 1880,	147,828
" " 1868,	131,420	" " 1881,	113,557
" " 1869,	125,672	" " 1882,	132,825
" " 1870,	140,220	" " 1883,	106,071
" " 1871,	179,880	" " 1884,	102,548
" " 1872,	282,481	" " 1885,	102,812
" " 1873,	136,873	" " 1886,	94,861
" " 1874,	139,587	" " 1887,	96,489
" " 1875,	137,340	" " 1888,	92,498
" " 1876,	114,487	" " 1889,	88,995

The number of cases of vaccination during the year ended the 30th of September last, as given above, is classified in the following table under the headings, "under one year old when vaccinated," "above one year old when vaccinated," and "other persons."

—	Under one year old when Vaccinated.	Above one year old when Vaccinated.	Other Persons.	Total.
Total of Ireland, . .	74,254	12,409	2,332	88,995

The number of cases of vaccination performed in workhouses during the same year was 1,104.

Vaccine Department.

24. During the year ended the 31st of March last, 3,522 applications were received from medical officers of workhouses and dispensaries and other public institutions, from military medical officers stationed in Ireland, and from private practitioners, for lymph; and 18,605 points, and 1,949 tubes charged with lymph were distributed. During the same period 1,585 vaccinations were performed at the stations in Sackville-street and York-street, Dublin.

Small-pox.

25. The number of deaths in workhouses from small-pox and the number of cases of the disease treated by dispensary medical officers in each of the last twenty-five years are given in the following table:—

DEATHS in WORKHOUSES from SMALL-POX, and NUMBER of CASES of SMALL-POX treated by DISPENSARY MEDICAL OFFICERS.

Deaths in Workhouses from Small-pox.		Number of Cases of Small-pox treated by Medical Officers of Dispensary Districts.	
PERIOD. 52 Weeks ended	Number of Deaths.	PERIOD. Year ended	Number of Cases.
10th February, 1866, . .	50	30th September, 1865, . .	2,000
9th February, 1867, . .	9	30th September, 1866, . .	879
8th February, 1868, . .	5	30th September, 1867, . .	105
6th February, 1869, . .	3	30th September, 1868, . .	155
5th February, 1870, . .	1	30th September, 1869, . .	27
4th February, 1871, . .	18	30th September, 1870, . .	51
3rd February, 1872, . .	462	30th September, 1871, . .	778
1st February, 1873, . .	677	30th September, 1872, . .	10,817
31st January, 1874, . .	110	30th September, 1873, . .	936
30th January, 1875, . .	142	30th September, 1874, . .	961
30th January, 1876, . .	41	30th September, 1875, . .	801
27th January, 1877, . .	2	30th September, 1876, . .	29
26th January, 1878, . .	12	30th September, 1877, . .	117
25th January, 1879, . .	254	30th September, 1878, . .	1,289
24th January, 1880, . .	112	30th September, 1879, . .	1,344
22nd January, 1881, . .	97	30th September, 1880, . .	863
21st January, 1882, . .	64	30th September, 1881, . .	114
20th January, 1883, . .	76	30th September, 1882, . .	479
19th January, 1884, .	11	30th September, 1883, . .	81
17th January, 1885, . .	1	30th September, 1884, . .	18
16th January, 1886, . .	2	30th September, 1885, . .	17
15th January, 1887, . .	1	30th September, 1886, . .	11
14th January, 1888, . .	3	30th September, 1887, . .	18
12th January, 1889, . .	1	30th September, 1888, . .	30
11th January, 1890, . .	-	30th September, 1889, . .	1

The following table shows in each province the quarters of the year when the disease most prevailed:—

SUMMARY of SMALL-POX cases attended by dispensary medical officers during the year ended 30th September, 1889,—taken from their quarterly returns.

PROVINCES.	Quarter, 31st Dec., 1888.	Quarter, 31st Mar., 1889.	Quarter, 30th June, 1889.	Quarter, 30th Sept., 1889.	Total.
Ulster, . . .	-	-	-	-	-
Munster, . . .	-	-	-	-	-
Leinster, . . .	-	-	-	1	1
Connaught, . .	-	-	-	-	-
Total Ireland,	-	-	-	1	1

Fever in dispensary districts.

26. The following table shows the number of cases of fever reported as attended by the medical officers of dispensary districts in each year ended on the 30th of September during the last twenty-five years, the number of cases in 1865 being 26,566, and in 1889 4,441.

Year ended 30th September.	Number of cases.	Decrease per Year.	Increase.
1865,	26,566		
1866,	22,287	4,279	
1867,	18,975	3,312	
1868,	17,400	1,575	
1869,	16,882	518	
1870,	15,744	1,138	
1871,	15,574	170	
1872,	15,654		80
1873,	14,454	1,150	
1874,	14,424	30	
1875,	13,280	1,144	
1876,	11,646	1,634	
1877,	11,396	258	
1878,	10,945	451	
1879,	10,999		54
1880,	11,211		212
1881,	9,713	1,498	
1882,	8,389	1,324	
1883,	8,031	358	
1884,	6,430	1,601	
1885,	5,780	650	
1886,	5,045	735	
1887,	5,092		47
1888,	4,357	735	
1889,	4,441		84

There were 1,838 cases of scarlatina treated by medical officers of dispensary districts in 1889, as compared with 3,800 cases in 1888, being a decrease of 1,962.

Influenza, 1889-90.

27. The epidemic of influenza which marked the close of 1889 and continued to prevail during the first quarter of 1890 constitutes the most remarkable event connected with the public health of Ireland since the publication of our last Report.

Influenza has been known in Ireland for many centuries and the earliest notice published respecting this disease in the

British Isles is contained in the "Annals of Ulster," A.D. 1326:—"Awful thunder and lightning this year, which destroyed the corn and produce of Erinn, so that it was blanched and waste. An epidemial disease common throughout all Erinn which was called *Slaedan* (prostration, influenza, which affected) during three or four days every person, so that it was second only to death."*

In 1328 influenza is recorded under the name of *Slaedan* in the "Annals of the Four Masters," and in the "Annals of Connaught," and under the name of *Murre* in the "Annals of Clonmacnoise." Several outbreaks of influenza are mentioned in the fourteenth century in Ireland. In 1580 the same disease is described as a strange kind of sickness called "the gentle correction" or influenza. Between 1650 and the end of the seventeenth century four outbreaks are mentioned, and between 1700 and 1800 thirteen epidemics of influenza visited Ireland. The great epidemic influenza of 1803 which overspread Europe began in Ireland. It was observed in Dublin and Armagh in January but is said to have appeared earlier in the south. It was at its height in April and began to decline in the middle of May. It was characterized by "cough, oppression of chest, vertigo (sic) of back and limbs, pain of face and jaws, noise of ears and deafness, extreme weakness and lowness, even fainting, but without serious consequences." There is considerable evidence that the lower animals, horses and cats especially, were simultaneously affected. The year 1801 was characterized by unusual heat, and respecting the year 1803 it is stated that "so much heat and long continued drought occurred that springs and even rivulets were dried up."† Between the epidemic of 1803 and the very general epidemic of 1847-8 there were eight visitations of influenza.

Continental outbreaks of influenza or "Grippe" are recorded at intervals in every century since the year 1400, but there appears to be a wide difference of opinion as to the precise route the disease followed in its progress. In 1580 it would appear to have travelled from west to east. The continental epidemic of 1733 is stated to have begun in Edinburgh, but since 1782 the tendency of influenza has been to move from east to west, starting from Russia, traversing Europe, and disappearing in America. In Russia influenza is considered to originate in China and to reach Russia by crossing the Ural mountains.‡

The influenza epidemic of 1889–90 prevailed at Tomsk (Siberia) on the 15th October (27th October) and during the first week in November at St. Petersburg, Moscow, Riga, and Sebastopol. In St. Petersburg it is thought that 650,000 persons, or nearly two thirds of the population of that city, were

* In connection with the high mean temperature preceding and accompanying the epidemic of 1889–90, it is interesting to note that Walsingham, the Chronicler of St. Albans, says that in 1325 and 1326, the seasons were so warm that the rivers were dried up, and many wild and tame animals died of thirst.—(Dean Butler's Notes to his translation of Grace's Annals)—Census of Ireland, 1851, Part V., Tables of Deaths, p. 83.

† Ibid., p. 164.

‡ Annales d'Hygiène, 3-Série, Vol. 23, No. 2, article "Influenza."

attacked. The epidemic fell rapidly upon every country in Europe, striking every important centre of population, and arrived in Paris in the early days of December. The Parisian outbreak attracted the serious attention of western Europe. It appeared suddenly in the great shops of the Louvre and in the central postal offices where large numbers of the hands employed were affected. Professor Brouardel and Dr. Proust were charged with the duty of inquiring into the nature of the outbreak. They reported in the middle of December that the epidemic was not a new disease, that it was not "dengue fever," but that, like the epidemic of 1837, it was one of influenza or "La Grippe." In the last week of December influenza was epidemic throughout all quarters of Paris, and, although the disease was itself of a mild type, its influence had largely increased the rate of mortality, it had in fact raised the death-rate of Paris from a weekly average of less than 900 in November to 2,683 in the last week of December. In France, as elsewhere on the continent, rich and poor were impartially attacked.

In London there is reason to believe that influenza was present during the last week of December, 1889. During the first week of January, 1890, it certainly prevailed in London, Birmingham, Liverpool, Bristol, and in other parts of England and Wales. In the first week of the present year its presence had also been recognised in Scotland.

Before proceeding to the consideration of the influenza of 1889–90 as it affected Ireland it may be well to refer briefly to the meteorological and other conditions present during the quarter preceding the general manifestation of its presence in this portion of the United Kingdom. The mean pressure of the barometer for the fourth quarter of 1889, as taken at eight Irish stations, was high, varying from 29·92 at Sligo to 30· at Valencia, and the mean temperature for the same three months was also high, ranging from 43·9 at Parsonstown and Sligo to 48·4 at Valencia.* In Dublin the mean barometrical pressure was 29·98 and the mean temperature 45·5 for the same period, and both were higher than the average for the corresponding quarter of the five years 1884–8. Out of 1,472 observations of the direction of the wind taken at the eight Irish meteorological stations during the last quarter of 1889 only 339 (or 23 per cent.) showed N., N.E., E. or S.E. winds, and December, the last month of the quarter, was remarkable for the absence of northerly and easterly winds. The average prices of

* Sir Arthur Mitchell and Dr. Buchan have made a laborious examination of the meteorological conditions attending five epidemics of influenza, extending over a period of forty-five years, and Sir Arthur Mitchell arrived at the conclusion that epidemics of influenza in the United Kingdom were connected with exceptionally warm weather, which manifested itself generally both before and during the epidemic. This observation is confirmed to a remarkable extent by the features of the Irish epidemic of 1889–90.

See also Dr. John William Moore's observations respecting the temperature and influenza in "The Influenza Epidemic of 1889–90, as observed in Dublin."—(Dublin, John Falconer.)

provisions for the fourth quarter of 1889 were lower than during the corresponding quarter of 1888. Thus the price of the 4lb. loaf was 6*d.* in 1889 as against 7*d.* in 1888. Potatoes in 1889 were from 1*s.* 11*d.* to 2*s.* 5*d.* per cwt. as against 2*s.* 6*d.* to 2*s.* 10*d.* in 1888, and beef was 4*s.* per cwt. lower in 1889 than in 1888. Lastly, the number of paupers relieved indoor and outdoor was lower in the last quarter of 1889 than in the last quarter of 1888. It will thus be seen that no climatic or economic conditions unfavourable to the public health existed in the quarter preceding the severe epidemic of influenza which set in with the first month of 1890, and the Registrar-General states that the statistics as to the health of the people, while not so satisfactory in the last quarter of 1889 as in the corresponding quarter of 1888, nevertheless compare favourably with the average results for the fourth quarter of the ten years 1879–88 as regards both the general death-rate and the rate represented by deaths from zymotic diseases.

We have obtained returns from about 780 dispensary medical officers in charge of the 720 districts into which Ireland is divided.* These returns are made up to the 15th of March, and, although influenza at that date was still present in many parts of the country, we believe the principal features of the epidemic may be gathered from the facts set forth in the returns completed up to that date.

It would appear that in a few districts on the east coast of Ireland cases of influenza were recognised in the month of October. In Banbridge union in the county of Down a case is reported as having occurred on the 8th of October. Farther north, in Ballymoney union in the county of Antrim, cattle suffered from influenza in the summer and autumn. In the county of Dublin a medical officer reports that he saw a case on the 28th of October in Howth. In Drogheda union in the county of Louth a case was noticed on the 11th of November. Cases are also returned as having occurred during November in the counties of Kilkenny, Meath, Kildare, and Wicklow. In November isolated cases are also returned from the counties of Mayo and Roscommon in the west of Ireland. During the month of December there can be no doubt that typical cases of influenza were treated in more than one county in each of the four provinces. It was, however, in the first week in January that influenza prevailed generally throughout Ireland, and the period of its maximum prevalence would appear to have been towards the close of that month and during the early part of February. The figures furnished to us fall short of the numbers affected, many medical officers having recorded that the cases returned represent only those who suffered so severely as to oblige them to seek medical advice, and that no record was kept respecting those lightly affected who did not consult the medical officers. The following table shows the population in 1881 and the number

* From 20 districts we have received no returns; and in 9 dispensary districts it is stated that no typical cases of influenza had occurred.

of cases of influenza made up to the 15th of March last in the four provinces of Ireland :—

Provinces.	Population in 1881.	Cases of Influenza.
Ulster, ...	1,743,075	25,561
Munster, . . .	1,331,115	21,513
Leinster, . . .	1,278,989	21,356
Connaught, . . .	821,657	7,879
Total, . .	5,174,836 *	76,309

What may be described as the severe cases of influenza amounted to a little more than 16 per 1,000 on the estimated population. (See note *.)

On the subject of the origin and mode of extension of the epidemic in Ireland the views expressed by medical officers differ, but there is a general concensus of opinion to the effect that the disease was of a miasmatic character, that it was air-borne, that it was preceded and accompanied by high temperature and moist atmosphere. A small number of observers considered it infectious and contagious, but the great majority were of opinion that it was not. There is no evidence to show that it manifested a preference for particular localities, and its incidence and progress were apparently uninfluenced by geological formations or geographical features. It does not appear to have followed the usual channels of communication; its spread was not influenced by valley lines,† by river-courses, by high or low levels, by undrained or marshy grounds, by drained lands or uplands, nor by the contour of the different areas attacked. No class of persons seem to have been exempt from attack, but several observers express the opinion that those whose occupations kept them in the open air suffered in larger numbers than persons who remained at home or worked under cover. ‡

In answer to our inquiry as to any observed uniform period of incubation a few medical officers state they have reason to think it has varied from six hours to forty-eight hours, or even longer, but the general expression of professional opinion is to the effect that the "*materies morbi*," whatever may be its nature, is received into the human system in a condition which produces immediate results, and that the attack of influenza is in the vast majority of instances sudden in its onset. A great

* The population of Ireland estimated to the middle of the year 1889, had fallen to 4,730,582. (Registrar-General's Returns.)

† In only one instance a medical officer reports that in his district the disease seemed at first to follow the valley lines, and then to spread right and left.

‡ One observer notes the exemption from influenza of persons working in the spinning rooms of flax-mills where the air is moist and the temperature averages 80° F.

many medical officers have themselves suffered from the disease and in almost every instance they state that they were in their usual health up to the moment when they were seized with rigors or severe chills.

The principal symptoms of the disease as detailed in the large mass of returns placed at our disposal admit of the following broad lines of classification:—first, a group of cases in which symptoms belonging to the nervous system predominated; second, a group presenting symptoms connected with the respiratory system; third, a group in which gastric symptoms were the most marked; and fourth, influenza with catarrhal symptoms. These four groups appear in many instances to have been attended with complications, amongst which bronchitis, pulmonary congestion, and pneumonia were the most frequent.

Relapses were very common especially amongst those who exposed themselves by going out of doors too soon, and in relapses pulmonary affections were very prominent. All observers agree that those who lay up from the first were most lightly affected and recovered best, and that the worst attacks were seen in persons who tried to follow their usual occupations and to battle against the disease.

The ordinary train of symptoms in the majority of cases of influenza may be described as follows:—sudden and severe rigors, or persistent chilliness, very frequently attended with vomiting. These symptoms were immediately succeeded by high temperature (from 100 to 103 or 104, in a few instances 105), intense and peculiar headache, principally in the forehead, across the vertex, and extending to the back of the neck. Pain or tenderness in the eyeballs. Severe muscular pains, principally in the muscles of the back, across the loins, and in the great flexor muscles of the lower limbs. Delirium was frequently an early symptom. Total loss of appetite with nausea. Sleeplessness was often present, and, on the other hand, great drowsiness and inclination to sleep have also been observed. Dry cough was frequently noticed. Tongue generally coated with a white or yellowish fur. The pulse has not been reported as high, rarely above 100. The skin has generally been dry, but perspiration has often been copious after the first forty-eight hours. The duration of the acute phase of the attack has generally been about four days Convalescence has been very slow.

It has been noted that the attack sometimes began amongst labouring men by their suddenly fainting at their work. Several observers have reported that the very young and the very old escaped influenza, and that when it attacked children it frequently began with convulsions.

There is a very general agreement amongst all observers of the disease in Ireland that the attack, whether light or severe, has been followed by most remarkable mental depression, loss of energy, and profound bodily prostration.

Diarrhœa has been present in the early stages in many parts of Ireland and early vomiting has been a marked symptom in most parts of the country. Influenza characterized by nervous symptoms, and especially neuralgia, appears to have been the most common, and the catarrhal variety the least common, type of the disease in Ireland.

Regarding the complications we gather from the reports sent to us that the disease has exhibited a marked tendency to search out and to affect any weak organ. In otherwise healthy subjects the complications most frequently recorded are the following:—an abnormally slow pulse, and, following the acute symptoms, sub-normal temperature (96). Otitis (inflammation of the ear) going on to suppuration, and sometimes deafness. Orchitis, this curious and inexplicable complication has been frequently noted. Cystitis has been recorded, and epileptic convulsions in adults have also been reported. Abortion has been observed in connection with influenza.

Rashes have been noticed by several medical officers; they have been described as resembling in some cases the rash of scarlatina, in others the rash of measles, in others that of erythema.

The mortality due directly to influenza in Ireland, as in other countries, has been very small, but this specific form of disease is remarkable by reason of the disturbing influence which its existence indirectly produces upon the public health. In the presence of influenza other diseases, and especially those of the respiratory organs, show a greatly increased tendency to end in death. The recent epidemic affords a further illustration of the truth that although influenza itself kills very few, a season of influenza is a season of high mortality. We have already pointed out that all the general conditions, meteorological and economic, which tell in favour of the public health were present during the quarter preceding the epidemic of 1889-90. We have reason to believe that conditions not less favourable continued to prevail during and after the subsidence of the epidemic which marked the close of the last and the early part of the present year. The death rate for the last quarter of 1889 was 16·5 per thousand, and, having regard to the favourable character of the weather in the three succeeding winter months, a death rate below the first-quarter average might have been expected in the first quarter of 1890; it has, however, increased to 24·5, the highest death rate recorded since the establishment of registration. So high a death rate has been approached, but not equalled, upon only two occasions, corresponding with two winters of unusual severity. The death rate for the first quarter of 1890 in fact exceeds by more than two per thousand the average first-quarter death rate of this part of the United Kingdom. We believe that when the Registrar-General's analysis of the tables of mortality for the period covered by the epidemic comes to be published it will be shown that the influenza of 1889-90 is indirectly accountable for a large excess over the average mortality of the period included in the three winter months of the year.

Diseases amongst the lower animals either preceded or accompanied influenza in human beings in nearly all parts of Ireland. In the province of Ulster horses and dogs were affected in the counties of Antrim, Armagh, Cavan, and Londonderry; horses only in Down, Fermanagh, and Monaghan, and dogs only in the county of Donegal. In Munster horses and dogs were affected in the counties of Clare and Kerry; horses, dogs, and cats in the county of Cork; horses, dogs, and horned cattle in the county of Limerick, and horses only in the counties of Tipperary and Waterford. In Leinster horses and dogs were affected in the counties of Carlow, Kildare, and Louth; horses and horned cattle in the county of Dublin; poultry and cats in the county of Westmeath; dogs and cats in the county of Wexford, and horses only in the counties of King's, Longford, Meath, Queen's, and Wicklow. In Connaught horses and dogs were affected in the county of Roscommon; horses only in the counties of Galway and Mayo, and dogs only in the county of Leitrim. Of the thirty-two counties in Ireland there are only two—Kilkenny and Sligo—from which we have not received reports of disease, supposed to have been influenza, amongst the lower animals.*

* The following is the description given by a medical officer of influenza in dogs:—"Great lassitude, very stiff on motion, thirst, vomiting of everything taken, and loss of flesh. Attack lasted about one week."

[TABLE.

28. The next table gives the expenditure under the Medical Charities Act and the Vaccination Acts in each of the last twelve years ended on the 29th of September.

MEDICAL CHARITIES EXPENDITURE.

Year ended 29th September	Ulster.	Munster.	Leinster.	Connaught.	Total.
	£	£	£	£	£
1878, .	39,584	42,274	44,030	19,024	144,912
1879, .	40,283	40,657	44,860	20,230	146,030
1880, .	43,298	43,168	45,805	21,114	153,375
1881, .	43,640	44,065	47,429	22,110	157,244
1882, .	44,839	44,663	47,569	21,957	159,028
1883, .	43,514	45,093	48,628	22,170	159,405
1884, .	42,333	44,768	48,865	22,397	158,363
1885, .	41,776	46,321	48,136	24,434	160,667
1886, .	42,264	44,018	49,809	22,021	158,112
1887, .	42,253	44,278	49,681	22,164	158,376
1888, .	43,412	46,713	48,102	20,769	158,996
1889, .	42,766	46,107	46,722	22,360	157,955

And the following shows in more detail, and under the usual heads, a comparative statement of the expenditure for the two years ended the 29th of September, 1888 and 1889, respectively:—

MEDICAL CHARITIES EXPENDITURE.

—	1888.	1889.
	£	£
1. Medicines and medical appliances, ...	26,964	26,877
2. Rent of dispensary buildings, ...	8,470	8,528
3. Books, forms, stationery, printing, and advertising,	940	1,031
4. Salaries of { medical officers, ...	89,844	69,722
{ apothecaries, ...	2,809	2,786
5. Fuel, porters, and incidental expenses, ...	19,423	16,949
6. Vaccination fees and other expenses:—		
Fees to medical officers, ...	9,256	8,834
Other expenses, ...	1,272	1,238
Total, ...	158,996	157,955

Dispensary houses and dwelling-houses for medical officers.

29. In paragraph 26 of our last Report we referred to the proceedings under the "Act to give facilities for providing Dispensary houses and Dwelling-houses for Medical Officers of Dispensary Districts in certain parts of Ireland."

Advantage still continues to be taken of the provisions of the Act, and certificates have been issued since our last Report in the following cases:—

—	Dispensary District.	Union.
Dispensary and Dispensary Residence, . .	Abbeyshrule, . .	Ballymahon.
Dispensary Residence, ...	Lusk, ...	Balrothery.
Do., ...	*Rafeagh, . . .	Carrickmacross.
Do., ...	Kilnaleck, . . .	Cavan.
Dispensary and Dispensary Residence, . .	Timoleague, . .	Clonakilty.
Dispensary, ...	Corofin, . . .	Corofin.
Do., ...	Whitechurch, . .	Dungarvan.
Dispensary and Dispensary Residence, . .	Ferns, ...	Enniscorthy.
Dispensary, ...	Fermoy, . . .	Fermoy.
Do., ...	Kenmare, . . .	Kenmare.
Dispensary and Dispensary Residence, . .	Dunmurry, . . .	Lisburn.
Dispensary, ...	Claudy, . . .	Londonderry.
Dispensary and Dispensary Residence, . .	Longford, . . .	Longford.
Do., do., . .	Cullen, ...	Millstreet.
Do., do., . .	Clane and Timahoe,	Naas.
Dispensary Residence, ...	Goleen, . . .	Skull.

* The certificate in this case was supplemental to another certificate granted for a loan which was found to be insufficient for the purpose required.

SANITARY ACTS.

Provisional Orders, &c.

30. Since our last Report we have made the following Provisional Orders:—

Date.	Place.	Purpose.
6th May, 1889, .	Killiney and Ballybrack Township.	Transferring the powers of the Grand Jury of the County of Dublin with respect to roads, bridges, footpaths, and public works, within the Urban Sanitary District of Killiney and Ballybrack to the Urban Sanitary Authority of Killiney and Ballybrack.
7th May, 1889, .	Listowel Town, .	Empowering the Town Commissioners of Listowel, the Urban Sanitary Authority, to put in force the provisions of the Lands Clauses Acts with reference to the purchase and taking of lands, otherwise than by agreement, required for the purpose of providing a supply of water.
22nd May, 1889, .	Tipperary Union, .	Empowering the Board of Guardians of Tipperary Union, the Rural Sanitary Authority, to put in force the provisions of the Lands Clauses Acts with reference to the purchase and taking of lands, otherwise than by agreement, required for the purpose of constructing Waterworks for the town of Tipperary.
24th May, 1889, .	Tralee Union, . .	Empowering the Board of Guardians of Tralee Union, the Rural Sanitary Authority, to put in force the provisions of the Lands Clauses Acts with reference to the purchase and taking of lands, otherwise than by agreement, required for the purpose of providing a supply of water for the Town of Castleisland.
29th April, 1889,	Youghal Town, . .	Forming a United District for the purpose of enlarging North Abbey Burial Ground.

Provisional Orders—continued.

We have received petitions for Provisional Orders in the following cases, and the petitions are under consideration.

Place.	Purpose.
Bangor Town, . . .	To put in force the provisions of the Lands Clauses Acts with reference to the purchase and taking of lands, otherwise than by agreement, required for the purpose of providing an additional supply of water, and for widening, opening, enlarging, and improving the streets.
Downpatrick Union, . .	To put in force the provisions of the Lands Clauses Acts with reference to the purchase and taking of lands, otherwise than by agreement, required for the purpose of providing a Water Supply for the Town of Downpatrick.
Drumcondra, Clonliffe, and Glasnevin Town.	To alter the Drumcondra, Clonliffe, and Glasnevin Township Act, 1878, by increasing the borrowing powers of the Township Commissioners.
Dungarvan Town, . . .	To put in force the provisions of the Lands Clauses Acts with reference to the purchase and taking of lands, otherwise than by agreement, required for the purpose of providing a supply of water.
Glin Union, ...	To put in force the provisions of the Lands Clauses Acts with reference to the purchase and taking of lands, otherwise than by agreement, required for the purpose of providing a Water Supply for the Town of Foynes.
Macroom Union, . . .	To put in force the provisions of the Lands Clauses Acts with reference to the purchase and taking of lands, otherwise than by agreement, required for the purpose of constructing sewerage works at Coachford.
Wexford Town, . . .	To put in force the provisions of the Lands Clauses Acts with reference to the purchase and taking of lands, otherwise than by agreement, required for the purpose of providing a new cemetery.

Bye-Laws.

31. The following is a list of Bye-laws submitted to and confirmed by us during the year 1889–90:—

Place.	Subject.
Coleraine Town, ...	Alteration in hours for holding pork market.
Cork City, ...	I. New streets and buildings. II. Slaughter houses. III. Conveyance of meat.
Dundalk Town, ...	Regulation of locomotives propelled by steam or by other than animal power.
Galway Union, ...	Common lodging-houses.
Kilkenny County, . . .	Regulation of locomotives propelled by steam or by other than animal power.
Kilmainham Township, . .	I. Removal of house refuse, cleansing of earth-closets, privies, ashpits, and cesspools. II. Nuisances arising from filth, ashes, and rubbish. III. New streets and buildings. IV. Regulation of the keeping of animals.
Kingstown Township, . .	Regulation of bathing-places.
Portadown Town, . . .	I. New streets and buildings. II. Cleansing of footways and pavements. III. Removal of house refuse. IV. Cleansing of privies, &c. V. Prevention of nuisances. VI. Regulation of the keeping of animals. VII. Slaughter-houses and knackers'-yards.

Burial Grounds.

32. Orders have been made and gazetted prohibiting further interments in the burial grounds named hereunder:—

1. The burial ground at Rathfarnham, in the South Dublin union.
2. The burial ground attached to the Protestant church in the town of Mallow.
3. The burial ground at Marshalstown, in the Enniscorthy union.
4. The Abbey burial ground at Naas, in the Naas union.
5. The Templecranny burial ground in the Downpatrick union.

Each of these Orders was made subject to certain exceptions mentioned therein.

SEWERAGE AND WATER SUPPLY.

33. Our report upon Public Health is continued from the last annual Report. Details were given therein of the operations in regard to sewerage and water-supply under the provisions of the Public Health Act, 1878, in continuation of the detail of proceedings under the Act of 1874; the extent of those operations is still in some degree measured in rural sanitary districts by the number of the Orders under seal fixing the area of charge for each such operation, and the loans borrowed for these purposes through the Public Works Commissioners.

The number of such Orders issued each year since 1875–6 is shown in the following table:—

Year.	Number of Orders issued declaring areas of charge for Sanitary expenses.
1875–6, . . .	79
1876–7, . . .	89
1877–8, . . .	122
1878–9, . . .	117
1879–80, . . .	126
1880–1, . . .	103
1881–2, . . .	79
1882–3, . . .	83
1883–4, . . .	79
1884–5, . . .	102
1885–6, . . .	87
1886–7, . . .	74
1887–8, . . .	80
1888–9, . .	65
1889–90, . . .	48
Total, . .	1,333

It will be seen from the foregoing that on the whole 1,333 Orders fixing areas of charge for sewerage or water-supply, or both, have been issued during the last fifteen years, the number for the year from the 26th of March, 1889, to the 25th of March, 1890, being 48, which were issued to the Guardians of 33 unions.

The above table relates to rural sanitary districts. In urban districts all sanitary expenses are chargeable upon funds levied from the whole district.

Loans.

34. In both urban and rural sanitary districts a considerable part of the expenditure on sewerage, water-supply, and other local improvements is carried out by means of loans which we recommend to be issued to the sanitary authorities by the Public Works Commissioners.

In the fourteen years ended the 31st of March, 1889, loans under the Sanitary Acts were sanctioned as follows :—

Year ended	Amount.		
	£	s.	d.
31st March, 1876, .	37,584	0	0
„ 1877, .	41,085	0	0
„ 1878, .	62,056	0	0
„ 1879, .	124,454	0	0
„ 1880, .	292,824	0	0
„ 1881, .	199,252	0	0
„ 1882, .	202,374	0	0
„ 1883, .	66,954	0	0
„ 1884, .	179,836	0	0
„ 1885, .	161,599	0	0
„ 1886, .	179,151	9	9
„ 1887, .	88,224	7	8
„ 1888, .	88,903	8	9
„ 1889, .	182,182	5	1
Total, . .	1,896,479	11	3

The following is a list of loans sanctioned by us during the year ended the 31st of March, 1890, in continuation of similar lists in previous Reports.

TABLE.]

LIST of LOANS sanctioned during the year ended the 31st of March, 1890, in continuation of similar lists in previous Reports.

Name of Sanitary District.		Amount of Loan. £	s.	d.	Purpose for which obtained.	Date of Sanction.
Antrim,	Rural, .	200	0	0	Completion of Antrim cemetery.	3rd February, 1890.
Ballinasloe,	Urban, .	800	0	0	To provide pumps, . .	25th April, 1889.
Do.,	Rural, .	100	0	0	To provide a pump at Lawrencetown.	1st November, 1889.
Balrothery,	do., .	450	0	0	Sewerage works at Rush. .	7th March, 1890.
Bangor,	Urban, .	240	0	0	Sewerage works, . .	18th March, 1890.
		230	0	0	Gas and water mains,	
Belfast,	Rural, .	800	0	0	Sewerage works at Sydenham.	18th February, 1890.
Do.,	do., .	200	0	0	Sewerage works at Green-Castle and Upper Whitehouse.	18th March, 1890.
Do.,	do., .	300	0	0	Sewerage works at Ballymisert.	10th March, 1890.
Blackrock,	Urban, .	780	0	0	Concreting footpaths, .	30th November, 1889.
Do.,	do., .	600	0	0	Sewerage works, . . .	20th March, 1890.
Castlerea,	Rural, .	1,500	0	0	Water supply, Ballaghaderreen.	2nd August, 1889.
Cavan,	do., .	2,000	0	0	Town Hall, Cavan (Loan to Town Commissioners).	24th December, 1889.
Clonakilty,	do., .	300	0	0	Fencing and enlarging Ross Abbey burial ground.	14th September, 1889.
Coleraine,	do., .	650	0	0	Sewerage works at Castlerock.	3rd May, 1889.
Do.,	do., .	350	0	0	Improvement of clear water basin, &c., Portrush waterworks.	7th August, 1889.
Cork,	Urban, .	20,000	0	0	Labouring Classes' Lodging Houses Acts.	12th September, 1889.
Do.,	do., .	482	0	0	Sewerage works, . . .	13th September, 1889.
Do.,	Rural, .	600	0	0	Monkstown water supply, .	4th June, 1889.
Corrofin,	do., .	70	0	0	To provide a pump at Kells, Co. Clare.	10th March, 1890.
Croom,	do., .	100	0	0	Disinfecting chamber, .	28th August, 1889.
Dalkey,	Urban, .	330	0	0	Sewerage works, and purchase of gas engine for pumping water to the high levels of the township.	15th August, 1889.
Drumcondra, Clonliffe, and Glasnevin.	do., .	695	0	0	Laying of water main and sewerage works.	24th April, 1889.
Do.,	do., .	200	0	0	Sewerage works, . . .	29th July, 1889.
Do.,	do., .	600	0	0	Concreting footpaths, .	29th July, 1889.
Fermoy,	do., .	175	0	0	Flagging footpaths, .	2nd August, 1889.
		100	0	0	Construction of sewers,	
Killiney and Ballybrack,	do., .	688	9	9	Costs, Provisional Order Confirmation Act, 1889.	7th February, 1890.
Kilmainham,	do., .	750	0	0	Water supply, .	7th August, 1889.

LIST of LOANS sanctioned during the year ended the 31st of March, 1890, in continuation of similar lists in previous Reports—*continued.*

Name of Sanitary District.	Amount of Loan.	Purpose for which obtained.	Date of Sanction.
	£ s. d.		
Kingstown, Urban, .	3,000 0 0	Concreting footpaths, .	23rd July, 1889.
Do., do., .	950 0 0	Sewerage works, . . .	17th July, 1889.
Do., do., .	500 0 0	Purchase of land for People's Park.	25th July, 1889.
Do., do., .	4,000 0 0	Laying out People's Park, .	10th December, 1889.
Kinsale, Rural, .	510 0 0	Waterworks at Crosshaven,	11th April, 1889.
Listowel, Urban, .	4,000 0 0	Water supply, . . .	28th February, 1890.
Londonderry, do., .	1,600 0 0	Completion of Waterside waterworks.	21st May, 1889.
Do., do., .	1,200 0 0	Filter bed, Creggan reservoir.	5th July, 1889.
Do., do., .	5,000 0 0	Completion of Creggan waterworks.	22nd August, 1889.
Lurgan, do., .	900 0 0	Purchase of store for street metal, stabling, &c.	16th September, 1889.
Do., do., .	100 0 0	Water supply, . . .	16th September, 1889.
Mallow, Rural, .	798 2 11	The sinking of wells and erection of pumps.	22nd August, 1889.
Newtownards, Urban, .	450 0 0	Re-erecting houses at gas works.	19th March, 1890.
	150 0 0	Laying gas mains, . .	
Parsonstown, do., .	200 0 0	Sewerage works, . . .	3rd August, 1889.
Pembroke, do., .	3,045 0 0	Sewerage works, . . .	13th June, 1889.
Do., do., .	600 0 0	Mortuary, ...	13th June, 1889.
Do., do., .	3,700 0 0	Water mains, . . .	6th July, 1889.
Portadown, do., .	1,900 0 0	Erection of municipal buildings.	7th September, 1889.
Sligo, Rural, .	190 0 0	Fencing and enlarging Ballisodare burial ground.	23rd September, 1889.
Strabane, do., .	1,100 0 0	Completion of Strabane waterworks.	3rd May, 1889.
Strokestown, do., .	530 0 0	Improvement of Strokestown waterworks.	1st August, 1889.
Tralee, Urban, .	2,000 0 0	To pay off gas debentures,	3rd June, 1889.
Do., do., .	450 0 0	Sewerage works, . . .	11th February, 1890.
Do., Rural, .	2,400 0 0	Castleisland waterworks, .	22nd March, 1890.
Waterford, Urban, .	2,300 0 0	Labouring Classes' Lodging Houses Acts.	30th May, 1889.
Do., Rural, .	188 0 0	Sewerage works at Tramore.	6th July, 1889.

The total amount of the loans included in the above list is £75,746 18*s.* 8*d.*, which, added to the previous sums, constitutes a total of £1,972,226 9*s.* 11*d.* for the fifteen years in question.

TOWNS IMPROVEMENT (IRELAND) ACT, 1854.

35. We have given our consent to the extension of the boundaries of the town of Mallow in pursuance of section 5 of the above-mentioned Act. The Town Commissioners of Lisburn desire to extend their town and we have the question at present under consideration.

Labourers Acts.

36. The following table shows the unions from which petitions for confirmation of improvement schemes were received by us from the inception of these Acts up to the 31st of March, 1890, the number of houses applied for in each case, the number actually authorized up to that date, and the number included in applications which remain to be disposed of. The amounts of the loans sanctioned by the Treasury for the purposes of the Acts are also given.

Table.

Unions.	Number of Cottages			Total amount of Loans sanctioned by the Treasury.		
	Applied for.	Authorised.	Included in applications which are still pending	£	s.	d.
Abbeyleix,	90	25	–	2,421	17	6
Ardee,	247	183	57	15,618	10	0
Athy,	301	123	–	12,941	0	0
Bailieborough,	43	15	–	1,788	0	0
Ballinasloe,	14	8	–	1,237	5	0
Ballycastle,	15	8	–	–		
Ballymahon,	266	115	–	9,935	0	0
Ballymena,	34	18	–	1,800	0	0
Ballyshannon,	20	–	–	–		
Balrothery,	171	53	76	6,450	0	0
Baltinglass,	170	60	22	7,270	0	0
Bandon,	220	133	–	13,000	0	0
Borrisokane,	78	41	–	3,400	0	0
Callan,	83	35	–	3,500	0	0
Carlow,	340	208	–	9,895	0	0
Carrickmacross,	45	–	32	–		
Carrick-on-Shannon,	21	10	–	790	0	0
Carrick-on-Suir,	71	46	–	5,770	0	0
Cashel,	358	255	28	22,120	0	0
Castlecomer,	47	23	–	2,162	0	0
Cavan,	107	23	–	2,760	0	0
Celbridge,	115	52	6	8,020	0	0
Clogheen,	197	100	–	11,006	0	0
Clonakilty,	170	123	–	12,950	0	0
Clonmel,	118	59	–	6,230	0	0
Cork,	433	287	–	30,310	0	0
Corrofin,	18	9	–	1,015	10	0
Croom,	354	187	118	14,335	0	0
Delvin,	318	185	39	22,090	0	0
Dingle,	20	10	–	1,000	0	0
Drogheda,	508	314	–	40,970	0	0
Dromore, West,	71	7	–	560	0	0
Dublin, North,	72	60	2	1,710	0	0
Dublin, South,	35	26	–	2,805	0	0
Dundalk,	149	54	–	7,504	10	0
Dungarvan,	60	47	–	4,070	0	0
Dunmanway,	304	187	–	18,700	0	0
Dunshaughlin,	134	75	–	9,080	0	0
Edenderry,	60	20	13	2,308	0	0
Ennis,	217	115	–	12,166	6	8
Enniscorthy,	296	161	1	15,295	0	0
Ennistymon,	104	27	–	3,380	0	0
Fermoy,	258	157	–	22,665	19	0
Glin,	186	131	–	18,436	0	0
Gorey,	180	96	25	9,290	0	0

TABLE—*continued.*

UNIONS.	Number of Cottages			Total amount of Loans sanctioned by the Treasury.		
	Applied for.	Authorized.	Included in applications which are still pending.			
				£	s.	d.
Gort, . . .	50	5	–	–		
Granard, . . .	274	96	81	9,000	0	0
Kanturk, . . .	463	320	–	32,600	0	0
Kells, . . .	425	193	34	22,725	0	0
Kilkenny, . . .	62	34	–	8,027	15	0
Killadysert, . . .	122	53	–	4,569	0	0
Killarney, . . .	286	131	–	11,000	0	0
Kilmacthomas, . .	359	123	–	11,162	0	0
Kilmallock, . . .	1,154	364	279	34,193	0	0
Kilrush, . . .	78	31	–	–		
Kinsale, . . .	103	42	–	4,620	0	0
Limerick, . . .	1,884	898	217	43,800	0	0
Lismore, . . .	253	124	–	14,180	0	0
Listowel, . . .	230	110	60	12,769	0	0
Longford, . . .	121	46	51	6,090	0	0
Loughrea, . . .	43	10	–	965	5	3
Macroom, . . .	697	318	277	30,580	0	0
Mallow, . . .	229	111	21	15,386	0	0
Manorhamilton, . .	43	17	–	1,666	10	0
Midleton, . . .	303	200	–	25,000	0	0
Millstreet, . . .	168	123	–	12,450	0	0
Mitchelstown, . .	274	163	8	18,008	0	0
Mohill, . . .	48	17	–	1,700	0	0
Mountmellick, . .	334	88	59	2,370	0	0
Mullingar, . . .	380	240	–	28,879	10	4
Naas, . . .	232	100	–	9,816	0	0
Navan, . . .	492	212	110	23,617	0	0
Nenagh, . . .	898	269	–	30,878	17	4
Newcastle, . . .	356	270	–	20,709	0	0
New Ross, . . .	202	157	–	2,808	13	3
Oldcastle, . . .	246	166	–	22,550	0	0
Parsonstown, . . .	77	46	–	4,060	0	0
Rathdrum, . . .	119	42	–	1,430	0	0
Rathkeale, . . .	834	152	–	18,325	0	0
Roscommon, . . .	7	8	–	360	0	0
Roscrea, . . .	4	–	4	–		
Scariff, . . .	77	85	–	8,915	0	0
Shillelagh, . . .	67	19	47	2,145	0	0
Skibbereen, . . .	513	160	166	17,848	0	0
Skull, . . .	47	18	–	1,235	0	0
Sligo, . . .	10	–	–	–		
Strokestown, . . .	24	1	–	–		
Thomastown, . .	72	60	–	5,992	0	0
Thurles, . . .	167	60	–	5,730	0	0
Tipperary, . . .	1,096	376	419	42,040	0	0
Tralee, . . .	420	228	–	19,632	0	0
Trim, . . .	330	170	65	21,012	10	0
Tulla, . . .	276	184	–	12,086	8	6
Tullamore, . . .	287	104	–	11,100	0	0
Urlingford, . . .	78	46	–	4,600	0	0
Waterford, . . .	488	167	–	5,000	0	0
Wexford, . . .	892	322	–	27,277	0	0
Youghal, . . .	381	215	–	22,575	0	0
Total, . .	22,210	10,687	2,446	£1,098,772	3	5

Following the course adopted in previous Reports, we now give tables showing what has been done by sanitary authorities under the improvement schemes authorized, and what is proposed to be done under further improvement schemes.

Table I. shows that out of the 10,637 houses authorized, 6,742 have been provided, and 6,463 of these actually let, and that 1,188 others are at present in progress of erection.

Table II. shows that further improvement schemes have been, or are, we understand, about to be, submitted to us, embracing 3,301 cottages at an estimated cost of about £398,661.

TABLE I.—RETURN showing what has been done under improvement schemes authorized.

UNIONS.	No. of Electoral Divisions in which the erection of houses has been authorized.	Number of Houses						
		Authorized.	Built.	In progress.	Not yet commenced.	Abandoned.	Actually Let.	Rent (Weekly.)
PROVINCE OF ULSTER.								
Co. ANTRIM.								
Ballycastle,	3	8			8			
Ballymena,	6	18	2	10	6			
Co. CAVAN.								
Bailieborough,	5	15	12	8			12	1s.
Cavan,	12	23			23			
Total for Ulster,	20	64	14	13	37		12	
PROVINCE OF MUNSTER.								
Co. CLARE.								
Corrofin,	6	9	9				9	1s. 0½d.
Ennis,	17	115	30	32	46	1	31	1s. and 1s. 2d.
Ennistymon,	13	27			26	1		
Kilrush,	11	50 and 3 to be repaired.	12		31 and 3 to be repaired.	7	12	10d.
Kilrush,	17	31			31			
Scariff,	13	35	35				31	1s.
Tulla,	17	134	66		52	14	67	9d.
Co. CORK.								
Bandon,	16	123 and 11 to be repaired.	68 and 6 repaired.	4	24 and 3 to be repaired.	6 and 2 to be repaired.	66	1s.
Clonakilty,	16	128	116	6	2	5	116	1s.
Cork,	20	230 and 1 to be repaired.	153	11	98 and 1 to be repaired.	24	153	1s.
Dunmanway,	15	187	173	6		6	160	10d.
Fermoy,	21	157	13	137	4	3	10	9d.
Kanturk,	32	320	288	33		3	264	10d.
Kinsale,	13	42	20		22		20	1s.
Macroom,	25	313	251	30	11	21	251	7½d. and 10d.
Mallow,	19	110 and 1 to be repaired.	66	31	11 and 1 to be repaired.	3	54	1s.

TABLE I.—RETURN showing what has been done under improvement schemes authorised—*continued.*

UNIONS.	No. of Electoral Divisions in which the erection of houses has been authorised.	Number of Houses						
		Authorised.	Built.	In progress.	Not yet commenced.	Abandoned.	Actually Let.	Rent (*Weekly*).
PROVINCE OF MUNSTER—*continued.*								
Co. CORK—*continued.*								
Midleton, . . .	19	200	190	4	4	2	126	1s.
Millstreet, . .	12	123	108	.	15	.	108	8d.
Mitchelstown, . .	17	150 and 4 to be repaired.	110	10 and 3 repairing.	23 and 2 to be repaired.	16	104	1s.
Skibbereen, . . .	23	155 and 5 to be repaired.	103 and 5 repaired.	.	48	4	105	9d.
Skull, ...	8	13	11	1	1	.	11	9d.
Youghal, . . .	14	215	48	49	111	7	47	1s.
Co. KERRY.								
Dingle, ...	5	10	.	.	10	.	.	.
Killarney, . . .	27	131	31	86	16	4	31	1s.
Listowel, . . .	51	110	66	15	25	8	60	11d. and 11½d.
Tralee, ...	28	222 and 1 to be repaired.	126	.	33 and 1 to be repaired.	61	125	Average, 9d.
Co. LIMERICK.								
Croom, ...	20	134 and 3 to be repaired.	115 and 3 repaired.	12	.	7	116	9d.
Glin, ...	15	131	66	.	60	5	60	10½d.
Kilmallock, . . .	36	364	286	.	.	78	286	10d. and 1s.
Limerick, . . .	32	393	205	13	42	43	282	11d.
Newcastle, . .	27	265 and 5 to be repaired.	240 and 3 repaired.	10 and 3 repairing	7	8	232	9d. and 10½d.
Rathkeale, . .	18	152	97	.	46	9	97	9d. and 10d.
Co. TIPPERARY.								
Borrisokane, . . .	9	41	28	5	1	7	28	1s. 1d.
Carrick-on-Suir, . .	12	45 and 1 to be repaired.	20	2	2	21 and 1 to be repaired.	19	1s.
Cashel, ...	34	253 and 2 to be repaired.	163 and 2 repaired.	21	20	49	163	10d., 11½d., and 1s. 1d.
Clogheen, . . .	14	107 and 3 to be repaired.	87	14	34 and 2 to be repaired.	9	48	1s.
Clonmel, . . .	11	54 and 6 to be repaired.	33	14	1 and 5 to be repaired.	6	33	1s.
Nenagh, . . .	27	269	246	15	.	8	246	1s.
Thurles, . . .	19	60	15	20	25	.	15	1s.
Tipperary, . . .	28	370	289	12	10	59	289	1s.
Co. WATERFORD.								
Dungarvan, . . .	23	47	46	1	.	1	45	10d.
Kilmacthomas, . .	14	123	103	.	.	20	103	9d.
Lismore, . . .	14	124	57	23	43	2	57	10d.
Waterford, . . .	26	167	54	.	109	4	54	1s.
Total for Munster, .	808	6,515 and 44 to be repaired.	4,327 and 18 repaired.	635 and 5 repairing.	1,055 and 15 to be repaired.	576 and 3 to be repaired.	4,138	.

TABLE I.—RETURN showing what has been done under improvement schemes authorized—*continued.*

UNIONS.	No. of Electoral Divisions in which the erection of houses has been authorized	Number of Houses						
		Authorized.	Built.	In progress.	Not yet commenced.	Abandoned.	Actually Let.	Rent (*Weekly*).
PROVINCE OF LEINSTER.								
CO. CARLOW.								
Carlow,	38	205 and 3 to be repaired.	58 and 1 repaired.	23	78 and 2 to be repaired.	46	59	1s.
CO. DUBLIN.								
Balrothery,	10	53	46	.	3	3	46	Average, 1s. 4d.
Dublin, North,	5	60	36	.	10	14	38	1s. 6d. and 2s.
" South,	8	26	.	26	.	.	.	.
CO. KILDARE.								
Athy,	38	126 and 2 to be repaired.	91 and 2 repaired.	13	4	19	93	1s.
Celbridge,	12	52	17	6	28	1	17	1s.
Naas,	24	104 and 3 to be repaired.	62	2	40 and 3 to be repaired.	.	62	1s.
CO. KILKENNY.								
Callan,	14	35	29	4	1	5	21	8d.
Castlecomer,	4	23	4	18	.	1	4	1s.
Kilkenny,	14	34	.	30	.	4	.	.
Thomastown,	19	60	45	2	13	.	43	8½d.
Urlingford,	15	46	.	.	45	.	.	.
KING'S CO.								
Edenderry,	8	30	.	30	.	.	.	.
Parsonstown,	11	42 and 4 to be repaired.	38 and 2 repaired.	3	.	1 and 1 to be repaired.	41	1s. 6d. and 2s.
Tullamore,	30	104	91	5	8	5	60	1s.
CO. LONGFORD.								
Ballymahon,	17	115	44	28	48	3	48	8d.
Granard,	20	06	58	24	8	1	67	11d.
Longford,	10	46	45	.	.	1	45	11d.
CO. LOUTH.								
Ardee,	13	125 and 3 to be repaired.	62	37	33	8 and 3 to be repaired.	55	1s. 3d.
Drogheda,	12	306 and 8 to be repaired.	239	43	21 and 6 to be repaired.	8	230	1s.
Dundalk,	9	53 and 1 to be repaired.	29	9	15 and 1 to be repaired.	.	18	1s. and 1s. 3d.
CO. MEATH.								
Dunshaughlin,	12	73	64	3	4	5	62	1s.
Kells,	22	198	79	50	69	15	77	1s. 1d.
Navan,	11	212	141	32	2	37	121	1s.
Oldcastle,	14	185	125	57	3	70	125	1s.
Trim,	26	169 and 1 to be repaired.	107 and 2 repaired.	54	20	8	107	1s.
QUEEN'S CO.								
Abbeyleix,	9	35	.	.	25	.	.	.
Mountmellick,	28	38	19	1	16	3	19	1s.

TABLE I.—RETURN showing what has been done under improvement schemes authorized—*continued.*

UNIONS.	No. of Electoral Divisions in which the erection of houses has been authorized.	Number of Houses						
		Authorized.	Built.	In progress.	Not yet commenced.	Abandoned.	Actually Let.	Rent (*Weekly*).
PROVINCE OF LEINSTER—*continued.*								
CO. WESTMEATH.								
Delvin,	19	188	111	12	38	24	111	1s.
Mullingar,	46	240	168	16	49	7	147	10d.
CO. WEXFORD.								
Enniscorthy,	27	156 and 8 to be repaired.	87	6	38 and 8 to be repaired.	23	87	10d.
Gorey,	28	96	60	35	.	2	57	10d.
New Ross,	31	157	20	36	97	14	20	1s.
Wexford,	33	322	258	.	.	64	258	1s.
CO. WICKLOW.								
Baltinglass,	18	68 and 1 to be repaired.	55	9 and 1 repairing	3	3	55	1s.
Rathdrum,	15	42	14	.	24	4	14	1s. 3d.
Shillelagh,	4	19	14	1	1	3	14	1s.
Total for Leinster,	651	3,903 and 33 to be repaired.	2,310 and 7 repaired.	635 and 1 repairing.	715 and 21 to be repaired.	334 and 4 to be repaired.	2,237	.
PROVINCE OF CONNAUGHT.								
CO. GALWAY.								
Ballinasloe,	8	8	1	2	5	.	1	1s. 6d.
Gort,	4	5	.	.	5	.	.	
Loughrea,	2	10	10	.	.	.	10	1s. 3d.
CO. LEITRIM.								
Carrick-on-Shannon,	7	10	4	6	.	1	4	1s.
Manorhamilton,	4	17	17	.	.	.	17	1s. 1d. and 1s. 4d.
Mohill,	7	17	17	.	.	.	17	1s. and 1s. 6d.
CO. ROSCOMMON.								
Roscommon,	2	3	1	2	.	.	.	.
Strokestown,	1	1	.	.	1	.	.	.
CO. SLIGO.								
Dromore West,	5	7	7	.	.	.	7	1s. 1½d.
Total for Connaught,	37	78	67	9	11	1	56	.
TOTAL FOR ALL IRELAND,	1,522	10,860 and 77 to be repaired.	6,717 and 25 repaired.	1,189 and 6 repairing	1,708 and 39 to be repaired.	363 and 7 to be repaired.	5,463	.

TABLE II.—RETURN showing what is proposed to be done under new improvement schemes.

NOTE.—This list includes the applications shown as still pending in the table given at page 37.

UNIONS.	No. of Electoral Divisions comprised in the Schemes.	No. of Cottages, &c., proposed to be provided.	Estimated Cost.
PROVINCE OF ULSTER.			
CO. ANTRIM.			£ s. d.
Ballycastle, ...	3	6	600 0 0
CO. MONAGHAN.			
Carrickmacross, . . .	9	32	4,243 0 0
Total for Ulster, . .	12	38	4,843 0 0
PROVINCE OF MUNSTER.			
CO. CLARE.			
Corrofin, ...	3	4	516 0 0
Ennis, ...	7	35 and 1 allotment,	3,233 0 0
Tulla, ...	13	40	4,021 0 0
CO. CORK.			
Bantry, ...	4	16	949 0 0
Clonakilty, ...	19	146	14,600 0 0
Cork, ...	16	100	14,840 0 0
Fermoy, ...	23	220	32,976 0 0
Macroom, ...	24	277	27,708 0 0
Mallow, ...	8	21	2,700 0 0
Millstreet, ...	8	38	3,880 0 0
Mitchelstown, . . .	1	8	1,040 0 0
Skibbereen, ...	22	166	19,920 0 0
CO. KERRY.			
Kenmare, ...	3	3	311 0 0
Listowel, ...	24	80	6,800 0 0
CO. LIMERICK.			
Croom, ...	30	100 & 8 to be repaired,	11,800 0 0
Kilmallock, ...	28	279 & 6 half-acre allotments.	31,660 0 0
Limerick, ...	28	294 & 13 to be repaired,	23,879 0 0
CO. TIPPERARY.			
Cashel, ...	10	28	2,800 0 0
Roscrea, ...	2	4	481 0 0
Tipperary, ...	39	419	54,470 0 0
CO. WATERFORD.			
Kilmacthomas, . . .	10	127	12,881 0 0
Total for Munster, . .	306	2,303, and 22 to be repaired, and 7 allotments to existing cottages.	£263,831 0 0
PROVINCE OF LEINSTER.			
CO. CARLOW.			
Carlow, ...	3	3	345 0 0
CO. DUBLIN.			
Balrothery, ...	10	78	10,400 0 0
Dublin, North, . . .	2	18	2,820 0 0

Table II.—Return showing what is proposed to be done under new improvement schemes—*continued.*

Note.—This list includes the applications shown as still pending in the table given at page 37.

Unions.	No. of Electoral Divisions comprised in the Schemes.	No. of Cottages proposed to be provided.	Estimated Cost.
PROVINCE OF LEINSTER—*continued.*			
Co. Kildare.			£ s. d.
Celbridge,	3	6	650 0 0
Co. Kilkenny.			
Castlecomer,	3	12	1,200 0 0
Urlingford,	4	4	400 0 0
King's Co.			
Edenderry,	10	13	1,838 11 0
Co. Longford.			
Ballymahon,	8	43	5,848 0 0
Granard,	22	81	8,100 0 0
Longford,	10	61	7,140 0 0
Co. Louth.			
Ardee,	10	58 & 1 to be repaired,	7,010 0 0
Drogheda,	12	72	9,880 0 0
Co. Meath.			
Kells,	11	34	4,875 0 0
Navan,	11	110	17,250 0 0
Trim,	16	65	8,450 0 0
Queen's Co.			
Mountmellick,	19	78	9,890 0 0
Co. Westmeath.			
Delvin,	14	39	5,335 0 0
Mullingar,	20	41	6,380 0 0
Co. Wexford.			
Enniscorthy,	1	1	115 0 0
Gorey,	9	21 & 4 to be repaired,	3,000 0 0
Co. Wicklow.			
Baltinglass,	7	22	2,640 0 0
Shillelagh,	5	32 & 15 to be repaired,	3,840 0 0
Total for Leinster,	209	835 & 20 to be repaired.	£119,097 11 0
PROVINCE OF CONNAUGHT.			
Co. Leitrim.			
Carrick-on-Shannon,	10	24	2,400 0 0
Manorhamilton,	3	9	900 0 0
Total for Connaught,	13	33	3,300 0 0
Total for all Ireland,	540	3,269 and 43 to be repaired, and 7 allotments to existing cottages.	£398,681 17 6

Housing of the Working Classes Act, 1885.

37. In paragraph 35 of our last Report we gave an account of the proceedings that were being taken under the Labouring Classes Lodging Houses and Dwellings Act of 1866, as incorporated with the Housing of the Working Classes Act of 1885, and since that Report we have sanctioned loans of £20,000 to the Corporation of Cork, and £2,200 to the Corporation of Waterford.

These sums, together with the sum of £70,721 19*s.* 8*d.* previously sanctioned, constitute a total of £92,921 19*s.* 8*d.* sanctioned up to the 31st March, 1890, to the various urban sanitary authorities in Ireland under the provisions of the Housing of the Working Classes Act.

In our last Report we mentioned that the Corporation of Dublin had under consideration tenders for the erection of houses for the working classes at Bow-lane, West, for which a loan of £10,325 had been previously sanctioned. These houses, which consist of 86 tenements, have now been completed, and the number of applicants for the dwellings largely exceeds the number of tenements. In Cork, Galway, New Ross, and Waterford, the works for which loans were sanctioned have not as yet been commenced. In Enniskillen a contract has been entered into for the erection of 12 houses. Thirty-seven houses have been completed in the city of Kilkenny and 26 in Wexford all of which are occupied. Nine additional cottages have been completed during the year in the city of Limerick and are occupied.

Artizans and Labourers Dwellings Improvement Acts, 1875 to 1885.

38. No Orders have been made under these Acts since our last annual Report.

Departmental arrangements.

39. Since our last Report we have lost by death the services of one of our medical inspectors, Dr. John Todd; another of our

medical inspectors, Dr. Stewart Woodhouse, resigned, having been appointed as medical member of the General Prisons Board, Ireland. The vacancies thus caused have been filled by the appointment of Dr. Thomas J. Browne, medical officer of the Dungannon dispensary district of Dungannon union, and Dr. Thomas J. Stafford, one of the medical officers of the Boyle dispensary district of Boyle union.

We have the honour to be,

Your Excellency's obedient servants,

ARTHUR JAMES BALFOUR.
HENRY ROBINSON.
GEORGE MORRIS.
F. MACCABE.

APPENDIX

TO THE

EIGHTEENTH ANNUAL REPORT

OF

THE LOCAL GOVERNMENT BOARD FOR IRELAND.

APPENDIX A.

ORDERS, CIRCULARS, AND CORRESPONDENCE UNDER THE POOR LAW ACTS AND OTHER ACTS NOT INCLUDED IN APPENDIX B OR C.

I.—ORDERS.

No. 1.—GENERAL ORDER ASSESSING upon UNIONS in IRELAND the amounts payable by them, respectively, under the Contagious Diseases (Animals) Act.

To the GUARDIANS of the POOR of the several Unions named in the Schedule hereunto annexed; to the Treasurer of each of such Unions, and to all persons whom it may concern.

WHEREAS, by an Act passed in the Forty-second year of the Reign of Her present Majesty, Queen Victoria, entitled "An Act for making better provision respecting Contagious and Infectious Diseases of Cattle and other Animals, and for other purposes," it is among other things enacted that on receipt of the Certificate of the Chief Secretary or Under Secretary to the Lord Lieutenant of Ireland to the effect that a sum equivalent to a certain Poundage, to be specified in such Certificate, on the net annual value of the property in all the Unions in Ireland is required for the purposes of the Act, the Local Government Board shall, by order under their Seal, assess that sum on the several Unions in proportion to the net annual value of the property therein, and the said Board shall transmit copies of the Order to the Guardians and to the Treasurer of each Union:

AND WHEREAS by the said Act it is further enacted that on receipt of such Order the Treasurer of each Union shall, out of the Union funds, pay over the amount assessed on the Union to the Bank of Ireland, to be placed to the General Cattle Diseases Fund, and the Guardians of each Union shall debit the several Electoral Divisions with proportions of that sum according to the net annual value of the property therein:

AND WHEREAS it is provided by the said Act that no larger sum shall be levied under the said Act at any one time than shall be equivalent to a poundage of One Halfpenny in the Pound on the net annual value of the property in all the Unions, nor shall any larger sum be levied under the said Act in the whole than shall be equivalent, taken with any money before the commencement of the said Act carried to the Cattle Plague Account, to a poundage of Fourpence in the Pound on the net annual value of the property in all the Unions:

And Whereas a Certificate under the hand of the Chief Secretary to the Lord Lieutenant, bearing date the Thirteenth day of April One Thousand Eight Hundred and Eighty-nine, has been received by Us, the Local Government Board for Ireland, in which it is certified that a sum of Fourteen Thousand Five Hundred and Twenty-three Pounds Thirteen Shillings and One Farthing sterling, being equivalent to a rating of One Farthing in the Pound on the net annual value of the property in all the Unions in Ireland, is required for the purposes of the said Act:

Now Therefore, in pursuance of the provisions of the said Act, We, the Local Government Board for Ireland, do hereby assess the said sum of Fourteen Thousand Five Hundred and Twenty-three Pounds Thirteen Shillings and One Farthing upon the several Unions in Ireland, in proportion to the net annual value of the property in each Union according to the Valuation thereof now in force as follows; that is to say, we assess upon each Union the amount set opposite to its name in the Schedule hereunto annexed.

Schedule.

Union.	Amount Assessed.			Union.	Amount Assessed.		
	£	s.	d.		£	s.	d.
Abbeyleix,	88	13	9¼	Claremorris,	44	8	2¼
Antrim,	120	18	0¼	Clifden,	18	4	3¾
Ardee,	98	8	0	Clogheen,	66	0	10¼
Armagh,	214	5	5	Clogher,	58	10	10¾
Athlone,	92	1	10	Clonakilty,	53	1	9¼
Athy,	115	13	10	Clones,	59	19	9¼
Bailieborough,	42	1	6	Clonmel,	74	13	2¼
Ballina,	51	10	7¾	Coleraine,	108	8	4½
Ballinasloe,	81	1	4¾	Cookstown,	68	8	6¼
Ballinrobe,	62	10	5¼	Cootehill,	76	6	10¼
Ballycastle,	47	0	4¼	Cork,	371	5	1¼
Ballymahon,	64	10	5¼	Corrofin,	21	4	8¼
Ballymena,	135	4	6¼	Croom,	65	16	10
Ballymoney,	80	16	10¼	Delvin,	55	4	4½
Ballyshannon,	52	13	6¼	Dingle,	25	17	1½
Ballyvaghan,	20	11	11¼	Donegal,	36	17	4
Balrothery,	90	17	0¼	Downpatrick,	185	7	2¾
Baltinglass,	70	16	9¼	Drogheda,	130	5	6½
Banbridge,	165	18	8¾	Dromore West,	38	8	6
Bandon,	70	17	4¾	Dublin North,	424	0	9½
Bantry,	23	5	8¾	Dublin South,	728	12	7¼
Bawnboy,	41	12	3¾	Dundalk,	118	12	9½
Belfast,	804	8	0¼	Dunfanaghy,	11	19	8
Belmullet,	11	0	3¾	Dungannon,	99	9	8
Borrisokane,	43	8	2	Dungarvan,	55	14	8
Boyle,	77	4	9¼	Dunmanway,	34	15	8
Caherciveen,	23	17	2¼	Dunshaughlin,	110	3	4
Callan,	75	5	10¼	Edenderry,	99	8	5¼
Carlow,	136	6	1¼	Ennis,	77	7	7¾
Carrickmacross,	52	10	8¼	Enniscorthy,	115	14	3
Carrick-on-Shannon,	50	4	9¼	Enniskillen,	112	0	11½
Carrick-on-Suir,	81	19	2¼	Ennistymon,	38	10	5
Cashel,	111	19	10¼	Fermoy,	107	13	3¼
Castlebar,	48	10	7½	Galway,	68	10	8
Castleblayney,	78	19	4¾	Glennamaddy,	33	1	4¾
Castlecomer,	33	8	3¾	Glenties,	21	8	8¾
Castlederg,	27	10	11¼	Glin,	29	12	8¼
Castlerea,	76	1	4¾	Gorey,	83	15	3¼
Castletown,	12	10	3	Gort,	44	18	1¼
Cavan,	119	0	2¾	Granard,	89	6	10¼
Celbridge,	119	7	6¾	Inishowen,	40	12	8¾

SCHEDULE—*continued.*

UNION.	Amount Assessed.			UNION.	Amount Assessed.		
	£	s.	d.		£	s.	d.
Irvinestown, . .	51	4	7	Nenagh, . . .	98	4	11½
Kanturk, . . .	80	11	9¾	Newcastle, . . .	65	15	9¼
Kells, . . .	100	13	0	New Ross, . . .	108	17	1½
Kenmare, . . .	20	8	1½	Newry, . . .	177	2	7½
Kilkeel, . . .	40	7	1½	Newtownards, . .	147	10	7½
Kilkenny, . . .	104	0	0½	Oldcastle, . . .	65	6	6½
Killadysert, . .	26	9	2¼	Omagh, . . .	111	14	3¾
Killala, . . .	21	4	10¾	Oughterard, . .	15	10	1¾
Killarney, . . .	80	2	10	Parsonstown, . .	106	18	0½
Kilmacthomas, . .	34	10	3¾	Portumna, . . .	86	16	7½
Kilmallock, . .	148	2	6¼	Rathdown, . . .	232	0	11½
Kilrush, . . .	55	0	8	Rathdrum, . .	133	12	9¼
Kinsale, . . .	62	11	0½	Rathkeale, . . .	58	8	11
Larne, . . .	108	13	9¾	Roscommon, . .	67	4	2¼
Letterkenny, . .	32	18	8½	Roscrea, . . .	93	5	9¼
Limavady, . . .	71	10	0½	Scariff, . . .	27	7	3
Limerick, . . .	205	8	11½	Shillelagh, . . .	52	6	8½
Lisburn, . . .	184	11	10¾	Skibbereen, . .	48	19	2½
Lismore, . . .	52	1	2¼	Skull, . . .	15	15	2
Lisnaskea, . . .	60	9	4	Sligo, . . .	103	5	6¾
Listowel, . . .	56	1	3	Strabane, . . .	112	9	1
Londonderry, . .	170	13	4½	Stranorlar, . .	31	12	11
Longford, . . .	63	4	2½	Strokestown, . .	52	18	3½
Loughrea, . . .	79	9	0	Swineford, . . .	42	14	8½
Lurgan, . . .	150	4	0¾	Thomastown, . .	68	17	9
Macroom, . . .	66	11	11½	Thurles, . . .	84	6	8½
Magherafelt, . .	96	1	8½	Tipperary, . .	148	17	11
Mallow, . . .	110	16	7½	Tobercurry, . .	42	9	4
Manorhamilton, . .	45	8	10¾	Tralee, . . .	91	7	4
Midleton, . . .	98	2	11½	Trim, . . .	113	10	4¾
Milford, . . .	31	4	10½	Tuam, . . .	80	0	7¼
Millstreet, . . .	29	3	5½	Tulla, . . .	34	16	1½
Mitchelstown, . .	51	2	11½	Tullamore, . . .	86	14	6½
Mohill, . . .	41	2	4½	Urlingford, . . .	50	14	4½
Monaghan, . . .	98	18	10¼	Waterford, . . .	160	7	2¼
Mount Bellew, . .	42	1	5¼	Westport, . . .	46	2	11
Mountmellick, . .	107	0	8	Wexford, . . .	112	18	5½
Mullingar, . . .	164	19	11½	Youghal, . . .	62	4	6½
Naas, . . .	159	11	4½				
Navan, . . .	103	7	2¼	Total, . . £	14,523	13	0½

Sealed with our Seal this Sixth day of May in the year of Our Lord One Thousand Eight Hundred and Eighty-nine.

(Signed), GEORGE MORRIS.
F. MACCABE.

LONDONDERRY.

We, Charles Stewart, Marquess of Londonderry, Lord Lieutenant-General and General Governor of Ireland, do hereby approve this Order.

By Command of His Excellency,

WEST RIDGEWAY.

No. 2.—General Order Assessing upon Contributory Unions under the National School Teachers Act their respective proportions of Results Fees for the year ending 31st March, 1890.

To the Guardians of the Poor of the several Unions named in the Schedule to this Order; to the Treasurer of each of such Unions, and to all persons whom it may concern:

Whereas We, the Local Government Board for Ireland, have received from the Commissioners of National Education an estimate for the year ending the 31st day of March, 1890, of the full amount payable as Results Fees in respect of Pupils attending the National Schools in each of the Unions which have become contributory Unions under an Act passed in the Thirty-ninth year of the Reign of Her present Majesty, Queen Victoria, entitled "An Act to provide for additional Payments to Teachers of National Schools in Ireland":

And Whereas the Unions which have become contributory under the said Act are those of which the names are placed in the first column of the Schedule hereto:

And Whereas by the said Act it is enacted that the Commissioners of National Education shall require the Local Government Board in every year to provide a sum equal to one-third of such full amount payable as Results Fees as aforesaid, and that the said Local Government Board shall thereafter provide such sum in the manner by the said Act prescribed; and the Local Government Board have received from the Commissioners of National Education a requisition to provide, in the year 1889–90, a sum equal to one-third of such full amount aforesaid:

And Whereas it is by the said Act further enacted that upon the receipt of every such estimate the Local Government Board shall by an Order under their Seal assess upon each contributory union a sum equal to one-third of the full amount payable as results fees in respect of pupils attending the National Schools in such contributory union, and shall transmit a copy of such Order to the guardians and likewise to the treasurer of such contributory union, stating the amount so assessed on such contributory union:

And Whereas it is by the said Act further enacted that forthwith on the receipt of such Order by the treasurer of any contributory union he shall, out of the funds then lying in his hands to the credit of the guardians of such union, or, if there shall be then no sufficient assets, out of the moneys next received by him and placed to the credit of such guardians, pay over the amount so assessed on such contributory union to the Bank of Ireland, to be there placed to the credit of the Commissioners of Education to a separate account, to be entitled "The Results Fees Account:" and that the guardians of such contributory union shall in their account with the electoral divisions of such contributory union debit each electoral division with its proportion of the said amount according to the net annual value for the time being of the property rateable to the rates for the relief of the destitute poor in each such division:

And Whereas it is provided by the said Act that if in any financial year the sum provided by the Local Government Board in respect of any contributory union exceeds the amount required for the purposes of the Act in such year in respect of such contributory union such overplus shall be carried to the credit of the next following financial year, and in such last-mentioned year only such sum shall be raised by assessment on such contributory union as shall be necessary in addition thereto to make up the sum which would in the ordinary course under the said Act be required to be provided by the Local Government Board in respect of such contributory union in such next following year:

AND WHEREAS we have received from the Commissioners of National Education a statement of the surplus of previous assessments, as set forth in the fourth column of the Schedule hereto:

NOW THEREFORE, in pursuance of the powers vested in us by the said Act, We do hereby assess upon each of the unions named in the first column of the Schedule hereto the amount set opposite to its name in the fifth column, such sum being equal to one-third of such full amount payable as Results Fees as aforesaid by such union as set forth in the second column of the said Schedule, less the amount of surplus of previous assessments as set forth in the fourth column.

SCHEDULE.—CONTRIBUTORY POOR LAW UNIONS.

Name of Union.	Full amount of Results Fees payable to the Teachers of National Schools situated in Union. (Estimated.)			Amount equal to one-third of the full amount of estimated Results Fees.			Surplus of previous Assessments.			Amount assessed on each Union, being one-third of the full amount of estimated Results Fees less amount of surplus of previous Assessments.		
1st Column.	2nd Column.			3rd Column.			4th Column.			5th Column.		
	£	s.	d.	£	s.	d.	£	s.	d.	£	s.	d.
Ballymahon,	933	11	8	311	3	10	14	3	10	297	0	0
Ballyvaghan,	474	0	0	158	0	0		—		158	0	0
Balrothery,	1,350	0	0	450	0	0		—		450	0	0
Belfast,	20,079	18	9	6,693	6	3	441	6	3	6,252	0	0
Castlecomer,	1,009	0	9	336	6	11	35	6	11	301	0	0
Clogheen,	1,739	7	6	579	15	10	67	15	10	512	0	0
Clogher,	974	15	9	324	18	7	16	18	7	308	0	0
Cork,	9,540	17	6	3,182	19	2	492	19	2	2,690	0	0
Croom,	1,378	19	3	459	13	1	49	13	1	410	0	0
Delvin,	643	3	0	214	7	8	42	7	8	172	0	0
Downpatrick,	3,276	1	6	1,092	0	6	51	0	6	1,041	0	0
Dungannon,	2,126	12	9	708	17	7	69	17	7	639	0	0
Edenderry,	943	17	3	314	12	5	143	12	5	171	0	0
Enniskillen,	2,848	14	6	949	11	6	66	11	6	883	0	0
Inishowen,	1,176	7	0	392	2	4	110	2	4	282	0	0
Irvinestown,	1,103	11	9	367	10	7	5	10	7	362	0	0
Kells,	1,610	1	6	536	13	10	106	13	10	430	0	0
Killarney,	4,419	0	0	1,473	0	0		—		1,473	0	0
Kilmallock,	2,979	0	0	993	0	0	152	0	0	841	0	0
Milford,	833	4	6	277	14	10	18	14	10	259	0	0
Mountmellick,	1,629	0	0	543	0	0		—		543	0	0
Mullingar,	2,025	8	0	675	2	8	23	2	8	652	0	0
Navan,	1,669	14	6	556	11	6	94	11	6	462	0	0
Newry,	3,238	5	9	1,079	0	7	134	8	7	945	0	0
Oldcastle,	1,707	0	0	569	0	0	99	0	0	470	0	0
Skibbereen,	3,510	0	0	1,170	0	0		—		1,170	0	0
Sligo,	3,607	9	0	1,203	9	8	68	9	0	1,134	0	0
Strabane,	1,924	7	9	641	9	3	70	9	3	571	0	0
Tipperary,	3,654	0	0	1,218	0	0	118	0	0	1,100	0	0
Trim,	1,454	17	6	484	19	2	49	19	2	435	0	0
Tullamore,	1,787	16	9	595	18	11	4	18	11	591	0	0

Sealed with our Seal this Eleventh day of May in the year of Our Lord One Thousand Eight Hundred and Eighty-nine.

(Signed), HENRY ROBINSON.
GEORGE MORRIS.
F. MACCABE.

LONDONDERRY.

We, CHARLES STEWART, Marquess of Londonderry, Lord Lieutenant-General and General Governor of Ireland, do hereby approve this Order.

By Command of His Excellency,

W. RIDGEWAY.

II. CIRCULARS.

No. 1.—The Poor Law Act, 1889.

Local Government Board, Dublin,
14th October, 1889.

Sir,—The Local Government Board for Ireland forward, for the information of the Board of Guardians, copies of the 1st and 9th sections of the Act 52 & 53 Vic., cap. 56, entitled "The Poor Law Act, 1889," which received the Royal Assent on the 30th of August last. The sections quoted apply to Ireland:—

1.—(1.) Where a child is maintained by the guardians of any union and was deserted by its parent, the guardians may at any time resolve that such child shall be under the control of the guardians until it reaches the age, if a boy, of sixteen, and, if a girl, of eighteen years, and thereupon until the child reaches that age all the powers and rights of such parent in respect of that child shall, subject as in this Act mentioned, vest in the guardians;

Provided that the guardians may rescind such resolution, if they think that it will be for the benefit of the child that it should be rescinded, or may permit such child to be either permanently or temporarily under the control of such parent, or of any other relative, or of any friend.

(2.) A court of summary jurisdiction, if satisfied on complaint made by a parent of the child that the child has not been maintained by the guardians, or was not deserted by such parent, or that it is for the benefit of the child that it should be either permanently or temporarily under the control of such parent, or that the resolution of the guardians should be determined, may make an order accordingly, and any such order shall be complied with by the guardians, and, if the order determines the resolution, the resolution shall be thereby determined as from the date of the order, and the guardians shall cease to have the rights and powers of the parent as respects such child.

(3.) For the purposes of this Act a child shall be deemed to be maintained by the guardians if it is wholly or partly maintained by them in a workhouse or in any district school, separate school, separate infirmary, sick asylum, hospital for infectious diseases, institution for the deaf, dumb, blind, or idiots, or any certified school under the Act of the session of the twenty-fifth and twenty-sixth years of the reign of Her present Majesty, chapter forty-three, or is boarded out by the guardians, whether within or without the limits of the union.

(4.) Where a parent is imprisoned under a sentence of penal servitude or imprisonment in respect of an offence committed against a child this section shall apply as if such child had been deserted by that parent.

(5.) Nothing in this section shall relieve any person from any liability to contribute to the maintenance of a child, but the fact of such contribution being made shall not deprive the guardians of any of the powers and rights conferred on them by this section.

(6.) Nothing in this section shall authorize the guardians to cause a child to be educated in any religious creed other than that in which the child would have been educated but for any resolution of the guardians under this section, nor affect the enactments respecting the religious education of a child maintained by the guardians, or respecting the right of any minister of the same religious persuasion as the child to visit and instruct the child, nor affect any of the enactments specified in the schedule to this Act, which enactments relate to the religious education of children maintained by guardians.

9. The section of this Act relating to the control of the guardians of a union over a child deserted by its parents, but no other section, shall apply to Ireland, and in such application of the said section to Ireland,—

(*a.*) The word "guardians" means the board of guardians of the poor for a union under the provisions of the Act of the session of the first and second years of the reign of Her present Majesty, chapter fifty-six, intituled an "Act for the more effectual relief of the destitute Poor in Ireland," and the Acts amending the same:

The word "union" means a union for the relief of the destitute poor under the provisions of the said Acts:

(*b.*) A court of summary jurisdiction shall be constituted of two or more justices of the peace in petty sessions, sitting at a place appointed for holding petty sessions, or of some magistrate or officer for the time being empowered by law to do alone any act authorized to be done by more than one justice of the peace, and sitting at some court or other place appointed for the administration of justice.

SCHEDULE.

Acts relating to Ireland.

Session and Chapter.	Title of Act.	Section referred to.
1 & 2 Vict., c. 56, . .	An Act for the more effectual relief of the destitute poor in Ireland.	Section forty-nine.
25 & 26 Vict., c. 83, .	An Act to amend the laws in force for the relief of the destitute poor in Ireland, and to continue the powers of the Commissioners.	Sections eight and eleven.
39 & 40 Vict., c. 38, .	An Act to extend the limits of age up to which, with the assent of boards of guardians, orphan and deserted pauper children may be supported out of workhouses in Ireland.	Section two

I am, sir, your obedient servant,

THOS. A. MOONEY, Secretary.

To the Clerk of each Union.

No. 2.—The Prevention of Cruelty to, and Protection of, Children Act, 1889; and the Technical Instruction Act, 1889.

Local Government Board, Dublin,
11th November, 1889.

Sir,

I am directed by the Local Government Board for Ireland to forward herewith, for the information of the Sanitary Authority, a copy of the "Prevention of Cruelty to, and Protection of, Children Act, 1889," 52 & 53 Vic., cap. 44, and of the "Technical Instruction Act, 1889," 52 & 53 Vic., cap. 76.

I am, sir, your obedient servant,
Thos. A. Mooney, Secretary.

To the Executive Sanitary Officer to each
Sanitary Authority, Urban and Rural.

No. 3.—National School Teachers (Ireland) Act.

Local Government Board, Dublin,
31st December, 1889.

Sir,—In pursuance of the 4th Section of "The National School Teachers (Ireland) Act, 1875," the Local Government Board for Ireland transmit to you herewith, to be laid before the Board of Guardians of   Union, the Notice which they are required by that Section to transmit, on or before the 1st day of January, to the Guardians of every Union which shall not at such time be a contributory Union within the meaning of the Act.

The Notice now transmitted, as in the case of the Notice which was transmitted on the 31st December, 1888, requires the Guardians within forty days from the receipt thereof to inform the Local Government Board whether, for the purpose of increasing the remuneration of the Teachers of National Schools within the Union, they are willing to make their Union a contributory Union within the meaning of the Act, and the Guardians will observe therefore that by the present Notice they are now called upon, in pursuance of the requirement of the Act, to decide whether they will become contributory for the year 1890-91, (that is for the year commencing on the 1st April next), and subsequent years, until the resolution to contribute be legally revoked.

The Board forwarded with their Circular of the 30th August, 1875, a copy of the Act and of various other Documents relating to this subject, and they desire to refer the Board of Guardians to that Circular and the Documents which accompanied it for any information which they may require before replying to the enclosed Notice.

The Board have to add that the Commissioners of National Education have furnished them with an estimate of the probable amount which will be payable by the Guardians of the several Unions in Results Fees to Teachers of National Schools within the respective Unions for the year 1890-91, and the liability which, according to this Estimate, the Guardians will incur by making their Union a contributory one is not expected to exceed £

In the event of the Guardians resolving to become a contributory Union within the meaning of the Act, you should, immediately upon the passing of such resolution, forward a copy of the same signed by the Chairman as well as by yourself to the Commissioners of National Education, and to the Local Government Board, in accordance with the terms of Section 6 of the Act.

I am, sir, your obedient servant,

THOS. A. MOONEY, Secretary.

To the Clerk Union.

ENCLOSURE TO THE FOREGOING.

Notice in pursuance of Section 4 of "The National School Teachers (Ireland) Act, 1875," 38 and 39 Vic., c. 96.

The Guardians of Union are hereby required, within forty days after the receipt hereof, to inform the Local Government Board for Ireland whether, for the purpose of increasing the remuneration of the Teachers of National Schools within the Union, they are willing to become a contributory Union within the meaning of "The National School Teachers (Ireland) Act," (38 and 39 Vic., c. 96).

By order of the Board,

THOS. A. MOONEY, Secretary.

31st December, 1889.

No. 4.—RECOUPMENT, FROM PARLIAMENTARY GRANT, IN RESPECT OF MEDICAL AND EDUCATIONAL EXPENDITURE IN UNIONS.

Local Government Board, Dublin,
14th February, 1890.

SIR,—I am directed by the Local Government Board for Ireland to state, for the information of Boards of Guardians, that their attention has been drawn to the fact that in some cases expenditure incurred in workhouses for articles such as whiskey, tobacco, snuff, and particular kinds of soap has been included under the head of "Cost of Medicine and Medical and Surgical Appliances" in the statement of Medical and Educational Expenditure furnished half-yearly to this Department with the view of obtaining recoupment in respect thereof from the Parliamentary Grant.

The Board think it necessary, therefore, to point out that no expenditure should be included in the statement referred to, under the heading above quoted, excepting the cost of Medicines and Drugs and Medical and Surgical Appliances, and they request that when preparing the statement in future for transmission to this Department you will be careful to observe this direction.

I am, sir, your obedient servant,

Thos. A. Mooney, Secretary.

To the Clerk of each Union.

No. 5.—Annual Election of Chairmen of Boards of Guardians.

Local Government Board, Dublin,
3rd March, 1890.

Sir,—The Local Government Board for Ireland have observed that it occurred in some Unions, upon the occasion of the election of Chairmen of the Board of Guardians after the last General Election of Guardians for the Union, that either the Clerk of the Union or some Guardian other than one of the Chairmen of the previous year acted as Chairman until the election of a Chairman for the current year took place.

The Board, therefore, consider it necessary to direct the attention of Boards of Guardians to article 3 of the General Order for regulating the Meetings and Proceedings of Boards of Guardians in Ireland, in which it is expressly provided that the Chairman, Vice-Chairman, and Deputy Vice-Chairman, when elected, shall, respectively, continue to hold their offices until the election of a Chairman, Vice-Chairman, and Deputy Vice-Chairman following the next Annual or General Election of Guardians shall take place, unless they shall previously die, resign, become incapable, or be disqualified by ceasing to be Guardians of the Union.

If, on the day fixed by the General Order above referred to for the election of Chairmen, the Chairman, Vice-Chairman, or Deputy Vice-Chairman of the previous year continues to be a Guardian and is present at the Meeting, he should preside until the Guardians elect a Chairman for the ensuing year, but if the Chairman, Vice-Chairman, and Deputy Vice-Chairman of the previous year have all ceased to be Guardians, or are absent from the Meeting, the Guardians present should elect one of themselves to preside, temporarily, at the Meeting until the election of a Chairman takes place.

On the Chairman being elected, he should, if present, take the Chair before the Guardians proceed to the election of Vice-Chairman and Deputy Vice-Chairman.

The Board request that you will bring this communication before the Guardians upon the occasion of the election of Chairmen for the ensuing year.

I am, sir, your obedient servant,

THOS. A. MOONEY, Secretary.

To the Clerk of each Union.

III.—CORRESPONDENCE, &c.

DISSOLUTION of BOARDS of GUARDIANS.

1, PORTUMNA UNION.—LETTER TO GUARDIANS.

Local Government Board, Dublin,
25th October, 1889.

SIR,—The Local Government Board for Ireland have had under consideration the financial condition of the Portumna Union, and a Report on the subject which they have received from their Inspector, Mr. Bourke.

The Local Government Board would refer to the letters addressed to the Board of Guardians on the 5th of April and 3rd of May last, in which they alluded to the Guardians' maladministration of the affairs of their Union, and the Board now regret to find that its condition continues to be in the highest degree unsatisfactory owing to the failure of the Guardians to make and levy sufficient rates in due time.

The rate to meet the requirements of the Union to the 29th of September last, which ought to have been put in course of collection early in the year, was not made by the Guardians till the month of June, and the Board observe from Mr. Bourke's Report that on the 14th instant the Guardians were in debt to contractors, officers, and others to the amount of about £1,900, while there was a balance of £72 against the Guardians at foot of the Treasurer's account in the Union ledger. To meet these debts there is only £1,937 of rate outstanding, with a further sum of about £280 payable to the Guardians this year in respect of the Parliamentary Grant and the sale of farm produce, and it will thus be seen that even if all these assets were now available the money at the disposal of the Guardians would only be about sufficient to meet existing liabilities, leaving barely any funds for the future expenditure of the Union.

Mr. Bourke also informs the Board that out-door relief ordered by the Guardians has not been paid from want of funds, and he makes the following statement in his Report:—

"The Union Treasurer refuses to honour any of the cheques issued by the Guardians unless there are funds in his hands sufficient to meet them, and I may mention that at this date a year's salary is due to both the chaplains of the Workhouse and to the Sisters of Charity (four in number) in the Hospital, and half a year's salary due to all the other officers of the Union, with the exception of one Relieving Officer who is owed only one quarter's salary. In consequence of the bad financial condition of the Union no one would tender for the supply of straw to the Union (a most necessary article), and the turf contractors are not sending in the supply of turf, which has to be bought from any one who brings it and is willing to wait for payment.

"A good supply of clothing, bedding, &c., is badly required, the children being almost in rags, and most of them dressed in their own clothes (such as they are) and not in suits belonging to the Union. Only one person has tendered for the supply of clothing, bedding, &c., and the Guardians have now advertised again for tenders for these articles in the expectation that others may be found ready to come forward. Meanwhile winter is approaching, and the inmates both healthy and sick must consequently suffer if the existing state of affairs continues."

Having regard to the manner in which the Union has been mismanaged and the state into which it has been brought by the present Board of Guardians, the Local Government Board are of opinion that the duties of the Guardians have not been duly and effectually discharged according to the intention of the Irish Poor Relief Acts, and the Local Government Board have therefore felt it necessary to make an order dissolving the Board of Guardians, and they will appoint paid officers to carry into execution the provisions of the Poor Law, Medical Charities, and Public Health Acts in the Portumna Union.

A copy of the Order is enclosed.

I am, Sir,

Your obedient servant

THOS. A. MOONEY, Secretary.

To the Clerk, Portumna Union.

ENCLOSURE REFERRED TO IN THE FOREGOING.

(ORDER DISSOLVING BOARD OF GUARDIANS.)

PORTUMNA UNION.

To the GUARDIANS of the POOR of the PORTUMNA UNION; To the CLERK of the said UNION, and to all other Persons whom it may concern:

WHEREAS, through the default of the Board of Guardians of the Portumna Union, the duties of the Board of Guardians of the said Union have not been duly and effectually discharged according to the intention of the Acts in force for the Relief of the Destitute Poor in Ireland:

NOW THEREFORE, We, the Local Government Board for Ireland, do hereby, in exercise of the powers by the said Acts vested in Us in this behalf, declare the said Board of Guardians to be dissolved, and the said Board is hereby dissolved accordingly.

Sealed with our Seal this Twenty-fifth day of October in the Year of Our Lord One Thousand Eight Hundred and Eighty-nine.

(Signed),

HENRY ROBINSON.

F. MACCABE.

2.—Cork Union.—Letter to Guardians.

Local Government Board,
Dublin, 22nd January, 1890.

Sir,

The Local Government Board for Ireland have had under consideration the proceedings of the Board of Guardians of the Cork Union at their meetings on the 9th and 16th instant, from which the Board find that on the former day the duties of the Guardians were not discharged by reason of the introduction of topics foreign to the administration of the business of the Union, and that on the latter the rules of the Local Government Board relating to the transaction of the Guardians' business were deliberately violated and set at naught.

The 14th Article of the General Order of the Local Government Board expressly directs that no matter or question shall be brought forward at a Guardians' meeting until all the business of the meeting comprised in the order of proceedings laid down in that rule shall first have been disposed of, but it appears that on the 9th instant a resolution unconnected with the business of the Union was proposed before the ordinary business was concluded, and on the Chairman very properly refusing to put the resolution the Guardians present adjourned the meeting. By reason of this course of action much of the ordinary business was postponed, and by a return obtained from the Clerk of the Union it appears that several important and pressing matters were not attended to.

On the 16th instant a resolution quite unconnected with the administration of the affairs of the Union was again proposed before the ordinary business was transacted, and on the Chairman very properly refusing to receive it a long and unseemly discussion took place which continued up to a late hour, and the Chairman and other Guardians having left the room the resolution referred to was then proposed and carried, and the General Order above mentioned was thus wilfully and deliberately infringed.

It must be borne in mind that on several former occasions the Local Government Board have found it necessary to remonstrate with the Guardians in regard to the manner in which the business of the Union was neglected in consequence of discussions having arisen on political and other questions altogether unconnected with their duties as Guardians. On the 18th of January and 14th of November, 1888, the Local Government Board addressed the Guardians in regard to their violation of the General Order regulating the meetings and proceedings of the Board of Guardians, and on the 7th of August, 1889, the Board had occasion to write again to the Guardians pointing out that owing to the disorderly opposition to the ruling of the Chairman at the meeting on the 1st of that month, and the consequent adjournment of the Board, the meeting broke up, leaving much important business undone. On that occasion the Local Government Board stated:—

"The Local Government Board are determined not to allow such a course of action to be pursued, or permit the business of the Union to be neglected by repeated attempts to infringe the provisions of the General Order regulating the Guardians' proceedings at their meetings, and the Board now warn the Guardians that if, through their default, the duties which devolve upon them are not in future duly and effectually discharged according to the intention of the Irish Poor Relief Acts, the Board will be reluctantly compelled to dissolve the Board of Guardians and appoint paid officers to administer the affairs of the Union."

Notwithstanding that communication, the Local Government Board were again obliged, on the 2nd of October, to address the Guardians respecting their continued disregard of the Order regulating their proceedings, and their neglect to discharge certain important duties devolving on them. In that letter the Local Government Board stated:—

"It is evident, however, that the legitimate business of a Union so important as that of Cork cannot be permitted to remain neglected to the detriment of the poor and the injury of the ratepayers, and the Local Government Board desire now to address a final warning to the Guardians, and to state that if without sufficient reason they continue to leave undischarged the important functions entrusted to them the Local Government Board will feel compelled to relieve them of duties which they appear unable or unwilling to continue to fulfil in the manner prescribed in the regulations governing their proceedings."

The Board regret now to find that their repeated warnings have had no effect, and they are compelled to abandon all hope that the management of the affairs of the Cork Union will be carried on with regularity and in accordance with law by the present Board of Guardians. The Local Government Board, therefore, feel it to be their duty, in the exercise of their powers under the 18th section of the Irish Poor Relief Extension Act, to dissolve the Board of Guardians and to appoint paid officers to carry into execution the provisions of the Poor Law, Medical Charities and Public Health Acts in the Cork Union.

A copy of the Order dissolving the Board of Guardians is forwarded to you herewith.

I am, sir, your obedient servant,

THOS. A. MOONEY, Secretary.

To the Clerk, Cork Union.

ENCLOSURE REFERRED TO IN THE FOREGOING.

(ORDER DISSOLVING BOARD OF GUARDIANS.)

CORK UNION.

To the GUARDIANS of the POOR of the CORK UNION; to the CLERK of the said UNION, and to all other persons whom it may concern:

WHEREAS, through the default of the Board of Guardians of the Cork Union, the duties of the Board of Guardians of the said Union have not been duly and effectually discharged according to the intention of the Acts in force for the Relief of the Destitute Poor in Ireland:

NOW THEREFORE, We, the Local Government Board for Ireland, do hereby, in exercise of the powers by the said Acts vested in Us in this behalf, declare the said Board of Guardians to be dissolved, and the said Board is hereby dissolved accordingly.

Sealed with our Seal this Twenty-second day of January in the Year of Our Lord One Thousand Eight Hundred and Ninety.

(Signed), HENRY ROBINSON.
GEORGE MORRIS.
F. MACCABE.

PROBATE DUTIES GRANT.

3.—REGULATIONS made under Section 4 of the Probate Duties (Scotland and Ireland) Act, 1888.

By the LORD LIEUTENANT-GENERAL and GENERAL GOVERNOR of IRELAND.

LONDONDERRY.

WHEREAS, by the "Probate Duties (Scotland and Ireland) Act, 1888," section 4, it is amongst other things provided that the sums paid or distributed under that Act in Ireland shall be paid and distributed in such manner and in accordance with such Regulations as the Lord Lieutenant for Ireland from time to time makes:

AND WHEREAS it is further provided, by the aforesaid section, that where any proportion or amount is to be certified, or where any question arises as to what costs, salaries, remuneration, allowances, or officers are to be included in ascertaining such proportion or amount, the proportion or amount shall be ascertained and the question determined in such manner as is for the time being directed by the Regulations made under that section:

NOW THEREFORE, We, Charles Stewart, Marquess of Londonderry, Lord Lieutenant-General and General Governor of Ireland, in pursuance of the powers vested in Us by the said Act, do hereby direct that the following Regulations shall be observed in the payment and distribution of all sums that shall be paid and distributed in Ireland under the provisions of the said Act:—

1. The sum of £5,000, named in the Probate Duties (Scotland and Ireland) Act, 1888, as payable to the Royal Dublin Society for the improvement of the breed of horses and cattle, shall be paid to that Society as soon after the 1st of January in each year as the Lord Lieutenant shall direct.

The sum of £5,000 shall be expended by the Royal Dublin Society under Regulations to be drawn up by the Council of the Society and submitted to the Lord Lieutenant each year for His Excellency's approval; and the Society shall submit to the Lord Lieutenant an annual account of the money so expended.

2. The Local Government Board for Ireland (hereinafter called the Local Government Board) shall prepare and submit to the Lord Lieutenant as soon after the 31st day of March, 1889, as may be practicable:—

(*a*) A certificate showing the amount expended by the Guardians of each Poor Law Union during the financial year ending the 29th day of September, 1887, on the salaries, remuneration, and superannuation allowances of officers of the Union in connexion with the Relief of the Poor, and under the Act 14 & 15 Vic., cap. 68, entitled an Act to provide for the better distribution, support, and management of Medical Charities in Ireland, &c.

(*b*) A certificate showing the amount expended out of any cess or rate by each Road Authority in Ireland on roads and bridges within its jurisdiction during the year ending the 31st day of December, 1887.

3[a]. * * * * * * * * *

a. See Regulation made on the 8th of July, 1889—pages 63–4.

4. The particulars for the preparation of the Certificates of Expenditure by Guardians of Poor Law Unions shall be taken from the Abstracts received by the Local Government Board of the Audited Accounts of the several Unions for the two half-years ended the 25th day of March, and the 29th day of September, 1887, respectively.

The particulars for the preparation of the Certificates of Expenditure by Road Authorities shall be obtained on a form to be prescribed by the Local Government Board, and to be issued to the several Road Authorities by that Board, which the several Road Authorities are hereby required to fill up and return to the Local Government Board within such time as shall be specified in the said form.

5. The Certificates to be furnished by the Local Government Board in accordance with the foregoing Regulations shall ascertain, and state in a column for the purpose, the amount of the Grant to which each Board of Guardians and Road Authority is entitled in respect of the financial year ending the 31st of March, 1889, such amounts to be calculated in the manner provided in section 3 of the said Act, and on receiving an intimation of the Lord Lieutenant's approval of such grants, the Local Government Board shall cause payment thereof to be made in the manner hereinafter provided.

6. In each subsequent year the Local Government Board shall, as soon after the 31st day of March as may be practicable, ascertain and submit to the Lord Lieutenant a statement showing the amount of the Grant to which each Board of Guardians and Road Authority is entitled in respect of the financial year ending on that day, such amounts to be calculated in the manner provided in section 3 of the said Act, and on receiving an intimation of the Lord Lieutenant's approval of such grants the Local Government Board shall cause payment thereof to be made in the manner hereinafter provided.

7[a]. * * * * * * *

Given at Her Majesty's Castle of Dublin, this 21st day of March, 1889.

By His Excellency's Command.

(Signed), W. S. B. Kaye

By the Lord Lieutenant-General and General Governor of Ireland.

Londonderry.

Whereas, by the "Probate Duties (Scotland and Ireland) Act, 1888," section 4, it is amongst other things provided that the sums paid or distributed under that Act in Ireland shall be paid and distributed in such manner, and in accordance with such Regulations as the Lord Lieutenant for Ireland from time to time makes.

a. See Regulation made on the 10th of April, 1889—page 63

And Whereas, Regulations for the purpose aforesaid were accordingly made on the 21st day of March, 1889*, which it is now deemed advisable to alter.

Now Therefore, We, Charles Stewart, Marquess of Londonderry, Lord Lieutenant-General and General Governor of Ireland, in pursuance of the powers vested in Us by the said Act, do hereby order and direct that paragraph 7 of the said Regulations be cancelled, and that the following paragraph be substituted therefor, and the Regulations therein contained shall be observed in the payment and distribution of sums payable to the several Boards of Guardians and Road Authorities in Ireland under the provisions of the said Act:—

7. To give effect to the foregoing Regulations, the Chief Secretary's Office shall, from time to time, on receipt from the Local Government Board of a statement, in accordance with the foregoing Regulations, of the amount of the Grant to which each Board of Guardians and Road Authority is entitled, and of negotiable Receipts drawn out by the Local Government Board, make orders requiring the Governor and Company of the Bank of Ireland to pay out of the Local Taxation (Ireland) Account in that Bank the sums payable to the several Boards of Guardians and Road Authorities: and the Governor and Company of the Bank of Ireland, after receipt of each such order, are hereby authorized to pay such sums accordingly. Upon making such orders the negotiable Receipts shall be signed by the Under Secretary or Assistant Under Secretary to the Lord Lieutenant, and returned to the Local Government Board for distribution to the several bodies referred to.

Given at Her Majesty's Castle of Dublin, this 16th day of April, 1889.

By His Excellency's Command.

(Signed), West Ridgeway.

By the Lords Justices-General and General Governors of Ireland.

Edward Saxe-Weimar, General.

Hedges Eyre Chatterton.

Whereas by the "Probate Duties (Scotland and Ireland) Act, 1888," section 4, it is amongst other things provided that the sums paid or distributed under that Act in Ireland shall be paid and distributed in such manner and in accordance with such Regulations as the Lord Lieutenant for Ireland from time to time makes.

And whereas Regulations for the purpose aforesaid were accordingly made on the 21st day of March, 1889*, which it is now deemed advisable to alter:

Now therefore, We, the Lords Justices General and General Governors of Ireland, in pursuance of the powers vested in Us by the said Act, do hereby order and direct that paragraph 8 of the said Regulations

* See pages 61–2.

be cancelled, and that the following paragraph be substituted therefor, and that the Regulations therein contained shall be observed in the payment and distribution of sums payable to the several Boards of Guardians and Road Authorities in Ireland under the provisions of the said Act:—

3. In the Certificates of Expenditure by the Guardians of the Poor Law Unions, to be furnished by the Local Government Board in pursuance of the foregoing Regulation, the following expenses shall be included:—

I. The salaries of Workhouse Officers, and the value of the rations allowed to them by the Guardians.

II. The salaries of Relieving Officers as such.

III. The salaries of Clerks of Unions as such.

IV. The salaries of Returning Officers.

V. The salaries of Medical Officers of Dispensary Districts as such.

VI. The salaries of Apothecaries and Midwives of Dispensary Districts.

VII. All Superannuation Allowances paid from the Poor Rates.

In the Certificates of Expenditure by Road Authorities, the following expenses shall be included:—

I. Expenses incurred in respect of roads and bridges within the jurisdiction of each Road Authority, whether in constructing new roads or bridges or in repairing or maintaining old ones, including the cost of cleaning and scavenging, but not of watering roads and bridges.

II. Payments made by a Road Authority on account of, or for interest on, any loan obtained by such Authority for, and expended on constructing, maintaining or repairing roads or bridges within its jurisdiction, but not any expenditure defrayed out of a loan.

If any question shall arise as to what costs, salaries, remuneration, allowances or officers are to be included in any such certificate, such question shall be determined by the Local Government Board.

Given at Her Majesty's Castle of Dublin, this 8th day of July, 1889.

By Their Excellencies' Command,

W. S. B. KAYE.

4.—Schedule of Sums authorized to be paid to Unions in Ireland, being the amounts payable to the Guardians in respect of the Probate Duties Grant for the year ended 31st of March, 1889.

Union.	Amount.			Union.	Amount.		
	£	s.	d.		£	s.	d.
Abbeyleix,	371	9	6	Donegal,	224	16	8
Antrim,	382	13	6	Downpatrick,	390	14	5
Ardee,	368	15	11	Drogheda,	435	10	4
Armagh,	409	17	9	Dromore, West,	182	18	9
Athlone,	382	13	8	Dublin, North,	1,848	7	5
Athy,	464	14	11	Dublin, South,	2,591	6	5
Bailieborough,	210	19	0	Dundalk,	418	0	1
Ballina,	257	4	8	Dunfanaghy,	147	7	5
Ballinasloe,	407	0	10	Dungannon,	295	4	8
Ballinrobe,	290	7	3	Dungarvan,	374	8	1
Ballycastle,	201	4	2	Dunmanway,	237	10	0
Ballymahon,	213	12	7	Dunshaughlin,	286	9	3
Ballymena,	463	1	4	Edenderry,	368	15	11
Ballymoney,	269	13	1	Ennis,	405	5	11
Ballyshannon,	223	2	7	Enniscorthy,	455	16	2
Ballyvaghan,	124	9	6	Enniskillen,	415	11	4
Balrothery,	427	19	10	Ennistymon,	233	2	4
Baltinglass,	311	6	2	Fermoy,	421	18	0
Banbridge,	358	1	7	Galway,	527	17	3
Bandon,	317	17	9	Glenamaddy,	186	6	11
Bantry,	189	15	2	Glenties,	270	12	7
Bawnboy,	199	0	3	Glin,	233	7	6
Belfast,	1,854	9	2	Gorey,	304	4	10
Belmullet,	220	9	0	Gort,	265	15	2
Borrisokane,	182	13	9	Granard,	360	10	4
Boyle,	381	14	2	Inishowen,	276	9	6
Cahirciveen,	262	6	11	Irvinestown,	214	12	1
Callan,	340	10	10	Kanturk,	427	14	11
Carlow,	551	4	11	Kells,	379	15	2
Carrickmacross,	200	0	6	Kenmare,	204	5	11
Carrick-on-Shannon,	300	13	7	Kilkeel,	197	15	11
Carrick-on-Suir,	361	0	0	Kilkenny,	573	18	0
Cashel,	435	5	11	Killadysert,	158	11	7
Castlebar,	229	14	1	Killala,	151	10	3
Castleblayney,	274	0	10	Killarney,	519	16	6
Castlecomer,	301	16	2	Kilmacthomas,	225	16	2
Castlederg,	153	14	1	Kilmallock,	778	5	6
Castlerea,	513	19	9	Kilrush,	326	8	3
Castletown,	170	0	6	Kinsale,	307	18	0
Cavan,	428	14	2	Larne,	317	12	10
Celbridge,	354	8	6	Letterkenny,	201	18	9
Claremorris,	226	10	9	Limavady,	272	11	7
Clifden,	277	4	2	Limerick,	1,044	0	8
Clogheen,	278	17	9	Lisburn,	370	5	2
Clogher,	216	0	3	Lismore,	301	1	7
Clonakilty,	207	5	11	Lisnaskea,	227	15	2
Clones,	211	8	9	Listowel,	297	18	3
Clonmel,	489	2	7	Londonderry,	492	6	0
Coleraine,	317	3	1	Longford,	270	2	10
Cookstown,	299	2	7	Loughrea,	266	14	11
Cootehill,	257	19	3	Lurgan,	473	1	1
Cork,	1,918	10	6	Macroom,	376	7	0
Corrofin,	138	16	11	Magherafelt,	295	19	3
Croom,	325	8	9	Mallow,	491	6	6
Delvin,	215	16	5	Manorhamilton,	268	18	6
Dingle,	310	1	10	Midleton,	420	18	6

SCHEDULE—*continued.*

Union.	Amount. £	s.	d.	Union.	Amount. £	s.	d.
Milford,	255	10	7	Scariff,	222	17	9
Millstreet,	222	12	10	Shillelagh,	241	8	1
Mitchelstown,	235	1	4	Skibbereen,	363	3	11
Mohill,	307	18	0	Skull,	145	3	7
Monaghan,	309	12	1	Sligo,	463	6	2
Mount Bellew,	203	17	9	Strabane,	376	7	7
Mountmellick,	474	10	4	Stranorlar,	218	8	2
Mullingar,	309	7	0	Strokestown,	218	15	11
Naas,	589	9	7	Swineford,	331	5	8
Navan,	334	4	2	Thomastown,	284	10	3
Nenagh,	407	0	10	Thurles,	425	9	6
Newcastle,	319	16	8	Tipperary,	469	3	2
New Ross,	571	19	1	Tobercurry,	216	6	2
Newry,	563	13	5	Tralee,	408	12	7
Newtownards,	360	5	5	Trim,	348	11	7
Oldcastle,	318	7	6	Tuam,	371	4	8
Omagh,	449	3	1	Tulla,	211	13	7
Oughterard,	214	16	11	Tullamore,	348	1	10
Parsonstown,	404	2	4	Urlingford,	245	1	1
Portumna,	179	5	6	Waterford,	765	7	3
Rathdown,	812	2	8	Westport,	405	11	7
Rathdrum,	482	6	3	Wexford,	403	8	3
Rathkeale,	308	2	10	Youghal,	354	8	6
Roscommon,	280	17	6				
Roscrea,	384	7	9	Total,	£60,500	0	0

5.—SCHEDULE of SUMS authorized to be paid to the Treasurers of Road Authorities in Ireland, being the amounts payable to such Authorities in respect of the Probate Duties Grant for the year ended 31st of March, 1880.

Road Authority.	Amount. £	s.	d.
The undermentioned Grand Juries, viz. :—			
Antrim County,	8,568	8	8
Armagh do.,	1,494	18	11
Carlow do.,	640	8	9
Carrickfergus, County of the Town,	105	16	6
Cavan County,	967	18	7
Clare do.,	1,650	18	4
Cork do.,	4,063	14	6
Donegal do.,	1,750	16	0
Down do.,	2,073	19	10
Drogheda, County of the Town,	45	2	7
Dublin County,	2,271	8	7
Fermanagh do.,	916	2	0
Galway do.,	1,346	5	0
Galway, County of the Town,	47	8	7
Kerry County,	2,315	10	5
Kildare do.,	819	7	10
Kilkenny do.,	1,451	5	11
Kilkenny, County of the City,	83	9	11
King's County,	908	8	5

SCHEDULE—*continued.*

Road Authority.	Amount.
The undermentioned Grand Juries, viz. :—	£ s. d.
Leitrim County,	542 0 2
Limerick do.,	1,827 9
Londonderry do.,	1,340 4 6
Longford do.,	896 16 9
Louth do.,	838 4 3
Mayo do.,	1,262 6 6
Meath do.,	1,196 13 4
Monaghan do.,	1,078 15 3
Queen's do.,	1,120 9 9
Roscommon do.,	858 17 9
Sligo do.,	774 17 1
Tipperary County, North Riding,	1,139 7 8
Do. South do.,	1,311 12 1
Tyrone County,	2,743 16 5
Waterford do.,	1,246 15 8
Waterford, County of the City,	1 17 1
Westmeath County,	794 18 9
Wexford do.,	1,453 5 11
Wicklow do.,	917 7 3
Cork City Corporation,	1,155 15 2
Dublin City do.,	4,170 3 7
Limerick City do.,	446 9 10
Ballymena Urban Sanitary Authority,	62 8 6
Belfast City Corporation,	2,562 7 0
Blackrock Township Commissioners,	181 19 8
Bray do., do.,	75 17 8
Carlow Urban Sanitary Authority,	50 10 10
Clonmel do., do.,	67 14 8
Clontarf Township Commissioners,	52 13 4
Dalkey do., do.	32 19 7
Drumcondra do., do.,	103 8 4
Dundalk Urban Sanitary Authority,	120 11 5
Dungarvan Town Commissioners,	23 14 8
Enniskillen do.,	48 10 0
Fermoy Urban Sanitary Authority,	25 0 10
Galway Town Commissioners,	104 0 11
Kilmainham Township Commissioners,	63 7 3
Kingstown do. do.,	299 0 4
Londonderry City Corporation,	880 1 10
Lurgan Urban Sanitary Authority,	74 11 0
Newry Town Commissioners,	136 7 1
Pembroke Township Commissioners,	205 17 10
Queenstown Town Commissioners,	50 3 5
Rathmines and Rathgar Township Commissioners,	298 8 6
Sligo Town Corporation,	86 14 1
Thurles Urban Sanitary Authority,	26 18 7
Tralee do. do.	56 19 0
Wexford do. do.	87 15 11
	£60,500 0 0

APPENDIX B.

Medical Charities Act and Vaccination Acts.

CIRCULARS.

No. 1.—Vaccination—Alleged Insusceptibility.

Local Government Board, Dublin,
20th March, 1890.

Sir,

The attention of the Local Government Board for Ireland has been requested to certain Statistical Tables laid before the Royal Commission on Vaccination, including returns of the "Number of persons insusceptible of Vaccination" throughout the Superintendent-Registrars' districts, or Poor Law Unions of Ireland.

The number of persons returned as insusceptible is in many Unions very large, and the Local Government Board have reason to believe that in some instances cases postponed have been entered in error under the heading of cases insusceptible. The result of the inquiries the Board have been able to make on this subject up to the present time leaves no doubt, however, that some public vaccinators have certified persons to be insusceptible before taking adequate measures to satisfy themselves that this very rare form of constitutional peculiarity really existed in the cases certified.

The Local Government Board have to request that before a public vaccinator certifies any person to be insusceptible of vaccination he will be good enough to make three attempts to vaccinate, and on three separate occasions, and on each occasion with fresh Liquid Lymph (that is Lymph conveyed directly from arm to arm), and that in vaccinating he will on each occasion proceed in strict accordance with the directions laid down in the Board's instructional Circular of the 30th of August, 1880.

I am, sir, your obedient servant,
Thos. A. Mooney, Secretary.

To each Medical Officer of a Dispensary District, and each Medical Officer of a Workhouse.

No. 2.—Committees of Management of Dispensary Districts.

Local Government Board, Dublin,
24th March, 1890.

Sir,

The Local Government Board for Ireland desire to call your attention to the Circular of the Poor Law Commissioners dated the 21st of March, 1862, relating to the annual appointment of Dispensary Committees and Wardens, and to the extracts from previous Circulars appended thereto, and they request that you will take the necessary steps, as pointed out in the Circular referred to, to place before the

Board of Guardians, after the annual election of Guardians, a correct list of the members of the Board entitled under section 7 of the Medical Charities Act (14 & 15 Vic., cap. 68) to be members of the respective Dispensary Committees in the Union. The Guardians should then, in each case in which it may be necessary to do so, elect a sufficient number of ratepayers possessing the qualifications prescribed by the section mentioned, so that the number of members of each Committee shall amount to the number authorized by Sealed Order.

This ought to be done by resolution and recorded on the minutes.

If it should appear from the Returning Officer's return of the election that there are any vacancies in the office of Guardian, the Board of Guardians should elect only such a number of qualified ratepayers to serve on the Dispensary Committees as would be necessary if the number of Guardians were complete, so that the persons who may be returned to supply the vacancies may become members of the respective Committees upon which they may be qualified and entitled to act.

As soon as the Committee shall have been completed for any Dispensary District, you should give notice to each member thereof of the day upon which the election of Chairman and Vice-Chairman and other honorary officers for the year will take place in accordance with Articles 6 & 7 of the Dispensary Regulations of 3rd November, 1885.

The Board enclose three copies of a form for a return of officers of the several Dispensary Committees in the Union to enable you to make the return in duplicate to this office and to retain a copy for the use of the Board of Guardians, and they request that you will procure the necessary information with the least possible delay and then forward the return to this office.

I am, sir, your obedient servant,

THOS. A. MOONEY, Secretary.

To the Clerk of each Union.

APPENDIX C.

ORDERS, CIRCULARS, &c., UNDER SANITARY ACTS.

I. ORDERS.

No. 1.—ORDER declaring proportions to be contributed by RIPARIAN NUISANCE DISTRICTS towards the cost of providing and maintaining an INTERCEPTING HOSPITAL at QUEENSTOWN.

To the GUARDIANS OF THE POOR OF THE CORK, KINSALE, AND MIDLETON UNIONS: to the MAYOR, ALDERMEN, and BURGESSES of the CITY of CORK; and to the TOWN COMMISSIONERS of the TOWN of QUEENSTOWN.

WHEREAS, We, the Local Government Board for Ireland did, by an Order under our Seal bearing date the Twentieth day of August, 1873, prescribe the Board of Guardians of the Cork Union to be the Nuisance Authority of the District (hereinafter referred to as the District), in which any ship, vessel, or boat being in any part of the port of Cork within the limits of Cork Harbour, should be deemed to be, and did direct that the expenses which might be incurred by the said Nuisance

Authority in carrying into effect the thirtieth section of the Sanitary Act, 1866, should be defrayed out of a common fund to be contributed by Riparian Nuisance Districts abutting on the district in the proportions which should thereafter be declared by Us to be in our opinion just and reasonable.

And whereas the following Unions, City, and Town are the Riparian Nuisance Districts abutting on the district, and are hereinafter referred to as the Riparian Nuisance Districts, viz.:—

1. The Cork Union, exclusive of the portions thereof comprised within the City of Cork and Town of Queenstown.
2. The Kinsale Union, exclusive of the portion thereof comprised within the Town of Kinsale.
3. The Midleton Union.
4. The City of Cork.
5. The Town of Queenstown.

And whereas the Guardians of the Poor of the Cork Union, acting as the Nuisance Authority prescribed as aforesaid, have provided an Intercepting Hospital at Queenstown for the reception and treatment of persons affected by dangerous contagious disease, and for the purpose of providing and maintaining the said Hospital have incurred, and may hereafter incur, certain expenses which, in accordance with the terms of our said order, are to be defrayed out of a common fund (hereinafter referred to as the common fund) to be contributed by the Riparian Nuisance Districts in such proportions as we think just.

Now Therefore, We, the Local Government Board for Ireland, do hereby declare that We think it just, and We do hereby order that the common fund shall be contributed by the Riparian Nuisance Districts in the following proportions, that is to say:—Each of the Riparian Nuisance Districts shall contribute to the common fund a sum bearing the same proportion to the whole amount of the expenses to be defrayed from the common fund as the valuation, in pursuance of the Acts in force for the valuation of rateable premises in Ireland, of the rateable premises contained in such Riparian Nuisance District bears to the total valuation, in pursuance of the said Acts, of the rateable premises contained in the Riparian Nuisance Districts collectively.

And We do hereby rescind an order under our seal bearing date the twentieth day of January, 1881, in regard to the expenses of providing the said Hospital.

Given under our hands and seal of office, this sixteenth day of April, in the year of Our Lord One Thousand Eight Hundred and Eighty-nine.

(Signed), Henry Robinson.
George Morris.
F. MacCabe.

No. 2.—ORDER prescribing FORM of CERTIFICATE to be given under Sub-section 1 (*b*) of Section 3 of the INFECTIOUS DISEASE (NOTIFICATION) ACT, 1889.

To the several URBAN and RURAL SANITARY AUTHORITIES in Ireland to whose Districts the Infectious Disease (Notification) Act, 1889, shall from time to time extend; and to all others whom it may concern.

WHEREAS by Sub-section (1) of Section 3 of the Infectious Disease (Notification) Act, 1889, it is, amongst other things, enacted that where an inmate (hereinafter referred to as "the patient") of any building used for human habitation within a District to which the Act extends is suffering from an infectious disease to which the Act applies, then, unless such building is a hospital in which persons suffering from an infectious disease are received, every medical practitioner attending on or called in to visit the patient shall forthwith, on becoming aware that the patient is suffering from an infectious disease to which the Act applies, send to the Medical Officer of Health for the District a certificate stating the name of the patient, the situation of the building, and the infectious disease from which, in the opinion of such medical practitioner, the patient is suffering:

AND WHEREAS by Sub-section (1) of Section 4 of the said Act it is enacted that "The Local Government Board may from time to time prescribe forms for the purpose of certificates under this Act, and any forms so prescribed shall be used in all cases to which they apply":

AND WHEREAS by Sub-section (1) of Section 18 of the said Act it is, amongst other things, enacted that in the application of the Act to Ireland the expression "Local Government Board" means the Local Government Board for Ireland, and the word "District" means Urban Sanitary District or Rural Sanitary District, as the case may be, within the meaning of the Public Health (Ireland) Act, 1878.

NOW THEREFORE, We, the Local Government Board for Ireland, in pursuance of the powers given to Us in that behalf, do, by this Our Order, Prescribe and Order as follows:—

The Form of Certificate contained in the Schedule hereto shall, until We otherwise prescribe, be the Form for the purpose of any Certificate to be given under Sub-section (1) (*b*) of Section 3 of the Infectious Disease (Notification) Act, 1889.

Schedule.

The Infectious Disease (Notification) Act, 1889.

Certificate of Medical Practitioner.

*———District.

To the Medical Officer of Health.(1)

I hereby certify and declare that in my opinion(2) ———, an inmate of(3) ———, is suffering from(4) ———.

Dated the ———day of———18——

(Signed),———
Medical Practitioner.

(Address)———

* Insert name of District of Rural or Urban Sanitary Authority, as the case may be.

(1.) Where in any District of a Sanitary Authority there are two or more Medical Officers of Health of such Authority the Certificate should be given to such one of those Officers as has charge of the area in which is the patient referred to in the Certificate, or to such other of those Officers as the Sanitary Authority may from time to time direct.

(2.) Insert name and age of person suffering from disease.

(3.) Insert No. or name of house and name of street if in a town, or if in a rural district, the name of occupier of house and name of townland. In the case of a ship, boat, tent, van, shed, or other similar structure, the name and description of the dwelling and the name of the place where it is situate, should be given.

(4.) Insert name of disease.

N.B.—This Certificate must (under a penalty not exceeding forty shillings) be sent to the Medical Officer of Health forthwith on the Medical Practitioner attending on or called in to visit the patient becoming aware that the patient is suffering from an infectious disease to which the Act applies, namely, any of the following diseases:—Small-pox, Cholera, Diphtheria, Membranous Croup, Erysipelas, the disease known as Scarlatina or Scarlet Fever, and the fevers known by any of the following names:—Typhus, Typhoid, Enteric, Relapsing, Continued, or Puerperal, and also any infectious disease to which the Act has been applied by the Sanitary Authority in manner provided by the Act.

Sealed with our Seal this Fifth day of December, in the year of our Lord One Thousand Eight Hundred and Eighty-nine.

(Signed),

Henry Robinson.
George Morris.
F. MacCabe.

II.—CIRCULARS.

No. 1.—Rules for the Regulation of Domestic Water Supply.

Local Government Board, Dublin,
13th June, 1889.

Sir,

The Local Government Board for Ireland have had their attention called to a misconception which seems to exist on the part of many Sanitary Authorities, both Rural and Urban, as to their power to make Rules or Bye-Laws regulating the domestic water supply in their respective districts.

Certain Corporate Authorities have been enabled by Local Acts to make special Bye-Laws with respect to water supply and the works connected therewith, but, except when so enabled, Sanitary Authorities have no power to make Bye-Laws for this purpose.

The object of a Sanitary Authority in framing such Rules as have in many cases been promulgated would appear to be met by the publication of the requirements of the Waterworks Clauses Acts, incorporated in the Public Health (Ireland) Act, 1878, by Section 67, which have to be complied with by persons taking a supply of water from a Sanitary Authority.

A suggested form of notice embodying the principal requirements referred to is enclosed, which may be found useful by Sanitary Authorities who are not empowered under Local Acts to make special Bye-Laws for this purpose.

I am, sir, your obedient servant,
Thos. A. Mooney, Secretary.

To each Executive Sanitary Officer.

Enclosure to the Foregoing.

Public Health (Ireland) Act, 1878, and the Waterworks Clauses Acts, 1847 and 1863.

The   of   acting as the Sanitary Authority for the town of   hereby give notice of certain requirements of the Waterworks Clauses Acts, 1847 and 1863, which must be complied with in respect of the supply of water provided by the said Sanitary Authority for public and domestic purposes:—

1. Upon the request of the owner or occupier of any house, the annual value of which shall not exceed ten pounds, in a district in which mains are laid by the Sanitary Authority, the Sanitary Authority shall lay a communication pipe from their pipes to such house in any district where the Sanitary Authority lay pipes for the supply of the inhabitants thereof. Waterworks Clauses Act, 1847, sec. XLIV., and Public Health Act, sec. 67.

2. The Sanitary Authority are entitled to charge a reasonable annual rent in addition to the water-rate for such communication pipes. [*The Sanitary Authority may here insert the charge they propose to make.*] Same sections.

Act of 1847, sec. XLVIII., and Public Health Act, sec. 67.

3. The owner or occupier of any house in a district in which mains are laid by the Sanitary Authority may lay the communication pipe on certain conditions, and after fourteen days' notice to the Sanitary Authority, but the strength and material of such pipe must be first approved of by the Sanitary Authority, or, in case of dispute, as settled by a Court of Summary Jurisdiction. [*The Sanitary Authority may here insert their requirements as to strength and material of communication pipes.*]

Act of 1847, sec. XLIX.

4. Before a householder makes any communication with the pipes of the Sanitary Authority two days' notice shall be given to the Sanitary Authority of the day and hour when such communication is intended to be made, and such communication shall be made under the superintendence and according to the directions of the officer appointed for that purpose by the Sanitary Authority.

Act of 1847, sec. L.

5. The bore of such communication pipe shall not exceed half an inch, except with the consent of the Sanitary Authority. [*The Sanitary Authority may here say whether or not and under what circumstances they will give such consent.*]

Act of 1847, sec. LVII.

6. Any person acting under the authority of the Sanitary Authority may, between the hours of 9 a.m. and 4 p.m., enter into any house or premises in order to examine if there be any waste or misuse of the water supplied to said house or premises.

Act of 1863, sec. 12.

7. A supply of water for domestic purposes shall not include a supply of water for cattle, or for horses, or for washing carriages where such horses or carriages are kept for sale or hire or by a common carrier, or a supply for any trade, manufacture, or business, or for watering gardens, or for fountains, or for any ornamental purpose.

Act of 1847, sec. LIV.

8. Every person supplied with water shall, when required by the Sanitary Authority provide a proper cistern to hold the water with which he shall be so supplied, with a ball and stop cock, and shall keep same in good repair so as to prevent waste.

Offences and Penalties.

Act.	Offence.	Penalty.
Act of 1847, sec. XXXIII.	For opening a street without notice and neglecting to restore same.	Not more than £5 for each offence and £5 each day after notice.
" LI.	For removing pipes without notice, . .	Not more than £5 for each offence.
" LIV.	For not providing or not keeping in good repair cisterns, ball or stop cocks.	Water may be cut off.
" LV.	For suffering a cistern, ball or stop cock to be out of repair.	Not more than £5 for each offence.
" LVII.	For obstructing inspection as to waste, &c., .	Water may be cut off.
" LX.	For breaking, injuring, or opening any lock, cock, valve, or pipe, or doing any other wilful act by which water may be wasted.	Not more than £5 for each offence.
" LXI.	For bathing in any stream or reservoir belonging to the sanitary authority.	Do., do.
	Or for washing, throwing, or causing to enter therein any animal.	Do., do.
	Or for throwing therein any rubbish, dirt, or filth.	Do., do.
	Or for washing or cleansing anything therein.	Do., do.
	And for causing the water of any sink, sewer, or drain, steam engine, boiler, or other filthy water to run or be brought therein.	Not more than £5 for each offence, and £1 for every day after during which the offence is continued.

OFFENCES AND PENALTIES—*continued.*

Act.	Offence.	Penalty.
Act of 1863, sec. 15,	For obstructing inspection of meters, . .	Not more than £5 for each offence.
„ 16, And Public Health Act, sec. 278.	For doing anything contrary to or omitting anything to be done according to the provisions of the Public Health (Ireland) Act, 1878, to prevent waste.	Water may be cut off.
Act of 1863, sec. 17,	For causing waste by failing to keep in repair any pipes, valves, cocks, cisterns, baths, soil-pans, water-closets, or using them so as to cause waste of water or return of foul air, or noisome or impure matter, into any pipe belonging to or connected with the pipes of the sanitary authority.	Not more than £3 for each offence.
„ 18,	For using water for other than domestic purposes without agreement; or, if with agreement, for other than agreed on purposes.	Not more than £2 for each offence.
„ 20,	For wrongfully taking or using any water belonging to the sanitary authority.	Not more than £5 for each offence.

RECOMMENDATIONS.

1. Lead service pipes should not be of less weight than as follows:—

Bore.	Weight per yard if with closed ends or under pressure.	Weight per yard if with open ends.
Inches.	lbs.	lbs.
[illegible] . .	4½	2
[illegible] . .	6	3
[illegible] . .	7½	4
[illegible] . .	9	5
[illegible] . .	10½	6
1 . .	12	7
1¼ . .	15	9

2. All pipes in contact with the ground should be of lead.

3. All joints of lead pipes should be wiped joints.

4. No pipe should be laid through any drain, sewer, ashpit, or similar place.

5. All pipes under open ground should be laid at a depth of at least two feet.

6. Screw-down high-pressure taps should be used.

7. There should be a screw-down stop-valve with cover and guard on the communication pipe outside of, but near to the premises.

8. All cisterns should be water-tight and covered.

9. Water-closets, urinals, and boilers should in *every case* be supplied through a cistern and not directly from the water-mains, such cisterns not to be drawn on for drinking purposes.

10. Each water-closet should be provided with a waste preventing apparatus, giving a flush of two gallons.

No. 2.—Sale of Horseflesh, &c., Regulation Act, 1889, 52 & 53 Vict., Cap. 11.

Local Government Board, Dublin,
12th September, 1889.

Sir,—I am directed by the Local Government Board for Ireland to forward herewith, for the information of the Sanitary Authority, a copy of the Sale of Horseflesh, &c., Regulation Act, 1889, 52 and 53 Vic., cap. 11.

The Sanitary Authority will observe that the Act comes into operation on the 29th instant.

I am, sir, your obedient servant,
Thos. A. Mooney, Secretary.

To the Executive Sanitary Officer of each Urban and Rural Sanitary District.

Enclosure to the Foregoing.

Sale of Horseflesh, &c., Regulation Act, 1889, 52 & 53 Vic., Chap. 11.

A.D. 1889.

An Act to Regulate the Sale of Horseflesh for Human Food, [24th June, 1889.]

Whereas it is desirable to make regulations with respect to the sale of horseflesh for human food:

Be it therefore enacted by the Queen's Most Excellent Majesty, by and with the advice and consent of the Lords Spiritual and Temporal, and Commons, in this present Parliament assembled, and by the authority of the same, as follows:

Signs on horseflesh shops.

1. No person shall sell, offer, expose, or keep for sale any horseflesh for human food, elsewhere than in a shop, stall, or place over or upon which there shall be at all times painted, posted, or placed in legible characters of not less than four inches in length, and in a conspicuous position, and so as to be visible throughout the whole time, whether by night or day, during which such horseflesh is being offered or exposed for sale, words indicating that horseflesh is sold there.

Horseflesh not to be sold as other meat.

2. No person shall supply horseflesh for human food to any purchaser who has asked to be supplied with some meat other than horseflesh, or with some compound article of food which is not ordinarily made of horseflesh.

Power of medical officer of health to inspect meat, &c.

3. Any medical officer of health or inspector of nuisances or other officer of a local authority acting on the instructions of such authority or appointed by such authority for the purposes of this Act may at all reasonable times inspect and examine any meat which he has reason to believe to be horseflesh, exposed for sale or deposited for the purpose of sale, or of preparation for sale, and intended for human food, in any place other than such shop, stall, or place as aforesaid, and if such meat appears to him to be horseflesh he may seize and carry away or cause to be seized and carried away the same, in order to have the same dealt with by a justice as hereinafter provided.

4. On complaint made on oath by a medical officer of health or inspector of nuisances, or other officer of a local authority, any justice may grant a warrant to any such officer to enter any building or part of a building other than such shop, stall, or place as aforesaid, in which such officer has reason for believing that there is kept or concealed any horseflesh which is intended for sale, or for preparation for sale for human food, contrary to the provisions of this Act; and to search for, seize, and carry away, or cause to be seized and carried away, any meat that appears to such officer to be such horseflesh, in order to have the same dealt with by a justice as hereinafter provided. Power of justice to grant warrant for search.

Any person who shall obstruct any such officer in the performance of his duty under this Act shall be deemed to have committed an offence under this Act.

5. If it appears to any justice that any meat seized under the foregoing provisions of this Act is such horseflesh as aforesaid, he may make such order with regard to the disposal thereof as he may think desirable; and the person in whose possession or on whose premises the meat was found shall be deemed to have committed an offence under this Act, unless he proves that such meat was not intended for human food contrary to the provisions of this Act. Power of justice with reference to disposal of horseflesh.

6. Any person offending against any of the provisions of this Act, for every such offence shall be liable to a penalty not exceeding twenty pounds, to be recovered in a summary manner; and if any horseflesh is proved to have been exposed for sale to the public in any shop, stall, or eating-house other than such shop, stall, or place as in the first section mentioned, without anything to show that it was not intended for sale for human food, the onus of proving that it was not so intended shall rest upon the person exposing it for sale. Penalty.

7. For the purposes of this Act "horseflesh" shall include the flesh of asses and mules, and shall mean horseflesh, cooked or uncooked, alone or accompanied by or mixed with any other substance. Definition of "horseflesh."

8. For the purposes of this Act the local authorities shall be, in the city of London and the liberties thereof, the Commissioners of Sewers, and in the other parts of the county of London the vestries and district boards acting in the execution of the Metropolis Local Management Acts, and in other parts of England the urban and rural sanitary authorities, and in Ireland the urban and rural sanitary authorities under the Public Health (Ireland) Act, 1878. Local authorities for purposes of Act. 41 & 42 Vic., c. 52.

9. In the application of this Act to Scotland the expression "justice" shall include sheriff and sheriff substitute, and the expression "local authority" shall mean any local authority authorized to appoint a public analyst under the Sale of Food and Drugs Act, 1875, and the procedure for the enforcement of this Act shall be in the manner provided in the thirty-third section of the said Sale of Food and Drugs Act, 1875. Application to Scotland. 38 & 39 Vic., c. 63.

10. This Act may be cited as the Sale of Horseflesh, &c., Regulation Act, 1889. Short title.

11. This Act shall come into operation on the 29th day of September, one thousand eight hundred and eighty-nine. Commencement of Act.

No. 3.—Infectious Disease (Notification) Act, 1889.
52 & 53 Vic., cap. 72.

Local Government Board, Dublin,
11th October, 1889.

Sir,

The Local Government Board for Ireland forward herewith, for the information of the Sanitary Authority, a reprint of the provisions applicable to Ireland of the "Infectious Disease (Notification) Act, 1889," which received the Royal assent on the 30th day of August last. This Act confers upon Sanitary Authorities important additional powers enabling them to acquire a knowledge of the existence of cases of infectious disease within their districts, and thus to put in force those provisions of the Public Health Act, 1878, intended to prevent the spread of infectious diseases. The following are the diseases specified in section 6 of the Act of 1889:—

Small-pox.
Cholera.
Diphtheria and Membranous Croup.
Erysipelas.
Scarlatina or Scarlet Fever.
The Fevers known as Typhus, Typhoid or Enteric, Relapsing Continued and Puerperal.

With respect to the diseases above-named it is enacted that where an inmate of any building used for human habitation, unless such building is a hospital in which persons suffering from infectious disease are received, the following provisions shall have effect:—

(a.) The head of the family to which such inmate (in this Act referred to as the patient) belongs, and in his default the nearest relatives of the patient present in the building or being in attendance on the patient, and in default of such relatives every person in charge of or in attendance on the patient, and in default of any such person the occupier of the building shall, as soon as he becomes aware that the patient is suffering from an infectious disease to which this Act applies, send notice thereof to the medical officer of health of the district:

(b.) Every medical practitioner attending on or called in to visit the patient shall forthwith, on becoming aware that the patient is suffering from an infectious disease to which this Act applies, send to the medical officer of health for the district a certificate stating the name of the patient, the situation of the building, and the infectious disease from which, in the opinion of such medical practitioner, the patient is suffering.

(2.) Every person required to give a notice or certificate who fails to give the same, shall be liable on summary conviction in manner provided by the Summary Jurisdiction Acts to a fine not exceeding forty shillings;

Provided that if a person is not required to give notice in the first instance, but only in default of some other person, he shall not be liable to any fine if he satisfies the court that he had reasonable cause to suppose that the notice had been duly given.

The Act does not extend to any urban, rural, or port sanitary district, until after its adoption by the "local authority," which is defined as meaning an urban or rural sanitary authority, within the meaning of the Public Health (Ireland) Act, 1878, and it is important sanitary authorities should observe that if they desire to extend the operation of the Act of 1889 to their district, it will be necessary to adopt the proceedings which are set forth in section 5 of the Act, in the following terms:—

Adoption of Act in urban or rural districts.

(1.) The local authority of any urban, rural, or port sanitary district may adopt this Act by a resolution passed at a meeting of such authority; and fourteen clear days at least before such meeting special notice of the meeting, and of the intention to propose such resolution, shall be given to every member of the local authority, and the notice shall be deemed to have been duly given to a member if it is either:

(*a*) given in the mode in which notices to attend meetings of the local authority are usually given, or

(*b*) where there is no such mode, then signed by the clerk of the local authority, and delivered to the member or left at his usual or last known place of abode in England, or forwarded by post in a prepaid letter addressed to the member at his usual or last known place of abode in England.

(2.) A resolution adopting this Act shall be published by advertisement in a local newspaper and by handbills, and otherwise in such manner as the local authority think sufficient for giving notice thereof to all persons interested, and shall come into operation at such time, not less than one month after the first publication of the advertisement of the resolution as the local authority may fix, and upon its coming into operation this Act shall extend to the district.

(3.) A copy of the resolution shall be sent to the Local Government Board when it is published.

In addition to the diseases specified in Section 6 of the Act power is given to sanitary authorities to extend the definition of infectious disease, from time to time, by an order passed after the observance of the prescribed conditions and approved by the Local Government Board.

The Act provides that the expenses incurred by a sanitary authority in the execution of the Act shall be paid as part of the expenses of such authority in the execution of the Acts relating to public health, and in the case of a rural authority shall be general expenses. Section 4 enacts that the Local Government Board may from time to time prescribe forms for the purpose of certificates under the Act, and any forms so prescribed shall be used in all cases to which they apply. It is further provided that the local authority shall gratuitously supply forms of certificate to any medical practitioner residing or practising in their district who applies for the same, and shall pay to every medical practitioner for each certificate duly sent by him in accordance with this Act a fee of two shillings and sixpence if the case occurs in his private practice, and of one shilling if the case occurs in his practice as medical officer of any public body or institution, and that where in any district of a local authority there are two or more medical officers of health of such authority a certificate under this Act shall be given to such one of those officers as has charge of the area in which is the patient referred to in the certificate, or to such other of those officers as the local authority may from time to time direct.

It is provided that a notice or certificate to be sent to a medical officer of health in pursuance of this Act may be sent by being delivered to the officer or being left at his office or residence, or may be sent by post addressed to him at his office or at his residence, and that where a medical practitioner attending on a patient is himself the medical officer of health of the district he shall be entitled to the fee to which he would be entitled if he were not such medical officer.

Section 13 enacts that the provisions of this Act shall apply to every ship, vessel, boat, tent, van, shed, or similar structure used for human habitation, in like manner as nearly as may be as if it were a building.

A ship, vessel, or boat, lying in any river, harbour, or other water not within the district of any local authority within the meaning of this Act shall be deemed for the purposes of this Act to be within the district of such local authority as may be fixed by the Local Government Board, and where no local authority has been fixed, then of the local authority of the district which nearest adjoins the place where such ship, vessel, or boat is lying.

Upon the receipt of a copy of the resolution of any sanitary authority adopting the Act, the Local Government Board will be prepared to prescribe the forms of certificates to be used under the Act.

I am, sir,

Your obedient servant,

Thos. A. Mooney, Secretary.

To the Executive Sanitary Officer of each Urban and Rural Sanitary District.

Enclosure to the Foregoing.

Extracts from the Infectious Disease (Notification) Act, 1889. 52 and 53 Vict., Cap. 72.

Short title. 1. This Act may be cited as the Infectious Disease (Notification) Act, 1889.

2. This Act shall extend—

Extent of Act. (a.) to every London district after the expiration of two months from the passing of this Act, and

(b.) to any urban, rural, or port sanitary district after the adoption thereof.

Notification of infectious disease. 3.—(1.) Where an inmate of any building used for human habitation within a district to which this Act extends is suffering from an infectious disease to which this Act applies, then, unless such building is a hospital in which persons suffering from an infectious disease are received, the following provisions shall have effect, that is to say:—

(a.) the head of the family to which such inmate (in this Act referred to as the patient) belongs, and in his default the nearest relatives of the patient present in the building or being in attendance on the patient, and in default of such relatives every person in charge of or in attendance on the patient, and in default of any such person the occupier of the building shall, as soon as he becomes aware that the patient is suffering from an infectious disease to which this Act applies, send notice thereof to the medical officer of health of the district;

(b.) every medical practitioner attending on or called in to visit the patient shall forthwith, on becoming aware that the patient is suffering from an infectious disease to which this Act applies, send to the medical officer of health for the district a certificate stating the name of the patient, the situation of the building, and the infectious disease from which, in the opinion of such medical practitioner, the patient is suffering.

(3.) Every person required by this section to give a notice or certificate who fails to give the same shall be liable on summary conviction in manner provided by the Summary Jurisdiction Acts to a fine not exceeding forty shillings;

Provided that if a person is not required to give notice in the first instance, but only in default of some other person, he shall not be liable to any fine if he satisfies the court that he had reasonable cause to suppose that the notice had been duly given.

As to forms and case of several medical practitioners.

4.—(1.) The Local Government Board may from time to time prescribe forms for the purpose of certificates under this Act, and any forms so prescribed shall be used in all cases to which they apply.

(2.) The local authority shall gratuitously supply forms of certificate to any medical practitioner residing or practising in their district who applies for the same, and shall pay to every medical practitioner for each certificate duly sent by him in accordance with this Act a fee of two shillings and sixpence if the case occurs in his private practice, and of one shilling if the case occurs in his practice as medical officer of any public body or institution.

(3) Where in any district of a local authority there are two or more medical officers of health of such authority a certificate under this Act shall be given to each one of those officers as has charge of the area in which is the patient referred to in the certificate, or to such other of those officers as the local authority may from time to time direct.

Adoption of Act in urban or rural district.

5.—(1.) The local authority of any urban, rural, or port sanitary district may adopt this Act by a resolution passed at a meeting of such authority; and fourteen clear days at least before such meeting special notice of the meeting, and of the intention to propose such resolution, shall be given to every member of the local authority, and the notice shall be deemed to have been duly given to a member if it is either:

(a.) given in the mode in which notices to attend meetings of the local authority are usually given, or

(b.) where there is no such mode, then signed by the clerk of the local authority and delivered to the member or left at his usual or last known place of abode in England, or forwarded by post in a prepaid letter addressed to the member at his usual or last known place of abode in England.

(2.) A resolution adopting this Act shall be published by advertisement in a local newspaper, and by handbills, and otherwise in such manner as the local authority think sufficient for giving notice thereof to all persons interested, and shall come into operation at such time, not less than one month after the first publication of the advertisement of the resolution, as the local authority may fix, and upon its coming into operation this Act shall extend to the district.

(3.) A copy of the resolution shall be sent to the Local Government Board when it is published.

Definition of infectious disease.

6. In this Act the expression "infectious disease to which this Act applies" means any of the following diseases—namely, small-pox, cholera, diphtheria, membranous croup, erysipelas, the disease known as scarlatina or scarlet fever, and the fevers known by any of the following names—typhus, typhoid, enteric, relapsing, continued, or puerperal, and includes as respects any particular district any infectious disease to which this Act has been applied by the local authority of the district in manner provided by this Act.

Power to local authority to extend definition of infectious disease.

7.—(1.) The local authority of any district to which this Act extends may, from time to time, by a resolution passed at a meeting of such authority where the like special notice of the meeting and of the intention to propose the resolution has been given as is required in the case of a meeting held for adopting this Act, order that this Act shall apply in their district to any infectious disease other than a disease specifically mentioned in this Act.

(2.) Any such order may be permanent or temporary, and, if temporary, the period during which it is to continue in force shall be specified therein, and any such order may be revoked or varied by the local authority which made the same.

(3.) An order under this section and the revocation and variation of any such order shall not be of any validity until approved by the Local Government Board.

(4.) When it is so approved, the local authority shall give public notice thereof by advertisement in a local newspaper and by handbills, and otherwise in such manner as the local authority think sufficient for giving information to all persons interested. They shall also send a copy thereof to each registered medical practitioner whom, after due inquiry, they ascertain to be residing or practising in their district.

(5.) The said order shall come into operation at such date not earlier than one week after the publication of the first advertisement of the approved order as the local authority may fix, and upon such order coming into operation, and during the continuance thereof, an infectious disease mentioned in such order shall, within the district of the authority, be an infectious disease to which this Act applies.

(6.) In the case of emergency three clear days' notice under this section shall be sufficient, and the resolution shall declare the cause of such emergency and shall be for a temporary order, and a copy thereof shall be forthwith sent to the Local Government Board and advertised, and the order shall come into operation at the expiration of one week from the date of such advertisement, but unless approved by the Local Government Board shall cease to be in force at the expiration of one month after it is passed, or any earlier date fixed by the Local Government Board.

(7.) The approval of the Local Government Board shall be conclusive evidence that the case was one of emergency.

Notices and Certificates.

8.—(1). A notice or certificate for the purposes of this Act shall be in writing or print, or partly in writing and partly in print; and for the purposes of this Act the expression "print" includes any mechanical mode of reproducing words.

(2.) A notice or certificate to be sent to a medical officer of health in pursuance of this Act may be sent by being delivered to the officer or being left at his office or residence, or may be sent by post addressed to him at his office or at his residence.

9. Any expenses incurred by a local authority in the execution of this Act shall be paid as part of the expenses of such authority in the execution of the Acts relating to public health, and in the case of a rural authority shall be general expenses. Expenses.

11. A payment made to any medical practitioner in pursuance of this Act shall not disqualify that practitioner for serving as member of the council of any county or borough, or as member of a sanitary authority, or as guardian of a union, or in any municipal or parochial office. Non-disqualification of medical officer by receipt of fees.

Where a medical practitioner attending on a patient is himself the medical officer of health of the district, he shall be entitled to the fee to which he would be entitled if he were not such medical officer.

13.—(1.) The provisions of this Act shall apply to every ship, vessel, boat, tent, van, shed, or similar structure used for human habitation, in like manner as nearly as may be as if it were a building. Application of Act to vessels, tents, &c.

(2.) A ship, vessel, or boat lying in any river, harbour, or other water not within the district of any local authority within the meaning of this Act shall be deemed for the purposes of this Act to be within the district of such local authority as may be fixed by the Local Government Board, and where no local authority has been fixed, then of the local authority of the district which nearest adjoins the place where such ship, vessel, or boat is lying.

(3.) This section shall not apply to any ship, vessel, or boat belonging to any foreign Government.

14. Where this Act is put in force in any district in which there is a local Act for the like purpose as this Act, the enactments of such local Act, so far as they relate to that purpose, shall cease to be in operation. Saving for local Act.

15. Nothing in this Act shall extend to any building, ship, vessel, boat, tent, van, shed, or similar structure belonging to Her Majesty the Queen, or to any inmate thereof. Exemption of Crown buildings.

18. This Act shall apply to Ireland, with the following modifications:— Application of Act to Ireland.

(1.) In this Act, unless the context otherwise requires—

The expression "Local Government Board" means the Local Government Board for Ireland:

The expression "local authority" means an urban or rural sanitary authority within the meaning of the Public Health (Ireland) Act, 1878: 41 & 42 Vic., c. 52.

The word "district" means urban sanitary district or rural sanitary district, as the case may be, within the meaning of the said Act:

The expression "clerk of the local authority" includes, in the case of an urban sanitary authority, town clerk and secretary:

(2.) References to a place of abode in England shall be construed to refer to a place of abode in Ireland.

(3.) Offences under this Act may be prosecuted, and fines under this Act may be recovered, in manner directed by the Summary Jurisdiction Acts, before a court of summary jurisdiction constituted in the manner mentioned in the two hundred and forty-ninth section of the Public Health (Ireland) Act, 1878. 41 & 42 Vic., c. 52.

No. 4.—INFLUENZA.

Local Government Board, Dublin,
28th February, 1890.

SIR,—The Local Government Board for Ireland desire to obtain accurate information respecting the date on which the specific disease commonly described as "Influenza" first made its appearance in different parts of Ireland, the extent to which it has prevailed, and the prominent symptoms of such cases as may have come under your personal observation. The Board request that you will be so good as to fill in answers to the accompanying questions and to return this document not later than the 15th of March.

The form is sent in duplicate in order that you may retain a copy of your reply.

I am, sir,
Your obedient servant,
THOS. A. MOONEY, Secretary.

To each Medical Officer of a Dispensary District.

ENCLOSURE TO THE FOREGOING.

QUESTIONS.	ANSWERS.
1. Give as accurately as possible the date on which you first saw a case of typical influenza. If you cannot fix the precise date please insert the word "about" before the date given.	1.
2. Name the Electoral Division in which the first case occurred.	2.
3. Date of the next case or subsequent cases. Have you observed any uniform period of incubation?	3.
4. Please give the leading symptoms in the cases seen by you—specifying premonitory signs, frontal headache, muscular pains, vomiting, high temperature, quick pulse, duration of attack. If succeeded by abnormally low pulse and sub-normal temperature, state the fact; and if followed by pulmonary complications state the fact. Please also mention if the attack was followed by marked nervous depression and prostration.	4.
5. Number of cases seen by you. Extent of mortality (*a*) from influenza, (*b*) from complications.	5.
6. Date of occurrence of last case.	6.
7. State any opinion you may have formed as to the origin of the disease, and the mode in which it spread through your district.	7.
8. Have you observed any unusual disease or complaint amongst domestic animals prevailing about the same time as Influenza?	8.
9 Please add any observations you may wish to make bearing upon the subject matter of this circular.	9.

No. 5.—Form of Bond for Collectors of Rents of Labourers' Cottages.

Local Government Board, Dublin,
12th March, 1890.

Sir,—The Local Government Board for Ireland have observed that in the Unions in which Cottages have been provided under the Labourers Acts the Boards of Guardians have usually appointed existing Union Officers to collect the rents of such tenements, and the Board desire to state, for the information of the Guardians, that the Bonds already entered into by these Officers as Collectors of Poor Rate, Relieving Officers, etc., would not cover any liability on their part in their capacity of Collectors of Rents.

The Board have, therefore, prepared a special Form of Bond for the purpose, a copy of which is enclosed, and they request that the Guardians will be good enough to cause the present Collectors of Rents to execute new Bonds accordingly, and to see that the form now forwarded is adopted in all cases in future.

I am, sir,
Your obedient servant,

Thos. A. Mooney, Secretary.

To

The Clerk,

—— Union.

Enclosure to the Foregoing.

Bond for Collection of Rents.

Know all Men by these Presents, that We, are jointly and severally held and firmly bound to the Guardians of the Poor of the Union, in the sum of of good and lawful money of the United Kingdom of Great Britain and Ireland, to be paid to the said Guardians of the Poor of the Union, or their certain solicitor, successors, or assigns, for which payment to be well and faithfully made, We bind ourselves jointly, and each of us bindeth himself severally, our and each and every of our heirs, executors, and administrators, and every of them, firmly by these presents, sealed with our seals. Dated this day of in the year of our Lord one thousand eight hundred and

Whereas the above bounden hath been duly appointed Collector of the rents of the cottages, plots, and tenements provided by the said Guardians of the Poor of the Union in pursuance of the provisions of the Labourers (Ireland) Acts, 1883 to 1886: and whereas the said hath been required to enter into security in a bond with two sureties to the said Guardians of the Poor of the Union, in the penalty hereinbefore mentioned to be conditioned as hereinafter is set forth, and hath requested the above bounden and to join with him as such sureties, in the above bond, subject to the condition hereinafter contained, to which they have assented: and the said Guardians have agreed to accept of them as such sureties accordingly.

NOW THE CONDITION of this obligation is such that if the above-bounden do and shall from time to time and at all times hereafter whilst he shall be employed in the said office of Collector of Rents as aforesaid, and until he shall be discharged therefrom by the said Guardians of the Poor of the Union, or by order of the Local Government Board for Ireland, or by and with the assent of the said Guardians shall cease and discontinue to hold the said office of collector, collect with all due diligence the rents aforesaid lawfully recoverable, on such rents becoming due, and pay the amount of the rents collected by him to the treasurer of the said Union, monthly, or oftener if required, and whenever the sum collected by him shall amount to Ten Pounds; and shall from time to time and at all times when required so to do, deliver to the person or persons authorised to require the same, true and perfect accounts in writing, under his hand, of all moneys which shall have been received by him by virtue of his said office of Collector of Rents as aforesaid, and of all moneys paid by him to the said treasurer, together with the proper vouchers for such payment, and shall verify his account upon oath when thereunto lawfully required, and shall deliver to such person or persons as aforesaid within three days after being thereunto required, all the books, papers, and writings, in his custody or power, relating to the affairs of the said Union, and shall immediately thereupon pay such moneys as upon the balance of any account or accounts shall appear to be in his hands, to the said treasurer; and shall in all other respects duly, fully, and faithfully observe, obey, perform, fulfil, and keep all the enactments, laws, rules, and regulations contained in the said Acts and in any Act or Acts or Order of the Local Government Board for Ireland, or the said Guardians touching and concerning the collection of the said rents; and if the said do not and shall not commit or cause or suffer to be done or committed any act, matter, or thing whatsoever, whereby or by means whereof the said Guardians of the Poor of the Union, shall or may or can be wronged, defrauded, or prejudiced in respect to any of the rents aforesaid, then the foregoing bond and obligation shall be void.

Signed, Sealed and delivered by the above-bounden } (*Seal.*)

(*Seal.*)

in presence of } (*Seal.*)

To , Gentlemen Solicitors of Her Majesty's High Court of Justice in Ireland, Queen's Bench Division, or either of them, or to any other solicitor of the same division, or to any other solicitor of any other division of Her Majesty's High Court of Justice in Ireland aforesaid, Great Britain, or elsewhere.

THESE are to authorize and appoint you, or either of you, to appear for us , or any or either of us, for the whole, jointly and severally, and confess one or more judgment or judgments, as of last Term, or of any Term or Time whatsoever, after the date of these presents, with stay of execution until breach shall be made in the performance of the condition of the Bond hereunto annexed, and bearing equal date herewith, in the said High Court of Justice in Ireland, Queen's Bench Division, or any other division of Her Majesty's High Court of Justice in Ireland, Great Britain, or elsewhere, by acknowledging the action, or otherwise, upon one or more declaration or declarations, there to be filed against us, or any or either of us, by himself for the whole, at the suit of the Guardians of the Poor of the Union, upon a Bond of sterling; and for your or any of your so doing this shall be your sufficient warrant and discharge.

AND THE CONDITION of the said Bond is such, that if the said do and shall from time to time and at all times hereafter, whilst he shall be employed in the office of Collector of Rents as in the said Bond mentioned, and until he shall be discharged therefrom by the said Guardians of the Poor of the Union, or by Order of the Local Government Board for Ireland, or by and with the assent of the said Guardians shall cease and discontinue to hold the said office of Collector, collect with all due diligence the rents aforesaid lawfully recoverable on such rents becoming due, and pay the amount of the rents collected by him to the treasurer of the said Union, weekly, or oftener if required, and whenever the sum collected by him shall amount to ten pounds; and shall from time to time and at all times when required so to do, deliver to the person or persons authorized to require the same, true and perfect accounts in writing, under his hand, of all moneys which shall have been received by him by virtue of his said office of Collector of Rents as aforesaid, and of all moneys paid by him to the said treasurer, together with the proper vouchers for such payment, and shall verify his account upon oath when thereunto lawfully required, and shall deliver to such person or persons as aforesaid, within three days after being thereunto required, all the books, papers, and writings in his custody or power, relating to the affairs of the said Union, and shall immediately thereupon pay such moneys as upon the balance of any account or accounts shall appear to be in his hands, to the said treasurer; and shall in all other respects duly, fully, and faithfully observe, obey, perform, fulfil, and keep all the enactments, laws, rules, and regulations contained in the Labourers (Ireland) Acts, 1883 to 1886, and in any Act or Acts or Order of the Local Government Board for Ireland or the said Guardians touching and concerning the collection of the said rents; and if the said do not and shall not commit or cause or suffer to be done or committed any act, matter, or thing whatsoever, whereby or by means whereof the said Guardians of the Poor of the Union shall or may or can be wronged, defrauded, or prejudiced in respect to any of the rents aforesaid, then the said Bond and Obligation shall be void.

AND KNOW ALL MEN BY THESE PRESENTS, that we the said do hereby for us, and each and every of us, by himself for the whole, and our and each, and every of our heirs, executors, administrators, and assigns, jointly and severally authorise you or any of you, to remise, release, and for ever quit claim, unto the said Guardians of the Poor of the Union, all and all manner of error or errors, or misprision of error or errors, or erroneous proceedings whatsoever, that are or may be in or about the entering or obtaining the said judgment or judgments, or any other the proceedings thereupon; and for what you the said solicitors, or any of you shall do in the premises, this shall be to you and every of you a sufficient authority; and we have expressly named , of , in the county of , a solicitor of Her Majesty's High Court of Justice in Ireland, and requested him to attend on our behalf to inform us of the nature and effect hereof before executing same, and to witness the due execution hereof by us; and we acknowledge that the said has accordingly attended and informed us of the true nature and effect hereof before such execution.

In witness whereof we have hereunto set our hands and seals, the day of , in the year of Our Lord

Signed, Sealed, and Delivered by the said , in the presence of me, , at , in the County of , a Solicitor of the High Court of Justice in Ireland, and I declare myself to be the Solicitor for the said , and attending at their request, and having previously to the execution of this warrant informed them of the nature and effect thereof, I hereunto subscribe my name as such Solicitor.	(*Seal.*) (*Seal.*) (*Seal.*)
Solicitor for the parties above-named.	

No. 6.—Tables for Calculating Outstanding Balances of Loans Obtained under the Labourers Acts.

Local Government Board, Dublin,
31st March, 1890.

Sir,—I am directed by the Local Government Board for Ireland to forward to you the accompanying copies of tables which have been prepared in this Department, by means of which the amount of principal of loans obtained by Boards of Guardians under the Labourers (Ireland) Acts outstanding at any time may be ascertained.

Examples are given in front of the tables for the guidance of Clerks of Unions.

I am, sir,
Your obedient servant,
Thos. A. Mooney, Secretary.

To the Clerk of——Union.

Enclosure to the Foregoing.

Tables by which the outstanding balances of Principal of Loans advanced under the Labourers (Ireland) Acts for terms of 35 years, 40 years, or 50 years, may at any time be readily ascertained.

Rule.—(1.) Multiply each instalment of the loan which has been received by the tabular number opposite to the number of financial years[a] (or financial years and half-year) in respect of which repayments shall have been made since the issue of the instalment, and the product will be the outstanding balance of principal in respect of such instalment.

a. By financial years or half-years are meant periods of twelve or six months commencing on a First day of May, or a First day of November.

(2.) Add together the products so obtained, and also the amount of any instalment in respect of which no repayment has been made (see Example 2), and the result will be the total amount of principal outstanding.

Example.—A Loan of £1,750 (repayable in 40 years) has been issued as follows:—

£
300 in January, 1885,
550 in September, 1886,
580 in July, 1887, and
320 in January, 1888.

(1.) Required: The outstanding balance of principal after the half-yearly repayment due on the 1st of November, 1892, shall have been made?

Answer:—

£		£	s.	d.
300 × ·900467 (7½ years paid)[a]	=	270	2	9
550 × ·922520 (6 years paid)	=	507	7	10
580 × ·936577 (5 years paid)	=	543	4	3
320 × ·943868 (4½ years paid)	=	301	17	6
Total, .		£1,032	12	4

(2.) Required: The outstanding balance after the half-yearly repayment due on the 1st of November, 1887, had been made?

Answer:—

£		£	s.	d.
300 × ·969597 (2½ years paid)	=	290	17	7
550 × ·988172 (1 year paid)	=	543	9	10
580 (no principal repaid)	=	580	0	0
Total, .		£1,414	7	5

---

a. In arriving at these numbers of years and half-years the broken period between the issue of an instalment and the first repayment should not be counted, as no part of the principal of a loan is included in such first repayment.

[Table.

35 Years. Rate of Interest, 3¼ per cent. Annuity covering Principal and Interest, £4 16s. 8d.				40 Years. Rate of Interest, 3½ per cent. Annuity covering Principal and Interest, £4 13s. 8d.				50 Years. Rate of Interest, 3½ per cent. Annuity covering Principal and Interest, £4 5s. 3d.			
Years.	Tabular No.	Years.	Tabular No.	Years.	Tabular No.	Years.	Tabular No.	Years.	Tabular No.	Years.	Tabular No.
½	·992123	25½	·388887	½	·994086	25½	·525334	½	·996463	25½	·706234
1	·984247	26	·371546	1	·988179	26	·511378	1	·992926	26	·697313
1½	·976114	26½	·353273	1½	·982052	26½	·496914	1½	·989254	26½	·688141
2	·967081	27	·335181	2	·975931	27	·482448	2	·985566	27	·678842
2½	·958584	27½	·316661	2½	·969597	27½	·467675	2½	·981779	27½	·669375
3	·951187	28	·297820	3	·963202	28	·452606	3	·977072	28	[illegible]
3½	·942617	28½	·278632	3½	·956705	28½	·437073	3½	·974021	28½	[illegible]
4	·933847	29	·259246	4	·950140	29	·421616	4	·970071	29	[illegible]
4½	·924896	29½	·239332	4½	·943308	29½	·405781	4½	·966078	29½	·629760
5	·915944	30	·219418	5	·936577	30	·389441	5	·961875	30	·619182
5½	·906701	30½	·198857	5½	·929653	30½	·372840	5½	·957633	30½	·608733
6	·897458	31	·178206	6	·922629	31	·355947	6	·953371	31	[illegible]
6½	·887915	31½	·157607	6½	·915206	31½	·338668	6½	·948759	31½	[illegible]
7	·878372	32	·135857	7	·907890	32	·321089	7	·944648	32	·575419
7½	·868516	32½	·113918	7½	·900467	32½	·304108	7½	·939971	32½	·564431
8	·858806	33	·091968	8	·892943	33	·286328	8	·935304	33	·552942
8½	·848489	33½	·069306	8½	·885160	33½	·267925	8½	·930648	33½	·541024
9	·838319	34	·046735	9	·877489	34	·249529	9	·925807	34	·529862
9½	·827815	34½	·023367	9½	·869300	34½	·230473	9½	·920971	34½	·516737
10	·817311	35		10	·861260	35	·211428	10	·916044	35	·504270
10½	·806465			10½	·852968	35½	·191714	10½	·910933	35½	·491541
11	·795029			11	·844590	36	·172000	11	·905822	36	·478513
11½	·784122			11½	·835939	36½	·151807	11½	·900619	36½	·465490
12	·773224			12	·827208	37	·131193	12	·895316	37	·452065
12½	·761062			12½	·818363	37½	·110075	12½	·889714	37½	·438227
13	·750109			13	·809427	38	·088958	13	·884219	38	·424465
13½	·738163			13½	·800178	38½	·067161	13½	·878694	38½	·410134
14	·726225			14	·790920	39	·045244	14	·872796	39	·394818
14½	·714009			14½	·781367	39½	·022622	14½	·866874	39½	·380644
15	·701574			15	·771785	40		15	·860842	40	·366079
15½	·688848			15½	·761877			15½	·854807	40½	·350683
16	·676182			16	·751970			16	·848643	41	·335223
16½	·663082			16½	·741710			16½	·842388	41½	·319241
17	·649842			17	·731461			17	·836013	42	·303279
17½	·636275			17½	·720840			17½	·829800	42½	·286826
18	·622708			18	·710236			18	·822936	43	·270049
18½	·608701			18½	·699251			18½	·816394	43½	·253029
19	·594608			19	·688060			19	·808903	44	·235536
19½	·580230			19½	·676807			19½	·801848	44½	·217731
20	·565737			20	·665528			20	·794735	45	·199627
20½	·550634			20½	·653701			20½	·787258	45½	·181873
21	·535601			21	·641964			21	·779963	46	·162788
21½	·520183			21½	·629815			21½	·772296	46½	·143528
22	·505604			22	·617637			22	·764537	47	·124147
22½	·490145			22½	·605039			22½	·756670	47½	·104330
23	·473320			23	·592487			23	·748718	48	·084373
23½	·456788			23½	·579381			23½	·740677	48½	·063859
24	·440332			24	·566334			24	·732528	49	·043940
24½	·423381			24½	·552832			24½	·723871	49½	·021463
25	·406410			25	·539029			25	·715115	50	

III.—CORRESPONDENCE, &c.

No 1.—INQUIRIES under SECTION 163 of the PUBLIC HEALTH (IRELAND) ACT, 1878, respecting the condition of BURIAL GROUNDS.

Instructional letter to Medical Inspectors.

Local Government Board, Dublin,
4th March, 1890.

SIR,—I am directed by the Local Government Board for Ireland to state that owing to changes which have recently taken place in the staff of Medical Inspectors the Board think it desirable to address you on the subject of inquiries under section 163 of the Public Health Act respecting the condition of burial grounds, and to express their opinion as to the manner in which such inquiries should be conducted.

The Board think that in the first instance evidence should be obtained on oath as to whether the requirements of section 163 with respect to the posting of the notices of the inquiry have been complied with. This evidence is important, and until it is shown that the necessary preliminaries have been properly carried out no evidence should be taken as to the condition of the graveyard.

The next stage in the proceedings is to take evidence as to the state of the burial ground, and the nature of this evidence must be left to your discretion as from your knowledge of the statements contained in the representation and the previous correspondence you will probably have given notice to attend to the persons capable of affording trustworthy testimony respecting the condition of the graveyard.

With respect to claims for right of interment it has been found that the questions put to witnesses vary considerably at inquiries held by different Inspectors, and with a view to securing greater uniformity in this respect in future the Board have to suggest to you that each applicant for reservation of right of interment should be required to supply satisfactory information on the following points before you recommend his name to be included in the Schedule of exceptions to the Order:—

1. What title—whether by purchase or by usage, and, if by usage, whether any other persons have equal rights in the grave. If obtained by purchase, documentary evidence ought to be forthcoming. If exclusive right is claimed, the nature of the claim should be fully set forth.

2. Precise size of grave or vault—any tombstone?—any inscription?—and if so, what is the degree of relationship of the applicant to the persons whose names are inscribed?

3. If there be a church in the graveyard which is actually used for Divine worship, and the right of interment is claimed in a vault, it will be necessary to ascertain whether the vault is under or adjoining any part of the church, and in the case of all vaults care should be taken to ascertain whether the opening of them would disturb the vaults or graves of other persons.

4. What is the number of persons already interred in the grave claimed? What was the date of the last interment? Was the applicant present thereat? If not, some person must attend who was present, and can swear to the depth of earth over the coffin, measuring from the natural surface of the ground.

5. In considering claims attention should be given to the nature of the soil. Human remains and the coffins in which they are enclosed are preserved for many years (from ten to fourteen) in wet and undrained clayey soils, whereas skeletons alone remain after an interval of from seven to ten years in dry, sandy, gravelly and well drained cemeteries. It must be borne in mind that no unwalled grave should be reopened within fourteen years after the burial of a person above twelve years of age, or within eight years after the burial of a child under twelve years of age, unless to bury another member of the same family, and if opened sooner to bury a member of the same family a layer of earth not less than one foot in depth should be left undisturbed above the previously buried coffin. It is well to bear in mind that coffins vary in depth from fourteen to eighteen inches. Sixteen inches may be taken as the average.

6. Where rights are proposed to be reserved in respect of a family group whose ages do not vary much it is to be borne in mind that if several lives expire within a short period of each other it may not be possible to bury all the bodies in the space claimed.

7. It is always expedient, when possible, to reserve to a widow or widower the right to be interred in the grave of a deceased husband or wife.

8. When a graveyard is surrounded by inhabited dwellings, or is situated within a town a very strong case should be established before admitting claims of exemption. The evidence given in the reports on intra-mural sepulture in a series of Parliamentary papers published from 1843 to 1850 clearly established that living in the vicinity of graveyards undermines the constitution, and when any epidemic touched the locality the people fell before it. Thus cholera has always attacked persons living in the vicinity of crowded graveyards.

The Board think that attention to the points indicated will greatly facilitate them in considering the question of closing burial grounds against future interments, especially in cases where the claims for reservation are numerous.

In some cases burial boards forward representations to the Local Government Board in favour of closing overcrowded graveyards without having taken any steps under section 172 to provide the public with burial ground accommodation as a substitute for the graveyard it is proposed should be closed. This is a point which should not be lost sight of by an Inspector holding an inquiry, and if no new burial ground has been provided it would be of great assistance to the Local Government Board if he would deal with this aspect of the matter in his report, pointing out whether it might not be possible for the burial board to extend the existing graveyard; he should also ascertain and state the space available for further interments in existing graveyards which may be within reasonable reach of the persons who have resorted to the burial ground which formed the subject of inquiry.

I am, sir,

Your obedient servant,

THOS. A. MOONEY, Secretary.

To each Medical Inspector.

No. 2.—STATEMENT of ORDERS issued under the 233rd Section of the PUBLIC HEALTH (IRELAND) ACT, 1878, determining the AREA of CHARGE on which the SPECIAL EXPENSES mentioned in such Orders respectively shall be chargeable (*in continuation of Statement in Seventeenth Annual Report, pages 90 to 104*).

NAME OF UNION, AND TOWN, VILLAGE, OR PLACE.	Date of Order.	Purposes for which incurred or to be incurred.		AREA OF CHARGE.
		Water Supply, &c.	Sewerage, &c.	
ARMAGH UNION:				
Keady.	14th July, 1889. .	—	Cleansing pond. .	The Townlands or portions of Townlands included within the limits or boundary of the Township of Keady, situate in the Commons Electoral Division
Do.	10th July, 1889. .	—	do. . . .	The Townlands or portions of Townlands included within the limits or boundary of the Township of Keady, situate in the Crossmore and Keady Electoral Divisions,—the above-mentioned Order of 14th July, 1889, being rescinded by this Order
BANBRIDGE UNION:				
Village of Lawrencetown.	20th July, 1889 .	Water supply . .	—	The Lawrencetown Electoral Division.
BALROTHERY UNION:				
Town of Malahide. .	15th November, 1889.	—	Sewerage. . .	The Townlands of Malahide, Malahide Demesne, and Malahide Demesne, situate in the Malahide Electoral Division.
Town of Rush. . .	16th December, 1889.	—	Constructing a main sewer.	The Townlands of Rush and Rush Demesne, situate in the Lusk Electoral Division.
[illegible] . . .	3rd January, 1890. .	Sinking a well and erect-	—	The Hollywood Electoral Division.

BANDON UNION:				
Kilbrittain National Schools.	6th December, 18[illegible].	Water supply	—	The Rathclarin, Kilbrittain, and Rourleigh Electoral Divisions.
BELFAST UNION:				
Ballymurphy.	19th January, 18[illegible].	—	Sewerage.	The portions of the Townlands of Ballymurphy and Strandtown consisting of the Tenements described in the Order, both the said Townlands being situate in the Ballyhackamore Electoral Division of the said Union.
CASTLEBAR UNION:				
Village of Balla.	22nd October, 18[illegible].	—	Maintenance of sewerage works.	The Townland of Balla, situate in the Balla Electoral Division.
CAVAN UNION:				
Kilnaleck.	6th April, 18[illegible].	Providing and maintaining a pump.	—	The portion of the Townland of Kilnaleck, situate in the Kilnaleck Electoral Division, consisting of the Tenements described in the Order.
CELBRIDGE UNION:				
Celbridge.	6th April, 18[illegible]	Water supply	—	The Townland of Alleswood, situate in the Clonsilla Electoral Division; and the Townlands of Coldblow, Laraghcon, St. Catherine's Park, and Westmanstown, situate in the Lucan Electoral Division.
Lucan.	8th April, 18[illegible]	—	Making and renovating sewers.	The Townlands of "Lucan Demesne" and "Lucan and Pettycannon," situate in the Lucan Electoral Division.
Town of Kilcock.	22nd January, 18[illegible]	Water supply.	Sewerage.	The Kilcock Electoral Division.
Town of Newcastle.	22nd January, 18[illegible].	Water supply	—	The Townlands of Greenogue, Glebe, and Newcastle South situate in the Newcastle Electoral Division.

STATEMENT of ORDERS issued under the 232nd Section of the PUBLIC HEALTH (IRELAND) ACT, 1878, determining the AREA of CHARGE on which the SPECIAL EXPENSES mentioned in such Orders respectively shall be chargeable—continued.

NAME OF UNION, AND TOWN, VILLAGE, OR PLACE.	Date of Order.	Purposes for which incurred or to be incurred.		AREA OF CHARGE.
		Water Supply, &c.	Sewerage, &c.	
COLERAINE UNION:				
Town of Castlerock.	3rd May, 188[illegible].	—	Sewerage works.	The Townland of Bogtown, situate in the Articlave Electoral Division and the Townlands of Freehall (Watson), and Freehall (Dunlop), situate in the Downhill Electoral Division—except the portions of said Townlands of Bogtown and Freehall (Watson) consisting of the Tenements described in the Order.
[illegible] UNION:				
Kells.	18th December, 188[illegible].	Sinking a well and erecting a pump.	—	The [illegible], [illegible], and [illegible] Electoral Divisions.
[illegible]	18th December, 188[illegible].	Do.	—	The [illegible] Electoral Division.
DROGHEDA UNION:				
Waterunder.	23rd September, 188[illegible].	In connection with the "Bully Well."	—	The Townlands and portions of Townlands included within the limits or boundaries of the West Ward of the St. Peter's Electoral Division, and not included in an Urban Sanitary District.

DUNFANAGHY UNION:				
Village of Creeslough. .	4th April, [illegible]. .	Water supply .	—	The portion of the Townland of Creeslough, situate in the Creeslough Electoral Division, consisting of the Tenements described in the Order.
DUNMANWAY UNION:				
Town of Ballineen. .	20th September, [illegible].	Water supply . .	—	The Ballineen Dispensary District.
Town of Dunmanway. .	18th September, [illegible].	Do. .	—	The Dunmanway Dispensary District.
Ballineen. . . .	18th December, [illegible].	—	Sewerage works. .	The Ballineen Dispensary District.
ENNIS UNION:				
Doora Electoral Division.	13th September, 1888.	Water supply. . .	—	The Doora Electoral Division.
GLIN UNION:				
Town of Foynes. . .	7th March, 1888. .	Water supply . .	—	The Shanagolden Electoral Division.
GORT UNION:				
Labane.	9th April, 1888. .	Sinking a well. . .	—	The Townlands of Ballyglass West, Ballylara, and Caherbelly, situate in the Ardrahan Electoral Division, the Townland of Ardgaine South, situate in the Castletaylor Electoral Division, and the Townlands of Ballymacgiff North and Ballymacgiff South, situate in the Skehanagh Electoral Division.
IRVINESTOWN UNION:				
Irvinestown. . . .	26th January, 1888. .	—	Constructing a sewer.	The Townlands of Brownhill, Hardfield, [illegible]

STATEMENT of ORDERS issued under the 232nd Section of the PUBLIC HEALTH (IRELAND) ACT, 1878, determining the AREA of CHARGE on which the SPECIAL EXPENSES mentioned in such Orders respectively shall be chargeable—*continued.*

NAME OF UNION, AND TOWN, VILLAGE, OR PLACE.	Date of Order.	Purposes for which Incurred or to be Incurred.		AREA OF CHARGE.
		Water Supply, &c.	Sewerage, &c.	
KILKENNY UNION:				
Townland of Ballyouskill. .	24th November, 1880	Sinking a well and erecting a pump.	—	The Ballyouskill Electoral Division.
KILMACTHOMAS UNION:				
Village of Stradbally. .	7th March, 1880. .	Water supply. . .	—	The Stradbally Electoral Division.
LISTOWEL UNION:				
Village of Ballyduff .	13th September, 1880.	Sinking a well and erecting a pump.	—	The Ballyduff Electoral Division.
MALLOW UNION:				

MOUNTMELLICK UNION:				
Town of Maryborough. .	[illegible] September, [illegible].	Repairing public pumps.	Making a sewer at Market Square, and scavenging the town.	The Townlands of [illegible] Little, [illegible], [illegible], [illegible], Maryborough, and [illegible], situate in the Maryborough Electoral Division.
[illegible], . . .	3rd January, [illegible]. .	Sinking a well and erecting a pump.	—	The Townland of [illegible], situate in the [illegible] Electoral Division, except the portion of said Townland consisting of the [illegible] described in the Order
[illegible] UNION:				
[illegible]. . . .	22nd January, [illegible]. .	Erecting a pump. .	—	The [illegible], [illegible], and [illegible] Electoral Divisions.
NAAS UNION:				
[illegible]. . . .	[illegible] December, [illegible].	Erecting a pump. .	—	The [illegible] North Electoral Division.
NAVAN UNION:				
Village of Yellow Furze.	[illegible] July, [illegible]. .	Providing a pump. .	—	The [illegible] and [illegible] Electoral Divisions.
NEWCASTLE UNION:				
[illegible]. . . .	27th October, [illegible]. .	Erecting a pump. .	—	The [illegible] Electoral Division.
NEW ROSS UNION:				
[illegible]. . . .	[illegible] July, [illegible]. .	Sinking a well and erecting a pump.	—	The [illegible] and [illegible] Electoral Divisions.
[illegible]. . .	10th January, [illegible]. .	Do. .	—	The [illegible], [illegible], and [illegible] Electoral [illegible]

STATEMENT of ORDERS issued under the 232nd Section of the PUBLIC HEALTH (IRELAND) ACT, 1878, determining the AREA of CHARGE on which the SPECIAL EXPENSES mentioned in such Orders respectively shall be chargeable—*continued.*

NAME OF UNION, AND TOWN, VILLAGE, OR PLACE.	Date of Order.	Purposes for which incurred or to be incurred.		AREA OF CHARGE.
		Water Supply, &c.	Sewerage, &c.	
[illegible] UNION:				
Town of [illegible] and Village of [illegible].	10th December, 18[illegible]	Providing pumps and maintaining them in repair and working order.	—	The Townlands of [illegible], Demesne, Glebe, [illegible], [illegible], [illegible], and [illegible], situate in the [illegible] Electoral Division.
TRIM UNION:				
Wardstown. . . .	17th October, 18[illegible].	Erecting a pump. . .	—	The Townlands of Wardstown and [illegible], situate in the [illegible] Electoral Division.
Castletown. . . .	3rd January, 18[illegible].	Do. .	—	The Townlands of [illegible] and Castletown, situate, respectively, in the Abbey and [illegible] Electoral Divisions.
URLINGFORD UNION:				
Townland of Rathlogan.	31st October, 18[illegible].	Sinking a pump and keeping it in repair	—	The Townland of Rathlogan, in the Parish of Rathlogan, and the Townland of [illegible], both the said Townlands being situate in the [illegible] Electoral Division.
Town of Urlingford. .		Keeping a pump in repair.	—	The Townland of Urlingford, situate in the Urlingford Electoral Division.

APPENDIX D.

TABLES CONNECTED WITH POOR RELIEF AND EXPENDITURE.

No. 1.—A Return (in pursuance of the 20th Section of the Act 10 Vic., cap. 31) Relieved in and out of the Workhouses, together with the Receipts in each Expenditure under the Medical Charities and Vaccination Acts, the National School Teachers, and the Parliamentary Voters, Jurors, and Expla. Poor Rates during the Year.

Part 1.—Return showing the Receipts and Expenditure

Names of Counties and Unions.	Receipts.					Seed Rate lodged.	Expenditure.			
	Amount of Poor Rate lodged.	Parliamentary Grants.	Other Receipts, including repayment of Relief by way of Loan, Grants, &c.	Amount of Loans.	Total Receipts during the year, exclusive of Seed Rate.		In-Maintenance.	Out-Relief.	Maintenance of [illegible]	Emigration Expenses.
1.	2.	3.	4.	5.	6.	7.	8.	9.	10.	11.
PROVINCE OF ULSTER.	£	£	£	£	£	£	£	£	£	£
Antrim.										
Antrim,	4,747	700	19	100	5,566	-	1,943	833	11	-
Ballycastle,	1,683	390	41	-	2,107	-	535	16	7	-
Ballymena,	8,429	1,156	1,220	630	6,436	-	1,217	1,309	147	-
Ballymoney,	3,841	554	337	-	4,732	-	638	646	58	-
Belfast,	40,184	3,744	1,164	2,480	53,012	-	21,780	2,077	678	-
Larne,	4,161	640	366	150	5,090	-	1,253	673	45	-
Lisburn,	6,560	756	55	-	6,390	-	1,118	1,131	64	-
Armagh.										
Armagh,	5,452	544	153	-	6,169	-	1,680	125	73	-
Lurgan,	7,325	1,217	170	-	8,715	-	2,430	533	207	-
Cavan.										
Bailieborough,	2,753	415	18	700	3,948	-	816	569	47	-
Bawnboy,	3,033	516	20	-	3,563		554	409	7	-
Cavan,	8,106	945	92	2,010	11,152	11	1,858	1,421	138	-
Cootehill,	3,155	465	27	-	3,648	-	508	782	23	-
Donegal.										
Ballyshannon,	3,998	532	45	1,000	6,675	-	1,001	490	14	-
Donegal,	1,720	444	20	-	2,209	-	546	125	-	-
Dunfanaghy,	935	250	14	-	1,199	-	271	13	4	-
Glenties,	2,341	577	80	-	2,907	-	564	229	19	-
Inishowen,	3,522	553	32	300	4,407	-	840	647	18	-
Letterkenny,	1,920	378	26	-	2,723	-	849	15	88	-
Milford,	2,170	439	22	-	2,077	-	677	62	-	-
Stranorlar,	1,555	421	9	-	1,985	-	285	23	10	-
Down.										
Banbridge,	6,405	681	46	-	6,132	-	1,312	1,702	129	-
Downpatrick,	6,022	789	64	-	6,775	-	1,499	247	102	-
Kilkeel,	2,093	408	30	-	2,521	-	414	199	22	-
Newry,	8,157	1,609	249	-	10,097	-	1,807	2,083	176	-
Newtownards,	6,915	1,003	65	-	7,982	-	2,185	1,160	71	-
Fermanagh.										
Enniskillen,	5,948	736	139	-	6,843	-	1,578	84	88	-
Irvinestown,	2,758	400	11	-	3,168	-	629	87	-	-
Lisnaskea,	1,791	390	4	-	2,185	-	459	171	-	-
Londonderry.										
Coleraine,	5,016	887	61	-	5,929	-	1,127	663	87	-
Limavady,	2,047	532	163	-	2,742	-	789	-	20	-
Londonderry,	6,143	1,464	197	299	7,093	-	1,600	142	145	-
Magherafelt,	3,262	594	34	-	3,870	-	1,236	467	59	-
Monaghan.										
Carrickmacross,	3,090	356	3	150	3,625	-	1,165	290	48	-
Castleblayney,	3,347	691	25	-	4,003	-	1,016	606	36	-
Clones,	2,066	306	21	-	2,444	-	541	11	1	-
Monaghan,	2,863	619	137	-	3,608	-	1,070	-	17	-
Tyrone.										
Castlederg,	1,351	296	2	-	1,648	-	243	5	-	-

of the EXPENDITURE on the RELIEF of the POOR, and of the TOTAL NUMBERS UNION in IRELAND, for the year ended the 29th of September, 1889; also showing the Registration, Public Health, Superannuation, Labourers, Contagious Diseases (Animals), sives Acts; the amount of LOANS repaid, and the TOTAL EXPENDITURE out of the

of Unions during the year* ended the 29th of September, 1889.

Expenditure.										(continued.)	
Salaries and Rations of Officers.	All other Poor Relief Expenditure.	Total Poor Relief Expenditure.	Expenses under Medical Charities and Vaccination Acts.	Expenses under the Acts for Registration of Births, Deaths, and Marriages.	Expenses under the Public Health Act. For Sanitary purposes.	Expenses under the Public Health Act. For Burial grounds.	Expenses under the Superannuation Acts.	Expenses under the Labourers Acts.	Expenses under Contagious Diseases (Animals) Act.	Payments under National School Teachers Act.	NAMES OF COUNTIES AND UNIONS.
12.	13.	14.	15.	16.	17.	18.	19.	20.	21.	22.	23.
£	£	£	£	£	£	£	£	£	£	£	PROVINCE OF ULSTER.
											ANTRIM.
805	690	3,612	809	[illegible]	102	300	57	-	167	-	Antrim.
427	213	1,220	502	21	92	–	99	–	84	–	Ballycastle.
1,658	768	5,209	1,213	125	154	36	–	186	147	–	Ballymena.
366	361	2,401	816	63	201	71	–	–	105	–	Ballymoney.
5,687	2,251	33,464	3,014	772	5,037	59	172	–	658	5,258	Belfast.
740	405	3,006	724	77	541	6	20	–	136	19	Larne.
739	471	3,443	1,150	127	213	2	–	–	213	–	Lisburn.
											ARMAGH.
785	1,009	3,682	1,846	118	278	–	60	–	254	–	Armagh.
941	839	5,490	1,027	141	101	60	197	–	205	–	Lurgan.
											CAVAN.
453	367	2,306	577	35	141	–	31	874	54	–	Bailieborough.
415	298	1,742	546	37	115	41	20	4	57	–	Bawnboy.
796	1,074	5,085	1,386	76	928	34	73	–	146	–	Cavan.
513	356	2,249	685	42	110	1	126	–	165	–	Cootehill.
											DONEGAL.
465	507	2,466	683	45	1,647	1	10	–	87	–	Ballyshannon.
494	286	1,391	742	38	174	12	–	–	61	–	Donegal.
283	178	670	462	31	67	5	17	–	32	–	Dunfanaghy.
414	270	1,580	1,098	66	132	–	76	–	44	–	Glenties.
604	366	2,301	860	50	474	–	–	–	44	282	Inishowen.
440	241	1,370	428	27	84	5	27	–	63	–	Letterkenny.
424	243	1,290	750	43	107	21	–	–	61	250	Milford.
467	196	1,060	483	31	135	–	110	–	38	–	Stranorlar.
											DOWN.
753	638	4,374	1,014	110	264	70	30	–	229	–	Banbridge.
755	507	3,207	1,210	97	425	–	40	–	197	1,057	Downpatrick.
435	212	1,272	648	29	321	2	–	–	116	8	Kilkeel.
973	1,029	5,900	1,407	186	283	–	72	–	260	946	Newry.
927	724	4,912	1,093	94	331	100	–	–	152	–	Newtownards.
											FERMANAGH.
796	607	3,180	1,164	87	184	12	74	–	205	894	Enniskillen.
451	386	1,444	580	26	150	6	17	–	71	366	Irvinestown.
417	213	1,260	674	35	90	–	61	–	78	–	Lisnaskea.
											LONDONDERRY.
668	690	3,387	941	70	255	9	60	–	185	–	Coleraine.
568	351	1,737	757	83	120	–	25	–	90	–	Limavady.
737	730	3,365	2,268	197	245	18	115	–	246	–	Londonderry.
373	481	2,815	927	91	172	11	–	–	136	–	Magherafelt.
											MONAGHAN.
496	252	2,557	1,600	31	98	2	–	13	99	–	Carrickmacross.
570	566	2,712	877	50	151	–	–	–	85	–	Castleblayney
403	254	1,208	494	31	93	–	106	–	79	–	Clones.
573	309	1,950	930	57	191	–	30	–	112	–	Monaghan.
											TYRONE.
490	145	794	366	24	155	1	–	–	40	–	Castlederg.
427	332	1,627	655	38	102	14	10	–	61	622	Clogher.
521	309	2,140	732	56	197	48	233	–	88	2	Cookstown.
611	525	2,849	1,090	71	350	6	15	–	151	639	Dungannon.
140	167	508	192	8	24	–	–	–	–	–	Gortin.
707	587	3,310	1,313	77	288	–	150	–	121	738	Omagh.
602	656	3,286	1,136	72	1,707	14	157	–	120	571	Strabane.
39,766	28,109	150,026	42,766	3,555	18,285	995	2,274	1,071	5,914	12,660	1889, Total,
39,665	26,103	143,398	43,412	3,681	13,934	707	2,120	668	5,696	11,310	1888, ULSTER.
101	2,006	6,628	–	–	4,351	288	154	403	218	1,350	Increase.
–	–	–	646	126	–	–	–	–	–	–	Decrease.

PART I.—RETURN showing the Receipts and Expenditure of unions during the year ended the 29th of September, 1889—*continued*.

Names of Counties and Unions.	Expenditure—(continued). Expenses under the Parliamentary Voters, Jurors, and Explosives Acts.	Repayment of Loans.	Total Expenditure during the year exclusive of repayments on account of Loans under seed supply Act.	Amount of Expenditure included in Columns 14 and 21 defrayed out of Loans. Poor Relief.	Other Expenditure.	Amount repaid to Commissioners of Public Works under Seed Supply Act.	Valuation on 29th Sept., 1889.	Poundage on the Valuation. Of Expenditure for Relief of the Poor (Col. 14), exclusive of the amount shown in Col. 28.	Of Total Expenditure, exclusive of the amounts shown in Cols. 28 and 29.
24.	25.	26.	27.	28.	29.	30.	31.	32.	33.
PROVINCE OF ULSTER.	£	£	£	£	£	£	£	s. d.	s. d.
ANTRIM.									
Antrim,	246	53	5,473	–	209	–	194,816	0 7	0 10
Ballycastle,	102	–	2,184	–	–	–	45,058	0 6½	0 11½
Ballymena,	125	16	7,214	–	180	–	124,731	0 9½	1 1
Ballymoney,	183	518	4,423	–	–	–	83,411	0 7½	1 0½
Belfast,	1,271	1,930	59,561	–	5,102	–	794,458	0 11½	1 4½
Larne,	234	450	5,418	–	100	–	102,820	0 7½	1 0½
Lisburn,	212	48	5,780	–	–	–	178,151	0 4½	0 7½
ARMAGH.									
Armagh,	247	183	6,710	–	–	–	207,785	0 4½	0 7½
Lurgan,	237	78	7,835	–	–	–	141,690	0 9	1 1½
CAVAN.									
Bailieborough,	82	21	4,181	–	874	–	40,303	1 10	1 7½
Bawnboy,	167	98	2,710	–	–	300	40,874	0 10½	1 4½
Cavan,	240	337	8,266	–	422	220	114,167	0 10½	1 4½
Cootehill,	106	–	3,310	–	–	–	73,391	0 7½	0 10½
DONEGAL.									
Ballyshannon,	137	77	5,390	–	1,180	–	60,500	0 11½	1 5½
Donegal,	108	–	2,128	–	–	–	31,447	0 0½	1 5½
Dunfanaghy,	40	43	1,075	–	–	62	11,604	1 2	2 4½
Glenties,	73	0	3,018	–	–	–	20,445	1 6½	2 11½
Inishowen,	112	176	4,484	–	290	–	84,046	1 2½	2 1½
Letterkenny,	85	–	2,000	–	–	–	31,728	0 10½	1 6
Milford,	75	60	2,771	–	–	–	20,979	0 10½	1 10½
Stranorlar,	90	–	1,022	–	–	–	30,619	0 8½	1 3½
DOWN.									
Banbridge,	232	–	6,403	–	–	–	160,381	0 6½	0 8½
Downpatrick,	173	147	6,666	–	–	–	177,004	0 4½	0 9
Kilkeel,	86	137	2,020	–	–	–	41,080	0 8½	1 2
Newry,	247	391	9,018	–	–	–	168,914	0 8½	1 1
Newtownards,	138	–	6,780	–	–	–	141,063	0 8½	0 11½
FERMANAGH.									
Enniskillen,	355	204	9,418	–	14	–	107,748	0 7	1 2½
Irvinestown,	101	34	2,765	–	–	–	49,157	0 7	1 1½
Lisnaskea,	110	26	2,352	–	–	–	84,081	0 5½	0 9½
LONDONDERRY.									
Coleraine,	251	814	5,880	–	–	–	101,084	0 7½	1 1½
Limavady,	152	807	3,257	–	–	–	68,692	0 0	0 11½
Londonderry,	217	9	6,620	–	219	–	163,098	0 0	0 9½
Magherafelt,	292	–	4,241	–	–	–	92,241	0 7½	0 11½
MONAGHAN.									
Carrickmacross,	95	–	3,180	–	500	–	50,307	0 10½	1 5½
Castleblayney,	144	–	4,178	–	–	–	75,885	0 8½	1 0½
Clones,	121	–	2,132	–	–	–	57,514	0 6	0 9
Monaghan,	154	–	3,102	–	–	–	94,080	0 6	0 9½
TYRONE.									
Castlederg,	90	48	1,577	–	–	–	24,835	0 7½	1 1½
Clogher,	144	–	3,215	–	–	–	66,180	0 7	1 2
Cookstown,	123	380	4,079	–	–	–	85,526	0 7½	1 2½
Dungannon,	252	1,072	6,563	–	213	–	98,001	0 7½	1 2½
Gortin,*	60	–	792	–	–	–	–	–	–
Omagh,	186	697	6,781	–	–	–	107,880	0 7½	1 3½
Strabane,	181	1,110	8,373	–	1,304	–	107,984	0 7½	1 3½
Total, ULSTER, 1889,	8,167	9,320	255,003	–	11,414	701	4,392,455	0 8½	1 1½
Total, ULSTER, 1888,	8,240	8,642	241,839	–	5,784	204	4,374,878	0 7½	1 1
Increase,	–	678	13,163	–	5,630	497	17,577	0 0½	0 0½
Decrease,	73	–	–	–	–	–	–	–	–

* See note at foot of pages 102 and 103.

PART I.—RETURN showing the Receipts and Expenditure of unions during the year ended the 29th of September, 1889—*continued.*

Names of Counties and Unions.	Receipts.						Expenditure—(*continued*).			
	Amount of Poor Rate lodged.	Parliamentary Grants.	Other Receipts, including repayment of Relief by way of Loan, Grants, &c.	Amount of Loans.	Total Receipts during the year, exclusive of Seed Rate.	Seed Rate lodged.	In-Maintenance.	Out-Relief.	Maintenance of Blind and Deaf and Dumb in Institutions, and cost of Relief in Extern Hospitals.	Emigration Expenses.
1.	2.	3.	4.	5.	6.	7.	8.	9.	10.	11.
PROVINCE OF MUNSTER.	£	£	£	£	£	£	£	£	£	£
CLARE.										
Ballyvaghan, .	4,064	259	68	-	4,385	-	878	3	24	-
Corrofin, .	2,172	303	6	50	2,531	1	743	389	0	13
Ennis, .	8,530	435	449	2,500	12,010	-	4,647	1,445	62	41
Ennistymon, .	4,234	541	50	-	4,845	-	2,278	512	53	5
Killadysert, .	3,418	296	26	102	3,842	4	1,235	600	-	10
Kilrush, .	9,410	616	137	273	10,447	-	2,668	2,040	30	8
Scariff, .	3,093	589	24	2,416	6,620	-	1,176	189	110	12
Tulla, .	4,054	532	118	-	4,704	-	1,320	328	3	-
CORK.										
Bandon, .	4,963	649	199	5,700	11,511	-	1,130	1,340	37	-
Bantry, .	2,222	370	88	900	3,580	-	703	928	-	-
Castletown, .	2,025	303	50	-	2,383	-	647	189	17	3
Clonakilty, .	4,576	375	206	3,750	9,007	-	1,688	706	82	5
Cork, .	55,016	4,806	2,027	5,751	67,601	-	19,744	16,779	1,702	67
Dunmanway, .	3,401	434	157	3,000	6,995	-	802	508	34	8
Fermoy, .	6,947	1,089	103	3,708	11,837	-	1,881	1,860	90	8
Kanturk, .	10,720	826	315	-	11,861	-	2,142	2,251	112	11
Kinsale, .	3,240	557	183	750	4,730	-	1,005	143	62	3
Macroom, .	9,071	870	310	4,447	14,810	-	2,772	1,117	210	-
Mallow, .	10,100	600	147	7,582	18,479	-	2,981	2,238	187	17
Midleton, .	8,218	1,182	128	14,000	23,528	-	2,840	1,074	175	5
Millstreet, .	4,670	400	9	-	5,079	-	1,125	1,081	5	8
Mitchelstown, .	4,450	429	226	3,400	8,505	-	1,622	927	64	-
Skibbereen, .	6,877	680	76	4,000	11,633	8	2,400	729	45	17
Skull, .	2,120	201	38	300	2,640	-	605	407	20	-
Youghal, .	5,724	918	158	100	6,930	-	3,023	1,111	108	-
KERRY.										
Cahersiveen, .	4,370	728	177	-	5,284	-	761	183	18	10
Dingle, .	3,602	810	44	183	1,609	-	1,403	218	49	-
Kenmare, .	3,135	705	8	-	3,846	2	618	831	15	-
Killarney, .	9,807	889	147	2,594	13,157	-	3,485	1,081	206	23
Listowel, .	6,310	779	190	3,278	10,553	-	1,839	2,407	71	28
Tralee, .	10,034	1,568	356	813	18,664	-	3,346	2,758	105	15
LIMERICK.										
Croom, .	7,151	609	178	1,780	9,707	-	1,830	1,741	70	1
Glin, .	4,014	563	171	-	5,648	-	1,033	1,068	92	10
Kilmallock, .	18,408	1,340	677	3,170	23,603	-	5,044	4,053	130	17
Limerick, .	24,202	2,126	1,695	4,414	32,437	-	12,656	6,916	384	18
Newcastle, .	7,209	839	245	4,101	12,174	-	1,727	1,845	97	18
Rathkeale, .	6,758	883	255	1,141	8,957	-	1,452	2,376	67	54
TIPPERARY.										
Borrisokane, .	2,606	354	74	760	3,744	-	658	020	15	-
Carrick-on-Suir, .	4,810	633	60	256	5,407	-	1,839	702	13	1
Cashel, .	9,604	845	266	3,021	13,736	-	3,307	2,981	146	1
Clogheen, .	4,465	616	153	2,102	7,246	-	2,310	810	15	27
Clonmel, .	8,733	872	303	2,619	12,187	-	2,778	1,002	73	6
Nenagh, .	7,296	472	401	4,060	12,229	-	2,180	2,019	44	-
Roscrea, .	4,424	884	37	-	5,345	-	1,885	687	49	-
Thurles, .	6,985	1,108	58	-	8,090	-	2,498	2,219	95	27
Tipperary, .	11,065	1,425	797	2,537	16,811	-	4,318	3,829	129	-
WATERFORD.										
Dungarvan, .	7,385	955	273	2,511	11,124	-	3,310	857	100	-
Kilmacthomas, .	4,088	306	186	1,000	5,580	-	1,138	300	26	-
Lismore, .	4,316	734	183	362	5,595	-	1,356	840	61	-
Waterford, .	18,418	1,866	364	373	21,021	-	7,317	3,656	216	-
Total, MUNSTER, 1889,	392,331	40,028	12,795	104,115	549,269	16	130,334	83,802	5,604	516
Total, MUNSTER, 1888,	374,964	29,292	8,689	156,915	579,190	53	131,654	87,093	5,144	564
Increase, .	17,367	10,736	4,106	-	-	-	-	-	560	-
Decrease, .	-	-	-	52,800	29,921	38	1,318	3,291	-	48

(*continued*.

PART 1.—RETURN showing the Receipts and Expenditure

Names of Counties and Unions.	[continued.] Expenditure. Salaries and Rations of Officers.	All other Poor Relief Expenditure.	Total Poor Relief Expenditure.	Expenses under Medical Charities and Vaccination Acts.	Expenses under the Acts for Registration of Births, Deaths, and Marriages.	Expenses under the Public Health Act. For Sanitary purposes.	For Burial grounds.	Expenses under the Superannuation Acts.	Expenses under the Labourers Acts.	Expenses under Contagious Diseases (Animals) Act.	Payments under National School Teachers Act.
12.	13.	14.	15.	16.	17.	18.	19.	20.	21.	22.	23.
PROVINCE OF MUNSTER.	£	£	£	£	£	£	£	£	£	£	£
CLARE.											
Ballyvaghan,	391	781	2,079	140	8	141	–	32	31	31	158
Corrofin,	305	240	1,773	170	10	92	11	91	12	21	–
Ennis,	1,129	1,027	7,704	815	27	182	113	121	2,345	93	–
Ennistymon,	903	691	4,072	482	87	196	31	33	–	55	–
Killadysert,	427	290	2,086	338	20	77	12	–	107	66	–
Kilrush,	648	810	5,419	742	70	170	17	14	8	87	–
Scariff,	598	260	2,810	438	26	168	2	13	8,241	47	–
Tulla,	509	420	2,789	478	16	213	6	12	118	58	–
CORK.											
Bandon,	747	400	3,743	770	53	231	–	24	6,000	125	–
Bantry,	381	202	1,703	643	22	518	62	8	–	43	–
Castletown,	116	201	1,479	345	26	130	10	66	–	25	–
Clonakilty,	530	390	3,376	329	44	131	2	80	4,068	136	–
Cork,	4,971	6,414	48,640	4,600	320	2,489	321	339	4,428	303	2,570
Dunmanway,	500	280	2,106	345	36	126	1	106	4,439	40	–
Fermoy,	1,135	623	6,810	1,630	45	311	8	82	3,400	195	–
Kanturk,	871	1,790	7,190	931	40	216	104	110	–	142	20
Kinsale,	371	396	2,185	671	34	125	12	183	490	97	–
Macroom,	700	504	5,987	1,003	54	105	31	204	6,185	73	–
Mallow,	1,401	884	7,271	1,351	51	805	112	137	6,434	148	–
Midleton,	894	1,275	7,902	1,130	42	725	25	311	14,700	164	–
Millstreet,	418	345	3,478	814	20	128	18	48	256	25	–
Mitchelstown,	767	425	3,442	654	30	108	11	33	3,709	84	–
Skibbereen,	743	785	4,604	771	60	240	46	104	2,267	152	1,170
Skull,	806	174	1,806	322	18	62	20	6	641	21	–
Youghal,	815	788	4,455	860	33	186	28	65	1,016	186	–
KERRY.											
Cahersiveen,	851	316	2,400	792	61	121	45	81	–	69	10
Dingle,	611	731	3,066	614	43	109	64	183	70	29	–
Kenmare,	570	390	2,340	748	31	178	21	107	–	36	–
Killarney,	1,963	1,472	8,642	1,068	86	606	83	194	1,626	189	1,423
Listowel,	729	576	6,267	788	67	212	47	136	3,290	169	–
Tralee,	1,586	1,343	8,631	1,476	91	307	24	189	454	144	–
LIMERICK.											
Croom,	978	663	4,818	638	22	334	3	75	1,691	127	418
Glin,	509	423	3,185	410	24	212	16	40	124	69	–
Kilmallock,	1,290	2,467	13,940	1,190	67	677	37	479	1,906	365	1,546
Limerick,	2,905	3,168	24,374	3,011	175	440	63	282	5,609	218	166
Newcastle,	778	648	5,011	658	63	186	10	60	7,217	146	–
Rathkeale,	806	619	5,303	777	20	343	46	4	390	183	–
TIPPERARY.											
Borrisokane,	431	219	1,968	471	16	134	–	28	1,260	74	–
Carrick-on-Suir,	907	653	3,462	747	43	108	13	96	369	121	–
Cashel,	1,106	888	7,787	911	48	230	12	86	2,630	304	–
Clogheen,	777	474	3,914	751	39	166	7	–	1,084	126	635
Clonmel,	1,206	1,364	6,992	969	45	256	5	40	1,850	160	–
Nenagh,	804	720	5,467	859	54	233	4	166	7,035	133	–
Roscrea,	728	727	3,676	809	37	175	8	330	3	115	6
Thurles,	932	859	6,416	987	33	226	61	30	1,940	134	–
Tipperary,	1,073	1,317	10,544	1,402	66	363	72	161	2,931	80	1,218
WATERFORD.											
Dungarvan,	835	1,786	6,870	738	34	130	6	146	2,176	167	–
Kilmacthomas,	494	348	2,598	336	18	184	–	15	1,171	68	–
Lismore,	674	519	3,194	644	32	304	5	47	686	96	–
Waterford,	2,094	2,479	15,092	1,631	116	634	53	187	81	283	–
Total Munster. (1869,	45,182	44,226	309,756	46,167	2,462	16,048	1,774	8,320	169,323	6,071	8,887
(1868,	45,250	38,632	308,537	46,715	2,636	18,260	2,070	8,415	163,502	5,885	2,094
Increase,	–	5,588	1,213	–	–	–	–	–	–	186	6,793
Decrease,	68	–	–	686	73	3,132	296	89	45,187	–	–

of Unions during the year ended the 29th of September, 1889—*continued.*

Expenditure.			Amount of Expenditure included in Columns 15 and 26 defrayed out of Loans.		Amount repaid to Commissioners of Public Works under Seed Supply Act.	Valuation on 29th Sept., 1889.	Poundage on the Valuation.		Names of Counties and Unions.
Expenses under the Parliamentary Voters, Jurors, and Explosives Acts.	Repayment of Loans.	Total Expenditure during the year, exclusive of repayments on account of Loans under Seed Supply Act.	Poor Relief.	Other Expenditure.			Of Expenditure for Relief of the Poor (Col. 15, exclusive of the amount shown in Col. 27).	Of Total Expenditure, exclusive of the amounts shown in Cols. 27 and 28.	
24.	25.	26.	27.	28.	29.	30.	31.	32.	33.
£	£	£	£	£	£	£	s. d.	s. d.	PROVINCE OF MUNSTER.
									CLARE.
194	259	3,003	-	-	-	10,751	2 1½	3 0¼	Ballyvaghan.
57	48	2,307	-	-	-	20,402	1 8½	2 3¼	Corrofin.
104	387	12,141	-	2,119	-	74,297	2 1	2 8¾	Ennis.
113	229	5,235	-	-	-	36,802	2 2½	2 10	Ennistymon.
60	73	3,309	-	127	339	25,401	2 0¾	2 6¼	Killadysert.
144	214	7,894	-	-	-	64,821	2 5½	2 11½	Kilrush.
60	98	5,302	-	2,241	401	26,266	1 9¾	2 4¾	Scariff.
78	865	4,133	-	-	-	33,414	1 8	2 5½	Tulla.
									CORK.
130	706	10,800	-	5,003	-	73,837	1 0¾	1 8¾	Bandon.
51	73	3,194	-	294	-	22,440	1 6¾	2 6¾	Bantry.
95	-	2,218	-	-	-	12,630	2 5¼	3 6¼	Castletown.
138	402	8,883	-	4,030	-	51,945	1 3¼	1 10¼	Clonakilty.
609	945	65,164	1,501	4,436	-	350,240	2 7¼	3 4¼	Cork.
133	632	8,258	-	4,130	-	33,534	1 3¼	2 3¼	Dunmanway.
346	234	11,164	700	3,498	-	103,299	0 11¼	1 4¼	Fermoy.
178	1,495	10,482	-	-	-	77,296	1 10¼	2 8¼	Kanturk.
163	180	4,105	-	403	-	60,003	0 6¾	1 2¾	Kinsale.
141	1,283	14,308	-	6,185	-	84,113	1 7¾	2 6¾	Macroom.
200	610	17,009	-	9,491	-	106,316	1 4¼	1 11½	Mallow.
124	635	25,016	-	14,790	-	84,172	1 6¾	2 2	Midleton.
108	519	9,194	-	236	-	28,142	2 5¼	3 8½	Millstreet.
90	450	8,061	-	3,686	-	40,114	1 4¾	2 0	Mitchelstown.
105	407	10,051	-	2,807	30	47,173	1 11¼	3 4	Skibbereen.
15	52	3,071	-	921	-	16,189	2 1½	2 10	Skull.
115	318	7,561	-	1,513	-	56,000	1 7½	2 2¼	Youghal.
									KERRY.
117	977	8,156	-	-	-	22,909	2 0½	4 0	Cahercivcen.
39	188	4,703	-	-	-	22,919	2 8	4 1½	Dingle.
18	101	3,554	-	-	-	19,802	2 4½	3 7¾	Kenmare.
216	395	14,720	-	2,217	-	76,757	2 3¼	3 3	Killarney.
100	501	10,081	-	5,278	-	53,868	2 0	2 6¾	Listowel.
342	1,919	12,946	-	327	494	87,060	1 11½	2 10¼	Tralee.
									LIMERICK.
139	838	8,021	-	1,672	-	62,000	1 8¼	2 3¼	Croom.
82	690	4,844	-	18	-	27,455	2 9¾	3 4¾	Glin.
242	1,428	21,963	-	1,670	-	137,241	1 10¼	2 0¾	Kilmallock.
385	1,851	37,361	-	7,881	-	190,845	2 5¼	3 0¼	Limerick.
117	828	14,495	-	7,083	-	63,167	1 7	2 4¾	Newcastle.
148	748	7,919	-	217	-	56,018	1 11	2 9	Rathkeale.
									TIPPERARY.
31	90	4,094	-	1,256	-	41,685	0 11½	1 4¼	Borrisokane.
135	108	5,732	-	354	-	78,548	1 0	1 4¼	Carrick-on-Suir.
167	610	12,734	-	2,380	-	107,605	1 5¼	1 11	Cashel.
121	160	6,868	-	1,200	-	63,419	1 2¾	1 9¼	Clogheen.
209	98	10,617	-	1,950	-	71,086	1 11¼	2 5¼	Clonmel.
160	1,089	16,874	-	6,098	-	91,424	1 2¾	1 9¾	Nenagh.
223	-	5,370	-	-	-	11,377	0 9¾	1 2½	Roscrea.
149	43	20,089	-	1,940	-	90,546	1 5	1 9¼	Thurles.
160	1,383	18,085	-	2,917	653	142,917	1 5¼	2 2¾	Tipperary.
									WATERFORD.
167	255	10,886	-	2,176	-	63,964	2 7	3 2¼	Dungarvan.
60	320	4,711	-	1,130	-	38,170	1 6¼	2 2	Kilmacthomas.
96	354	5,380	-	608	-	49,921	1 3¼	1 11	Lismore.
251	250	19,385	-	470	-	154,394	2 0¼	2 5¼	Waterford.
7,249	24,964	535,933	2,201	109,597	1,923	3,444,485	1 9¼	2 6¼	1889, Total, MUNSTER.
7,256	17,032	569,708	-	154,665	739	3,444,784	1 9¾	2 5	1888, Total, MUNSTER.
-	7,932	-	2,201	-	1,184	-	-	0 0¼	Increase.
6	-	33,775	-	45,068	-	299	-	-	Decrease.

PART 1.—RETURN showing the Receipts and Expenditure

Names of Counties and Unions.	Receipts.					Road Rate lodged.	Expenditure.			
	Amount of Poor Rate lodged.	Parliamentary Grants.	Other Receipts, including repayment of Relief by way of Loan, Grants, &c.	Amount of Loans.	Total Receipts during the year, exclusive of Road Rate.		In-Maintenance.	Out-Relief.	Maintenance of Blind and Deaf and Dumb in Institutions, [illegible]	Emigration Expenses.
1.	2.	3.	4.	5.	6.	7.	8.	9.	10.	11.
PROVINCE OF LEINSTER.	£	£	£	£	£	£	£	£	£	£
CARLOW.										
Carlow,	13,094	1,185	210	1,194	16,600	–	4,770	2,211	56	9
DUBLIN.										
Balrothery,	6,162	436	216	545	7,351	–	1,490	1,418	63	4
Dublin, North	51,191	4,572	3,510	1,515	61,316	–	23,677	4,690	781	27
Dublin, South	50,257	4,155	1,730	1,270	67,421	–	27,087	3,042	1,109	94
Rathdown,	17,140	1,918	1,124	2,000	22,182	–	5,750	419	249	–
KILDARE.										
Athy,	10,415	1,098	381	3,000	14,799	–	3,175	1,062	118	3
Celbridge,	7,283	600	8	250	8,141	–	1,761	1,645	–	–
Naas,	10,281	1,655	731	1,850	13,800	–	2,768	2,831	39	13
KILKENNY.										
Callan,	6,790	522	19	400	7,711	–	2,281	1,858	37	13
Castlecomer,	4,271	561	28	630	5,130	–	1,241	782	–	3
Kilkenny,	9,109	1,085	181	1,018	12,285	–	4,158	2,178	75	14
Thomastown,	5,171	510	251	985	6,919	–	1,720	1,184	34	–
Urlingford,	4,420	621	211	1,101	6,304	–	1,390	668	48	–
KING'S CO.										
Edenderry,	6,292	782	8	518	6,870	–	1,303	880	135	–
Parsonstown,	4,816	1,641	206	1,310	7,989	–	2,005	344	78	31
Tullamore,	8,124	930	211	1,045	10,345	–	2,951	2,080	17	20
LONGFORD.										
Ballymahon,	4,881	840	110	1,700	7,081	–	1,230	634	17	3
Granard,	5,214	694	83	4,300	10,371	–	1,440	2,195	76	15
Longford,	4,185	582	181	3,150	9,131	–	2,084	1,258	51	6
LOUTH.										
Ardee,	5,884	772	88	3,420	10,165	–	1,881	1,441	21	–
Drogheda,	11,138	1,158	410	8,194	20,870	–	3,193	5,273	115	–
Dundalk,	9,741	810	250	1,024	12,815	–	2,487	2,811	102	–
MEATH.										
Dunshaughlin,	5,098	393	865	–	6,306	–	1,316	877	30	–
Kells,	9,989	638	273	921	12,034	–	2,030	2,414	52	–
Navan,	8,162	657	462	6,077	15,808	–	2,378	3,220	36	–
Oldcastle,	5,245	649	277	5,958	12,042	1	1,201	901	46	–
Trim,	8,180	519	251	6,701	15,641	–	1,682	2,500	73	–
QUEEN'S CO.										
Abbeyleix,	5,030	926	8	–	5,967	–	1,712	1,705	41	3
Mountmellick,	6,064	1,180	130	2,010	10,282	–	2,289	2,114	84	5
WESTMEATH.										
Athlone,	6,017	1,130	181	–	7,228	–	1,803	1,224	42	8
Delvin,	4,411	497	276	3,300	8,114	–	881	707	28	–
Mullingar,	11,109	948	304	4,810	16,028	–	2,009	3,308	231	8
WEXFORD.										
Enniscorthy,	18,068	404	202	210	18,942	–	3,714	2,723	85	23
Gorey,	4,391	810	70	1,840	7,120	–	1,794	605	25	–
New Ross,	9,071	988	83	1,060	11,702	–	3,011	1,646	30	15
Wexford,	7,907	759	838	2,098	12,022	–	3,080	1,800	187	–
WICKLOW.										
Baltinglass,	6,231	803	148	1,030	7,867	–	1,772	1,161	45	6
Rathdrum,	7,586	1,366	105	290	9,846	–	2,435	2,300	47	–
Shillelagh,	3,744	333	80	1,990	6,210	–	1,703	463	24	–
Total, Leinster, [illegible],	365,530	37,009	14,708	83,787	522,960	1	137,638	70,703	4,065	293
Total, Leinster, [illegible],	340,181	29,163	14,146	99,497	503,580	5	139,988	72,907	4,406	217
Increase,	25,158	8,416	620	–	19,400	–	–	–	–	16
Decrease,	–	–	–	15,710	–	4	2,330	2,204	341	–

of Unions during the year ended the 29th of September, 1889—*continued.*

Expenditure.										(*continued.*)	
Salaries and Rations of Officers.	All other Poor Relief Expenditure.	Total Poor Relief Expenditure.	Expenses under Medical Charities and Vaccination Acts.	Expenses under the Acts for Registration of Births, Deaths, and Marriages.	Expenses under the Public Health Act. For Sanitary purposes.	For Burial grounds.	Expenses under the Superannuation Acts.	Expenses under the Labourers Acts.	Expenses under Contagious Diseases (Animals) Act.	Payments under National School Teachers Act.	Names of Counties and Unions.
12.	13.	14.	15.	16.	17.	18.	19.	20.	21.	22.	23.
£	£	£	£	£	£	£	£	£	£	£	PROVINCE OF LEINSTER.
											CARLOW.
1,187	1,751	10,714	1,480	75	331	185	182	2,133	206	-	Carlow.
											DUBLIN.
709	791	4,266	1,227	35	580	131	150	463	277	450	Balrothery.
5,061	8,033	41,340	3,930	452	745	690	821	102	1,788	63	Dublin, North.
7,093	8,612	47,691	4,451	858	791	81	1,015	1,642	2,101	-	Dublin, South.
1,713	3,700	11,900	2,100	118	2,742	617	198	-	1,415	-	Rathdown.
											KILDARE.
1,085	1,449	7,247	1,499	54	516	42	111	2,508	203	-	Athy.
721	874	4,637	910	30	108	313	107	2,290	176	-	Celbridge.
1,142	852	7,350	1,030	72	545	47	46	2,543	201	-	Naas.
											KILKENNY.
780	787	6,602	660	33	309	14	48	896	117	-	Callan.
771	841	3,196	480	21	185	6	-	1,092	64	300	Castlecomer.
1,307	1,303	9,122	972	89	234	4	-	552	133	-	Kilkenny.
696	545	4,290	473	30	210	2	60	975	117	-	Thomastown.
540	352	3,012	552	23	121	1	17	-	76	-	Urlingford.
											KING'S CO.
512	691	3,800	1,100	34	164	177	186	941	227	171	Edenderry.
702	661	3,754	1,141	46	261	4	100	1,540	142	10	Parsonstown.
817	680	6,767	1,041	40	346	43	-	066	200	501	Tullamore.
											LONGFORD.
825	428	3,038	480	24	155	63	30	1,431	135	287	Ballymahon.
703	564	5,081	141	53	253	4	112	3,554	147	-	Granard.
786	826	4,751	843	41	785	32	-	1,775	134	-	Longford.
											LOUTH.
778	619	4,540	970	24	217	8	34	3,970	396	10	Ardee.
973	1,387	8,073	1,223	70	207	30	86	18,308	254	-	Drogheda.
923	919	6,075	1,304	73	312	3	105	900	314	-	Dundalk.
											MEATH.
644	563	3,010	680	17	104	-	-	2,653	626	-	Dunshaughlin.
681	820	6,834	917	28	141	17	180	1,721	156	434	Kells.
780	743	5,804	681	35	448	60	10	5,005	37	1,084	Navan.
585	668	3,600	755	81	184	11	206	5,708	130	400	Oldcastle.
730	665	5,873	674	91	300	20	86	2,469	146	435	Trim.
											QUEEN'S CO.
899	807	4,914	825	43	217	22	119	13	130	51	Abbeyleix.
536	664	5,917	1,080	62	420	8	233	1,614	137	643	Mountmellick.
											WESTMEATH.
751	677	4,705	1,182	61	213	83	55	-	167	-	Athlone.
494	419	2,180	600	17	160	10	4	1,792	22	-	Delvin.
996	1,087	8,033	1,440	97	685	157	242	4,013	230	665	Mullingar.
											WEXFORD.
973	1,131	7,570	1,279	74	211	61	44	144	210	-	Enniscorthy.
721	481	5,840	914	87	225	1	23	1,871	128	-	Gorey.
971	1,098	7,714	1,298	85	224	6	104	2,128	227	-	New Ross.
861	763	6,030	1,030	78	186	4	-	2,617	130	-	Wexford.
											WICKLOW.
870	645	4,494	881	34	143	1	180	2,241	60	-	Baltinglass.
936	878	6,605	1,480	67	417	80	20	198	315	-	Rathdrum.
886	421	3,257	400	29	320	22	130	836	104	-	Shillelagh.
43,092	48,002	303,763	46,722	2,798	14,772	2,064	5,014	74,854	11,966	5,613	1890, } Total,
42,616	48,433	308,596	46,102	3,072	16,384	1,970	4,698	88,697	14,148	3,871	1889, } LEINSTER.
477	-	-	-	-	-	984	316	-	-	1,042	Increase.
-	431	4,833	1,380	274	1,612	-	-	13,843	2,182	-	Decrease.

Part I.—Return showing the Receipts and Expenditure of Unions during the year ended the 29th of September, 1889—*continued.*

Names of Counties and Unions.	Expenditure—(continued). Expenses under the Parliamentary Voters, Jurors, and Explosives Acts.	Repayments of Loans.	Total Expenditure during the year, exclusive of repayments on account of Loans under Seed Supply Act.	Amount of Expenditure included in Columns 14 and 27 defrayed out of Loans. Poor Relief.	Other Expenditure.	Amount repaid to Commissioners of Public Works under Seed Supply Act.	Valuation on 29th Sept., 1889.	Poundage on the Valuation. Of Expenditure for Relief of the Poor (Col. 14), exclusive of the amount shown in Col. 28.	Of Total Expenditure, exclusive of the amounts shown in Cols. 28 and 29.
24.	25.	26.	27.	28.	29.	30.	31.	32.	33.
PROVINCE OF LEINSTER.	£	£	£	£	£	£	£	s. d.	s. d.
CARLOW.									
Carlow,	285	181	15,883	-	2,115	-	150,004	1 8¼	1 10
DUBLIN.									
Balrothery,	147	250	8,090	-	345	-	95,856	0 11	1 7½
Dublin, North,	958	2,001	56,401	1,018	406	-	407,498	2 1½	2 [illegible]
Dublin, South,	1,200	1,861	61,027	-	1,024	-	701,773	1 4½	1 8¾
Rathdown,	736	353	20,243	-	8,000	-	271,633	0 10¾	1 4
KILDARE.									
Athy,	313	408	12,071	-	2,800	-	111,030	1 3¾	1 10½
Celbridge,	160	28	8,851	-	2,224	-	114,603	0 9¾	1 1½
Naas,	104	311	13,170	-	2,348	-	151,216	0 11¾	1 4¾
KILKENNY.									
Callan,	158	107	7,374	-	354	-	72,107	1 6¼	1 11¾
Castlecomer,	96	80	5,650	-	1,091	-	37,072	2 0	2 [illegible]
Kilkenny,	175	15	11,377	-	589	-	90,798	1 10	2 1
Thomastown,	180	107	6,301	-	971	-	66,118	1 3¾	1 8¾
Urlingford,	98	72	4,158	-	-	-	48,656	1 2¾	1 8¾
KING'S CO.									
Edenderry,	100	65	6,307	-	-	-	98,374	0 9¼	1 4
Parsonstown,	160	113	7,200	-	1,507	-	102,040	0 8¾	1 1½
Tullamore,	176	321	10,069	-	1,523	-	90,247	1 7¾	2 3¾
LONGFORD.									
Ballymahon,	77	209	5,014	-	1,217	-	61,814	0 11¾	1 5¾
Granard,	155	118	10,380	-	3,256	311	85,420	1 3	1 7
Longford,	98	108	8,115	-	2,988	401	60,707	1 8¾	1 11¾
LOUTH.									
Ardee,	70	210	10,478	-	3,070	-	94,391	0 11¾	1 4¾
Drogheda,	208	851	22,310	-	10,011	-	125,294	1 8¾	1 11¾
Dundalk,	201	97	10,290	-	950	-	100,498	1 8¾	1 8¾
MEATH.									
Dunshaughlin,	50	249	7,067	-	2,559	-	105,790	0 8	1 0¾
Kells,	133	410	10,022	-	1,279	-	90,560	1 6	1 11¾
Navan,	133	737	15,127	-	6,085	-	90,237	1 4¾	2 0¾
Oldcastle,	101	405	11,995	-	5,700	695	92,718	1 1¾	1 [illegible]
Trim,	120	370	10,721	-	2,160	-	100,041	1 1¾	1 6¾
QUEEN'S CO.									
Abbeyleix,	131	50	8,898	-	9	-	85,115	1 1¾	1 6¾
Mountmellick,	83	120	10,317	-	1,588	-	102,687	1 8	1 [illegible]
WESTMEATH.									
Athlone,	224	65	8,006	-	-	-	98,356	1 0¾	1 [illegible]
Delvin,	81	842	5,582	-	1,760	-	51,010	1 0	1 [illegible]
Mullingar,	207	708	17,076	-	4,675	-	138,412	1 0¾	1 7
WEXFORD.									
Enniscorthy,	290	393	10,225	-	144	-	111,018	1 4¾	1 [illegible]
Gorey,	131	195	7,086	-	1,682	-	90,457	0 10¾	1 [illegible]
New Ross,	254	88	12,111	-	2,120	-	104,361	1 8¾	1 [illegible]
Wexford,	398	1,110	12,148	-	2,363	-	108,374	1 2¾	1 8¾
WICKLOW.									
Baltinglass,	238	208	8,450	-	2,222	-	73,727	1 8¾	1 [illegible]
Rathdrum,	197	81	9,511	-	193	-	128,316	1 0¾	1 [illegible]
Shillelagh,	109	40	5,402	-	1,006	-	80,281	1 3¾	1 9
Total, Leinster, { 1889,	8,972	14,741	492,389	1,018	77,350	1,294	4,763,449	1 3¾	1 [illegible]
Total, Leinster, { 1888,	8,649	14,282	512,467	-	85,837	288	4,757,155	1 3¾	1 [illegible]
Increase,	323	459	-	1,018	-	992	6,294	-	-
Decrease,	-	-	20,308	-	8,487	-	-	0 0¾	0 0¾

PART I.—RETURN showing the Receipts and Expenditure of Unions during the year ended the 29th of September, 1889—*continued.*

Names of Counties and Unions.	Receipts.					Seed Rate lodged.	Expenditure—(*continued*).			
	Amount of Poor Rate lodged.	Parliamentary Grants.	Other Receipts, including repayments of Relief by way of Loans, Grants, &c.	Amount of Loans.	Total Receipts during the year, exclusive of Seed Rate.		In-Maintenance.	Out-Relief.	Maintenance of Blind and Deaf and Dumb in Institutions, and cost of Relief in Fever Hospitals.	Emigration Expenses.
1	2.	3.	4.	5.	6.	7.	8.	9.	10.	11.
PROVINCE OF CONNAUGHT.	£	£	£	£	£	£	£	£	£	£
GALWAY.										
Ballinasloe,	6,747	1,009	35	616	8,436	-	2,402	925	38	8
Clifden,	3,160	732	60	-	3,967	195	708	535	-	-
Galway,	6,407	980	301	206	8,394	-	2,490	539	45	6
Glennamaddy,	2,083	186	40	-	2,309	20	843	612	16	-
Gort,	3,450	607	47	-	4,103	13	1,307	641	81	26
Loughrea,	5,431	651	73	664	6,819	-	1,101	1,021	55	18
Mountbellew,	2,864	303	11	-	3,259	87	867	335	32	95
Oughterard,	2,564	365	14	-	2,969	24	661	117	40	-
Portumna,	2,176	636	23	-	2,835	-	1,252	411	16	-
Tuam,	6,167	773	103	-	7,048	12	1,704	1,631	30	4
LEITRIM.										
Car.-on-Shannon,	4,154	527	62	1,000	6,023	-	1,294	634	28	60
Manorhamilton,	4,500	867	93	1,118	6,508	-	1,236	309	37	16
Mohill,	4,476	520	32	750	5,730	-	1,806	679	20	6
MAYO.										
Ballina,	6,040	850	44	-	6,943	-	1,490	714	73	9
Ballinrobe,	1,780	501	40	-	6,301	-	1,158	801	3	-
Belmullet,	2,517	496	210	-	3,271	-	532	67	16	111
Castlebar,	3,180	376	46	-	3,751	32	568	607	75	-
Claremorris,	4,016	808	40	-	4,864	240	814	640	7	12
Killala,	2,158	507	61	-	2,967	-	581	316	10	18
Swineford,	8,293	911	117	-	9,357	98	1,571	403	108	49
Westport,	5,127	1,085	54	-	6,366	-	2,070	108	77	-
ROSCOMMON.										
Boyle,	5,818	1,061	129	-	7,010	10	1,573	1,127	44	25
Castlerea,	5,408	333	106	-	6,286	-	1,612	738	75	11
Roscommon,	4,013	531	108	320	5,870	16	2,110	843	31	26
Strokestown,	4,848	601	2	-	5,201	-	2,360	1,110	45	19
SLIGO.										
Dromore West,	2,040	515	55	-	3,210	12	477	158	30	-
Sligo,	6,475	1,106	140	-	8,021	104	2,480	1,015	17	-
Tobercurry,	4,459	660	67	-	5,186	61	840	607	142	-
Total, Connaught, 1889,	127,128	18,800	2,319	4,028	152,835	850	38,220	18,112	1,298	413
Total, Connaught, 1888,	125,203	12,310	2,051	4,028	144,605	497	38,083	18,405	1,313	216
Increase,	1,925	6,371	268	600	8,230	353	137	-	-	197
Decrease,	-	-	-	-	-	-	-	293	15	-

SUMMARY OF PROVINCES.

	2.	3.	4.	5.	6.	7.	8.	9.	10.	11.
Ulster,	200,408	30,707	5,027	10,070	257,081	12	63,101	23,460	2,194	3
Munster,	398,321	40,658	12,705	101,113	610,849	16	130,336	83,602	5,094	516
Leinster,	386,630	37,908	14,756	85,787	532,040	1	137,038	70,703	4,063	293
Connaught,	127,128	18,800	2,319	4,028	152,835	850	38,220	18,112	1,298	413
Total, Ireland, 1889,	1,114,936	127,963	35,396	203,579	1,481,894	887	369,245	196,070	11,581	1,225
Total, Ireland, 1888,	1,072,275	96,420	30,274	264,749	1,463,718	657	369,197	201,152	11,260	1,102
Increase,	42,661	31,543	5,122	-	18,176	230	148	-	312	123
Decrease,	-	-	-	61,167	-	-	-	5,082	-	-

[*continued.*

Part 1.—Return showing the Receipts and Expenditure

Names of Counties and Unions.	*continued.* Expenditure. Salaries and Rations of Officers.	All other Poor Relief Expenditure.	Total Poor Relief Expenditure.	Expenses under Medical Charities and Vaccination Acts.	Expenses under the Acts for Registration of Births, Deaths, and Marriages.	Expenses under the Public Health Act. For Sanitary purposes.	For Burial grounds.	Expenses under the Superannuation Acts.	Expenses under the Labourers Acts.	Expenses under Contagious Diseases (Animals) Act.	Payments under National School Teachers Act.
12.	13.	14.	15.	16.	17.	18.	19.	20.	21.	22.	23.
PROVINCE OF CONNAUGHT.	£	£	£	£	£	£	£	£	£	£	£
GALWAY.											
Ballinasloe,	868	1,238	4,761	1,121	39	207	23	132	409	136	–
Clifden,	624	318	1,873	829	28	158	26	–	–	63	–
Galway,	1,171	1,131	5,787	1,234	80	210	387	128	–	118	–
Glennamaddy,	455	492	2,428	409	30	112	7	84	–	63	–
Gort,	504	845	3,116	588	10	287	6	70	–	48	–
Loughrea,	606	608	3,600	809	41	208	28	34	839	106	–
Mountbellew,	461	290	1,880	806	30	122	0	–	–	63	–
Oughterard,	482	340	1,831	880	17	107	17	10	–	26	–
Portumna,	488	236	2,324	835	18	92	7	–	–	28	–
Tuam,	798	712	4,820	1,033	60	311	186	111	14	145	–
LEITRIM.											
Car.-on-Shannon,	793	604	3,970	664	43	320	30	84	118	85	–
Manorhamilton,	848	458	2,688	1,818	58	148	4	188	864	84	6
Mohill,	848	814	3,188	079	44	144	10	88	884	82	10
MAYO.											
Ballina,	708	429	3,123	710	40	104	72	63	–	103	–
Ballinrobe,	810	696	3,370	833	52	212	63	19	–	175	–
Belmullet,	380	377	1,673	538	24	60	16	34	–	48	–
Castlebar,	886	410	2,311	873	61	210	–	28	–	134	–
Claremorris,	682	373	2,496	636	63	361	81	38	–	64	–
Killala,	383	280	1,630	348	12	128	10	63	–	66	–
Swinford,	722	1,608	4,870	1,047	98	347	46	190	–	140	6
Westport,	606	881	3,803	1,938	85	230	24	201	–	76	–
ROSCOMMON.											
Boyle,	757	768	4,275	1,103	71	148	24	11	–	139	–
Castlerea,	683	601	3,539	723	72	667	18	237	–	104	–
Roscommon,	677	806	4,625	867	20	410	7	60	98	107	–
Strokestown,	638	388 *	3,406	800	80	118	6	32	–	76	–
SLIGO.											
Dromore West,	425	418	1,805	840	22	86	102	18	–	85	–
Sligo,	907	801	5,434	1,776	92	237	117	30	86	190	–
Tobercurry,	677	486	2,911	714	19	189	8	17	–	71	–
Total, Connaught, 1890,	17,747	16,648	90,373	23,800	1,290	6,412	1,238	1,781	2,780	2,618	21
Total, Connaught, 1889,	18,137	15,677	89,721	20,700	1,371	6,060	1,190	1,884	3,548	2,670	17
Increase,	–	1,406	652	1,091	–	348	98	–	–	–	4
Decrease,	380	–	–	–	73	–	–	103	770	58	–

SUMMARY OF

	13.	14.	15.	16.	17.	18.	19.	20.	21.	22.	23.
Ulster,	30,786	33,109	190,036	42,788	3,528	18,280	008	2,374	1,071	8,914	12,089
Munster,	48,182	44,220	300,790	48,107	2,482	19,046	1,774	5,828	108,328	6,071	6,387
Leinster,	48,002	48,005	303,763	46,723	2,788	14,772	2,054	5,044	74,834	11,086	4,511
Connaught,	17,747	16,683	90,373	23,860	1,298	6,412	1,223	1,781	2,780	2,618	28
Total, Ireland, 1890,	136,777	130,014	883,012	157,868	10,101	54,517	6,061	14,428	186,998	28,586	27,086
Total, Ireland, 1889,	136,387	122,348	880,282	158,906	10,043	54,467	5,008	14,118	246,873	29,798	17,322
Increase,	390	7,869	3,030	–	–	50	956	310	–	–	9,960
Decrease,	–	–	–	1,041	648	–	–	–	60,883	1,888	–

* A further sum of £111 has been excluded from the expenditure shown in columns 15 and 24, in the case of emigration clauses of the Arrears of Rent (Ireland) Act.

of Unions during the year ended the 29th of September, 1889—*continued.*

Expenditure.			Amount of Expenditure included in Columns 15 and 26 defrayed out of Loans.		Amount repaid to Commissioners of Public Works under Seed Supply Act.	Valuation on 29th Sept., 1888.	Poundage on the Valuation.		Names of Counties and Unions.
Expenses under the Parliamentary Voters, Jurors, and Explosives Acts.	Repayment of Loans.	Total Expenditure during the year, exclusive of repayments on account of Loans under Seed Supply Act.	Pure Relief.	Other Expenditure.			Of Expenditure for Relief of the Poor (Col. 15), exclusive of the amount shown in Col. 27.	Of Total Expenditure exclusive of the amounts shown in Cols. 27 and 28.	
24.	25.	26.	27.	28.	29.	30.	31.	32	33.
									PROVINCE OF CONNAUGHT.
£	£	£	£	£	£	£	s. d.	s. d.	GALWAY.
138	128	7,187	-	331	300	77,827	1 2¼	1 3½	Ballinasloe.
185	88	3,310	-	-	126	17,404	3 3	3 0½	Clifden.
229	660	8,729	-	-	-	85,737	1 0½	1 7½	Galway.
30	39	3,236	-	-	823	31,748	1 0½	2 0½	Glennamaddy.
73	102	4,822	-	-	224	48,118	1 8½	2 0	Gort.
315	236	3,918	-	035	48	70,350	0 11½	1 4	Loughrea.
81	-	2,816	-	-	401	40,383	0 11½	1 5½	Mountbellew.
82	-	3,831	-	-	39	14,846	3 0½	3 1½	Oughterard.
74	72	3,481	-	-	-	35,341	1 4½	1 8½	Portumna.
87	67	6,943	-	-	800	70,818	1 3½	1 0½	Tuam.
									LEITRIM.
134	70	3,927	-	700	-	48,182	1 6½	2 1½	Car.-on-Shannon.
107	89	3,391	-	1,110	-	42,037	1 3½	1 11½	Manorhamilton.
33	48	3,140	-	864	837	38,523	1 7	3 2	Mohill.
									MAYO.
43	1,302	6,310	-	-	-	40,504	1 4½	2 3½	Ballina.
104	78	4,984	-	-	-	60,394	1 1½	1 7½	Ballinrobe.
64	188	2,671	-	-	-	10,838	3 10½	4 8½	Belmullet.
83	-	3,880	-	-	830	48,883	0 11½	1 3½	Castlebar.
118	101	3,790	-	-	510	42,678	1 2	1 9½	Claremorris.
31	60	2,230	-	-	-	30,369	1 3	2 3½	Killala.
223	886	7,088	-	-	700	41,022	2 3½	3 5½	Swineford.
106	87	6,018	-	-	-	44,183	1 3½	2 8½	Westport.
									ROSCOMMON.
228	83	3,091	-	-	840	74,337	1 1½	1 7½	Boyle.
143	358	3,868	-	31	708	72,488	1 6	1 7½	Castlerea.
114	88	3,108	-	303	777	64,827	1 3½	1 0½	Roscommon.
140	030	3,108	-	-	-	80,782	1 4½	2 0½	Strokestown.
									SLIGO.
44	78	2,779	-	-	610	36,010	0 11½	1 6	Dromore West.
229	318	6,439	-	-	417	90,770	1 1½	1 8½	Sligo.
141	93	4,140	-	-	706	40,768	1 3½	2 0½	Tobercurry.
3,337	5,008	187,771	-	4,102	7,906	1,305,840	1 3½	1 11½	1889, } Total,
3,265	3,930	184,310	-	3,541	3,913	1,305,038	1 3½	1 11	1888, } CONNAUGHT.
72	1,069	3,481	-	561	4,203	-	-	0 0½	Increase.
-	-	-	-	-	-	79	-	-	Decrease.

PROVINCES.

24.	25.	26.	27.	28.	29.	30.	31.	32	33.
8,167	8,830	288,008	-	11,414	701	4,832,455	0 9½	1 1½	ULSTER.
7,940	24,964	588,903	2,901	109,907	1,038	3,444,490	1 9½	2 0½	MUNSTER.
8,973	14,741	402,009	1,018	77,380	1,264	4,763,440	1 3½	1 8½	LEINSTER.
3,337	5,308	187,771	-	4,102	7,906	1,305,840	1 3½	1 11½	CONNAUGHT.
27,723	54,623	1,430,963	3,919	203,408	11,874	12,908,263	1 9½	1 9	1889, } TOTAL,
27,409	43,804	1,468,282	-	240,837	4,358	12,942,712	1 2½	1 8½	1888, } IRELAND
316	10,723	-	3,919	-	6,616	28,835	-	0 0½	Increase.
-	-	37,317	-	47,394	-	-	0 0½	-	Decrease.

Belmullet Union, expenditure to this amount having been defrayed by the Board of Guardians from a grant under the

No. 1. Part 2.—Return of the number of persons who received relief during the year ended the 30th of September, 1880, together with the expenditure for provisions, necessaries and clothing of workhouse inmates during the year, and the average weekly cost per head in the workhouse.*

Names of Counties and Unions.	Number of persons who received relief under the Poor Relief Acts during the year: In Workhouse.	Out-door.	In Blind and Deaf and Dumb Institutions.	Total.	Collective number of days for all persons relieved in the workhouse during the year.*	Average number of days of relief to each person in workhouse.	Average daily number of persons in workhouse.	Cost of provisions, necessaries, and clothing: Provisions and necessaries.	Clothing.	Total.	Average weekly cost per head: Provisions and necessaries.	Clothing.	Total.
PROVINCE OF ULSTER.								£	£	£	s. d.	s. d.	s. d.
Antrim.													
Antrim, . .	1,318	2[illegible]	1	1,[illegible]39	63,048	47	174	1,6[illegible]	246	1,953	[illegible]	0 3½	2 10
Ballycastle, . .	456	1[illegible]	—	470	24,068	60	77	480	96	658	[illegible]	0 4	2 [illegible]
Ballymena, . .	1,711	1,08[illegible]	13	2,784	111,326	60	304	1,107	13[illegible]	1,007	1 [illegible]	0 3	1 [illegible]
Ballymoney, . .	1,076	07[illegible]	4	1,805	42,110	35	115	448	110	658	1 7½	0 8	2 11
Belfast, . .	19,870	009	8[illegible]	20,514	1,604,850	60	4,743	18,804	2,078	21,700	2 [illegible]	0 8	[illegible]
Larne, . .	1,343	881	4	2,130	6[illegible]	63	188	1,010	204	1,224	2 1	0 3	2 [illegible]
Lisburn, . .	2,018	[illegible]	8	3,1[illegible]	61,017	31	104	850	282	1,118	2 0¼	0 0½	1 [illegible]
Armagh.													
Armagh, . .	944	189	8	1,0[illegible]8	75,310	80	205	1,800	234	1,900	2 4½	0 7½	3 0
Lurgan, . .	3,407	009	10	4,056	127,01[illegible]	43	300	2,371	270	2,630	2 [illegible]	0 3½	3 3½

Milford,	300	98	–	402	30,671	68	114	187	100	411	[illegible]	[illegible]	[illegible]	[illegible]	[illegible]	[illegible]
Stranorlar,	270	17	1	298	48,017	41	115	413	[illegible]	456	[illegible]	[illegible]	0	[illegible]	[illegible]	[illegible]
DOWN.																
Banbridge,	2,089	769	6	2,864	66,729	98	290	1,134	278	1,816	3	3½	0	4½	2	[illegible]
Downpatrick,	694	139	6	889	72,690	86	109	1,831	650	1,496	0	[illegible]	0	6	2	10½
Kilkeel,	807	98	6	682	26,460	67	79	373	63	414	1	11	0	4	0	8½
Newry,	2,926	1,104	9	4,036	99,089	39	327	1,600	347	1,607	2	[illegible]	0	8½	2	7½
Newtownards,	1,404	409	1	1,904	104,147	73	371	1,790	412	2,169	[illegible]	[illegible]	0	1½	2	10½
FERMANAGH.																
Enniskillen,	1,273	32	8	1,313	99,925	71	248	1,258	240	1,274	2	7½	0	4½	1	3½
Irvinestown,	373	30	–	804	13,701	84	118	431	110	540	3	4½	0	4½	2	[illegible]
Lisnaskea,	640	90	–	630	25,128	45	71	366	54	431	2	1	0	4½	4	5½
LONDONDERRY.																
Coleraine,	900	363	2	1,265	32,981	64	185	904	319	1,147	0	4½	0	7	2	11½
Limavady,	1,840	–	2	1,842	41,267	37	118	608	100	788	2	0½	0	3½	2	8½
Londonderry,	3,018	81	6	3,076	95,640	41	230	1,410	300	1,600	1	1½	0	7	2	4½
Magherafelt,	1,436	134	6	1,602	86,183	60	106	1,056	231	1,290	2	1½	0	7	0	3½
MONAGHAN.																
Carrickmacross,	3,000	172	5	3,140	47,116	94	130	960	224	1,167	2	8½	0	8	2	8½
Castleblayney,	1,387	481	4	1,836	66,344	37	188	911	095	1,218	1	6½	0	8½	3	10
Clones,	364	9	1	371	26,763	78	78	470	71	511	1	7½	0	4½	2	3½
Monaghan,	862	–	6	806	66,089	106	100	941	180	1,070	2	2½	0	4	2	7½
TYRONE.																
Castlederg,	390	9	–	392	13,011	79	37	302	41	343	2	1	0	9	2	0
Clogher,	646	41	2	798	30,267	67	80	620	137	757	3	9½	0	7	3	0½
Cookstown,	612	190	3	804	44,373	73	182	489	180	779	3	0½	0	4½	0	4½
Dungannon,	1,738	601	1	2,080	90,677	41	148	730	470	1,000	1	0½	0	0½	2	1½
*Gortin,	203	27	1	241	7,121	29	40	167	61	163	1	11½	1	7½	2	3
Omagh,	1,362	245	4	1,570	79,477	60	125	1,300	140	1,440	0	9½	0	4½	1	7½
Strabane,	1,610	160	5	1,791	90,263	57	200	1,434	334	1,762	2	3½	0	6	2	7½
Total Ulster, 1860,	60,210	11,709	167	81,216	3,246,2[illegible]	37	8,699	64,109	10,750	96,114	4	4½	0	6½	2	9½
Do. do. 1859,	71,616	12,127	164	83,353	3,304,918	37	8,810	60,436	11,450	92,474	4	1½	0	3½	4	7
Increase,	–	–	–	–	–	–	–	1,668	–	2,078	0	2½	–	–	0	2½
Decrease,	1,311	416	–	2,128	40,630	–	61	–	727	–	–	–	–	–	–	–

No. 1. Part 2.—Return of the number of persons who received relief during the year ended the 29th of September, 1859, together with the expenditure for provisions, necessaries and clothing of workhouse inmates during the year, &c.—*continued.*

Names of Counties and Unions.	Number of persons who received relief under the Poor Relief Acts during the year: In Workhouse.	Out-door.	In Blind and Deaf and Dumb Institutions.	Total.	Collective number of days for all persons relieved in the workhouse during the year	Average number of days of Relief to each person in workhouse	Average daily number of persons in workhouse.	Cost of provisions, necessaries, and clothing: Provisions and necessaries.	Clothing.	Total.	Average weekly cost per head: Provisions and necessaries.	Clothing.	Total.
PROVINCE OF MUNSTER.								£	£	£	s. d.	s. d.	s. d.
CLARE.													
Ballyvaughan,	450	22	2	474	30,988	86	106	666	219	873	3 8½	0 2½	3 8½
Corrofin,	1,211	283	1	1,497	32,904	27	90	686	47	733	3 11½	0 2½	3 2
Ennis,	2,417	888	1	3,306	182,164	78	480	3,311	736	4,047	2 6½	0 5¼	3 1½
Ennistymon,	1,318	472	6	1,796	96,286	71	264	1,871	207	2,078	3 0½	0 7	3 4½
Kildysart,	375	307	–	682	44,773	119	122	1,429	187	1,616	3 2½	0 7	3 2½
Kilrush,	2,180	1,802	2	3,984	116,134	103	314	2,384	304	2,688	3 10½	0 4½	3 2½
Scariff,	1,061	321	8	1,390	44,080	38	121	1,046	130	1,176	3 4	0 5	3 0
Tulla,	2,403	379	–	2,782	60,098	24	167	1,383	217	1,600	3 2½	0 3¼	3 3½
CORK.													
Bandon,	1,267	1,209	4	2,480	47,980	38	131	961	169	1,130	3 0½	0 7	3 8½
Bantry,	661	1,003	1	1,665	36,318	44	100	643	166	799	3 8½	0 7	3 0½
Castletown,	347	172	–	519	22,821	67	69	577	70	647	3 5	0 3½	2 9
Clonakilty,	1,138	839	3	1,970	74,169	65	203	1,306	380	1,686	2 7½	0 4½	3 1
Cork,	11,430	10,861	102	22,393	622,984	73	2,271	17,290	2,348	[illegible]	2 11½	0 4½	3 4
Dunmanway,	694	436	2	1,132	39,101	44	107	677	127	804	3 3	0 3½	3 10½
Fermoy,	4,533	1,010	6	5,549	[illegible]	21	208	1,650	341	1,991	3 2½	0 5	3 9½
Kanturk,	2,190	1,350	7	3,547	172,743	[illegible]	394	1,648	463	2,112	2 8	0 7	2 3
Kinsale,	1,316	122	4	1,442	62,046	40	143	895	110	1,005	3 4½	0 3½	3 9
Macroom,	1,870	589	5	2,464	92,870	60	261	[illegible]	684	[illegible]	3 7½	0 5½	3 9
Mallow,	4,389	1,374	7	5,768	116,677	27	340	2,040	634	2,664	3 0	0 5	3 6
Midleton,	4,916	1,044	7	5,966	114,627	27	314	2,639	611	3,249	2 10½	0 7½	3 6½

Skull, . . .	268	368	5	986	52,696	58	93	627	70	605	1 3	0 4	1 7
Youghal, . .	2,549	708	4	3,707	67,820	90	245	1,706	250	2,063	0 7½	0 6	1 2½
KERRY.													
Cahersiveen, .	480	760	1	1,280	37,218	76	158	703	70	798	2 7½	0 3½	2 11½
Dingle, . . .	685	298	0	983	64,407	96	170	1,297	168	1,464	1 10	0 [illegible]	1 [illegible]
Kenmare, . .	523	584	1	1,104	32,177	61	90	616	90	618	2 0	0 6½	2 [illegible]
Killarney, . .	1,480	1,117	0	2,600	142,401	90	294	2,763	612	3,415	3 2½	0 9	2 [illegible]
Listowel, . .	1,094	1,533	4	2,671	72,339	94	108	1,339	220	1,659	5 6½	0 6½	0 11½
Tralee, . . .	2,397	2,042	11	4,442	167,465	62	480	2,401	378	3,146	4 0½	0 4½	3 0½
LIMERICK.													
Croom, . . .	2,030	794	4	2,800	78,171	96	204	1,348	296	1,690	0 4½	0 7	3 0½
Glin, . . .	1,016	627	0	1,640	64,406	46	196	818	210	1,028	0 [illegible]	0 7½	1 1
Kilmallock, . .	5,796	2,090	10	7,896	200,059	45	649	4,193	987	4,046	3 11½	0 7½	3 6½
Limerick, . .	10,340	3,101	33	13,424	647,530	63	1,660	11,009	2,147	12,164	3 0½	0 6	3 3½
Newcastle, . .	1,014	1,056	6	2,075	76,348	73	280	1,436	271	1,747	3 6	0 6	2 2
Rathkeale, . .	2,210	912	8	3,130	92,067	49	170	1,167	296	1,480	3 4½	0 7	3 2½
TIPPERARY.													
Borrisokane, .	977	326	1	1,304	29,414	98	61	629	94	693	2 10½	0 4½	5 3½
Carrick-on-Suir, .	2,650	516	1	3,166	53,041	92	634	1,201	236	1,438	2 1	0 9	0 [illegible]
Cashel, . . .	3,101	2,911	[illegible]	6,014	142,876	63	391	2,616	633	3,247	1 [illegible]	0 9½	0 [illegible]
Cloghleen, . .	4,134	198	7	4,321	97,631	24	280	1,692	476	2,310	2 0	0 7	1 [illegible]
Clonmel, . .	2,101	904	6	3,200	130,144	44	367	2,236	347	2,778	6 4	0 7	0 11
Nenagh, . .	1,330	1,096	6	2,434	91,492	69	281	1,730	401	2,160	3 [illegible]	0 7½	3 0
Roscrea, . .	1,153	327	–	1,480	94,878	90	177	1,306	270	1,540	3 10	0 7½	3 5
Thurles, . .	2,380	1,030	6	3,900	207,984	40	362	2,050	400	2,446	2 9½	0 7	3 4
Tipperary, . .	5,168	2,516	6	7,640	187,204	32	466	3,610	607	4,310	3 0½	0 7	3 7½
WATERFORD.													
Dungarvan, . .	3,410	734	7	4,941	199,240	30	309	3,168	744	3,310	3 11	0 10	3 0
Kilmacthomas, .	1,136	440	–	1,649	35,441	45	142	1,041	91	1,132	1 7½	0 7½	2 10½
Lismore, . .	4,901	614	4	4,519	88,480	16	174	1,066	294	1,360	3 4½	0 7½	2 1½
Waterford, . .	6,103	6,304	14	8,416	260,444	66	888	6,460	1,048	7,317	5 6	0 6	2 11
Total Munster, 1880,	189,881	94,859	388	177,288	5,803,203	48	19,404	109,611	20,185	130,336	5 0½	0 6	3 2½
Do. do. 18[illegible]	132,110	98,734	368	190,874	5,[illegible],130	46	20,286	108,467	21,762	131,884	5 7½	0 6½	3 1½
Increase, . .	–	–	7	–	–	1	–	–	–	–	0 1½	–	0 1½
Decrease, . .	8,900	4,048	–	13,606	316,803	–	882	56	2,352	1,516	–	0 0½	–

No. 1. Part 2.—Return of the number of persons who received relief during the year ended the 29th of September, 1889, together with the expenditure for provisions necessaries and clothing of workhouse inmates during the year, &c.—*continued.*

Names of Counties and Unions.	Number of persons who received relief under the Poor Relief Acts during the year: In Workhouse.	Out-door.	In Blind and Deaf and Dumb Institutions.	Total.	Collective number of days for all persons relieved in the workhouse during the year.	Average number of days of relief to each person in workhouse.	Average daily number of persons in workhouse.	Cost of provisions, necessaries, and clothing: Provisions and necessaries.	Clothing.	Total.	Average weekly cost per head: Provisions and necessaries.	Clothing.	Total.
PROVINCE OF LEINSTER.								£	£	£	s. d.	s. d.	s. d.
Carlow.													
Carlow, . . .	4,100	1,582	8	5,736	177,035	43	486	4,039	137	4,176	3 2½	0 7	3 11½
Dublin.													
Balrothery, . .	664	804	8	1,507	47,017	87	129	1,206	107	1,[illegible]	3 10	[illegible] 7	4 7
Dublin, North, .	16,041	4,845	67	20,953	879,984	61	2,040	22,015	2,003	33,877	3 1½	0 5	3 7½
Dublin, South, .	10,470	8,112	67	13,164	1,105,016	104	3,097	24,242	2,190	27,061	3 10½	0 4½	4 3
Rathdown, . .	2,811	1,283	20	6,104	213,448	60	589	4,971	397	5,160	1 7	0 6½	3 8½
Kildare.													
Athy, . . .	2,970	2,190	7	5,164	107,495	37	295	2,000	314	2,116	3 4½	0 8	4 0½
Celbridge, . .	1,602	380	—	1,930	55,104	35	151	1,287	127	1,604	3 9½	0 6	4 3½
Naas, . . .	2,244	1,647	8	4,083	110,060	17	304	3,199	200	3,704	2 11½	0 6½	3 6

											s. d.	s. d.	s. d.
Longford.													
Ballymahon, . .	2,331	884	1	2,446	68,317	39	119	1,087	171	1,730	2 2½	0 7½	4 0
Granard, . .	1,771	1,084	5	6,090	89,821	45	154	1,854	143	1,449	2 11½	0 7½	5 4½
Longford, . .	4,090	906	0	6,294	97,039	39	276	1,209	194	2,070	2 0½	0 5½	5 8½
Louth.													
Ardee, . .	3,880	780	8	4,541	86,212	15	190	1,187	188	1,881	3 1½	0 4½	4 0½
Drogheda, . .	5,896	2,016	7	7,430	128,280	32	308	2,790	471	3,373	3 0	0 6½	4 0½
Dundalk, . .	3,470	1,338	0	4,804	96,344	28	204	1,461	548	2,487	2 1½	0 11	3 7½
Meath.													
Dunshaughlin, . .	2,870	808	0	4,000	40,189	11	130	1,228	132	1,318	1 11	0 8	4 7
Kells, . .	2,538	779	3	6,570	84,464	37	231	2,713	335	2,830	3 10	0 5½	4 4½
Navan, . .	4,530	1,304	8	5,763	77,011	17	213	1,073	402	2,070	2 0½	0 5½	3 0
Oldcastle, . .	2,661	678	4	3,143	62,040	38	144	1,131	220	1,101	0 1½	0 7	3 8½
Trim, . .	1,708	1,214	0	3,813	67,530	34	180	1,708	284	1,844	0 3½	0 7	1 10½
Queen's Co.													
Abbeyleix, . .	2,880	613	0	4,470	73,708	10	190	1,400	308	1,318	2 8½	0 7	3 3½
Mountmellick, . .	3,818	790	0	4,011	82,118	41	252	1,092	388	2,590	3 0½	0 3½	3 8½
Westmeath.													
Athlone, . .	3,086	882	2	5,084	94,981	15	309	1,708	196	1,303	0 4½	0 8½	4 4
Delvin, . .	2,020	881	1	2,900	40,409	16	111	731	100	1,151	2 8½	0 6½	4 0½
Mullingar, . .	2,819	1,268	0	4,106	93,840	39	344	2,870	179	2,082	4 4½	0 6½	3 11½
Wexford.													
Enniscorthy, . .	3,190	1,801	8	5,092	139,272	22	318	2,229	490	2,314	2 5½	0 7	3 8½
Gorey, . .	1,253	783	0	1,930	78,340	48	790	1,440	370	1,724	2 5½	0 9½	3 2½
New Ross, . .	5,004	1,131	4	6,137	107,000	21	440	2,102	748	2,711	3 7½	0 7½	3 3½
Wexford, . .	3,168	1,353	0	4,540	160,180	46	402	2,241	458	4,009	3 6½	0 3½	0 10½
Wicklow.													
Baltinglass, . .	908	400	3	1,330	61,083	64	190	1,142	290	1,572	3 1	0 5½	0 9½
Rathdrum, . .	2,093	1,874	3	4,080	97,194	38	320	1,980	460	2,440	3 9	0 5½	0 11½
Shillelagh, . .	2,747	880	2	2,079	67,873	23	100	1,830	267	1,763	2 9½	0 8½	3 0½
Total Leinster, 1860,	144,879	40,487	388	189,866	4,421,226	37	14,882	180,367	19,844	147,844	3 5½	0 0	3 8½
Do. do. 1859,	154,087	43,347	395	201,810	5,016,794	35	10,882	112,912	22,676	150,300	2 11½	0 0½	3 0
Increase, . .	—	—	—	—	—	3	—	873	—	—	0 1½	—	0 0½
Decrease, . .	10,470	3,010	13	12,044	599,331	—	400	—	4,000	2,400	—	0 0½	—

No. 1, Part 2.—Return of the number of persons who received relief during the year ended the 29th of September, 1889, together with the expenditure for provisions, necessaries, and clothing of workhouse inmates during the year, &c.—continued.

Names of Counties and Unions.	Number of persons who received relief under the Poor Relief Acts during the year. In Workhouse.	Out-door.	In Blind and Deaf and Dumb Institutions.	Total.	Collective number of days for all persons relieved in the workhouse during the year.	Average number of days of relief to each person in workhouse.	Average daily number of persons in workhouse.	Cost of provisions, necessaries, and clothing. Provisions and necessaries.	Clothing.	Total.	Average weekly cost per head. Provisions and necessaries.	Clothing.	Total.
PROVINCE OF CONNAUGHT.								£	£	£	s. d.	s. d.	s. d.
Galway.													
Ballinasloe, .	2,975	408	6	[illegible]	90,702	43	286	2,094	381	2,472	2 11¼	0 6¼	3 6
Clifden, . .	888	683	—	1,570	41,919	114	116	640	156	796	5 1½	0 6¼	[illegible]
Galway, . .	2,213	689	6	[illegible]	102,841	98	287	2,624	272	2,896	2 3¾	0 3½	2 1½
Glennamaddy, .	968	602	4	1,570	38,608	42	106	773	90	863	2 5¾	0 4	3 1½
Gort, . . .	2,760	438	7	3,209	60,848	66	166	1,111	196	1,307	2 4½	0 5	2 9½
Loughrea, . .	2,087	606	4	2,737	80,309	34	180	1,033	168	1,201	2 10½	0 3½	[illegible]
Mount Bellew, .	677	105	2	944	34,888	64	95	712	146	867	2 10½	[illegible] 7	[illegible] 6½
Oughterard, . .	221	117	6	344	28,431	140	78	804	87	891	2 11	0 4	3 3
Portumna, . .	1,151	606	3	[illegible]	61,108	46	140	1,002	160	1,162	3 0	0 5½	3 4½
Tuam, . . .	1,448	794	4	2,246	60,254	[illegible]	200	1,610	144	1,754	2 8	0 3½	2 6½
Leitrim.													

Roscommon.													
Boyle, . . .	1,366	646	4	1,846	77,600	60	312	1,576	301	1,873	2 9½	0 4½	2 10
Castlerea, . .	1,189	806	6	1,710	91,271	71	283	1,800	262	1,618	3 4	0 5½	2 0¼
Roscommon, .	1,066	436	6	2,895	60,638	46	346	2,100	240	2,416	3 3½	0 5½	3 9
Strokestown, .	1,439	633	3	2,071	56,841	36	147	1,791	145	1,304	3 3	0 4½	3 0½
Sligo.													
Dromore West, .	344	398	2	734	28,861	56	65	405	73	477	2 6½	0 5½	2 11
Sligo, . . .	1,620	848	5	2,498	104,013	71	260	3,008	431	3,400	3 0	0 7	3 4
Tobercurry, . .	946	726	4	1,662	85,529	41	100	757	93	849	2 9	0 4	3 1
Total, Connaught, {1896,	32,783	14,358	186	47,238	1,692,831	46	4,440	31,446	4,778	38,190	2 9½	0 6	3 1¼
{1895,	34,748	14,751	184	50,496	1,781,238	46	4,650	30,807	5,264	38,043	2 9½	0 6¼	2 11¼
Increase, . .	–	–	–	–	–	1	–	661	–	157	0 3½	–	0 2
Decrease, . .	2,972	393	1	3,257	88,407	–	212	–	484	–	–	0 0¼	–

SUMMARY OF PROVINCES.

Ulster, . .	89,346	11,706	184	61,726	3,284,330	47	9,000	54,168	20,749	85,131	3 3½	0 4½	2 8¾
Munster, . .	123,831	54,806	389	177,288	5,454,288	46	16,494	140,841	28,494	190,036	3 8¾	0 8	3 4¾
Leinster, . .	144,579	40,497	290	185,364	6,134,320	37	14,883	118,747	50,331	177,130	3 0¼	0 6	3 6¼
Connaught, . .	32,786	14,202	303	47,203	1,692,831	49	4,446	32,446	4,772	38,280	2 8¼	0 8	3 1½
Total, Ireland, {1896,	384,570	120,400	877	481,202	16,364,089	43	43,925	324,478	84,397	488,545	3 6	0 0¼	3 3¾
{1895,	389,697	130,150	866	520,786	16,848,448	43	46,317	309,063	96,136	488,107	3 7¾	0 6	3 1½
Increase, . .	–	–	–	–	–	1	–	5,438	–	188	0 1¼	–	0 1¾
Decrease, . .	27,127	9,480	11	39,580	484,781	–	2,306	–	8,998	–	–	0 0¼	–

No. 2.—Classification of persons relieved in workhouses in Ireland, during each of the half-years ended the 25th of March and the 29th of September, 1889, respectively.

	Classes of persons relieved in workhouses.	No. in the half-year ended 25th March, 1889.	No. in the half-year ended 29th September, 1889.
	ABLE-BODIED AND THEIR CHILDREN.		
1	Adults, — Married couples, — Males,	6,454	6,769
2	Adults, — Married couples, — Females,	6,454	6,769
3	Adults, — Other males,	80,848	74,862
4	Adults, — Other females,	26,516	29,088
5	Children under 15, of able-bodied inmates, — Illegitimate,	5,814	6,651
6	Children under 15, of able-bodied inmates, — Other children,	20,525	22,937
	NOT ABLE-BODIED.		
7	Adults, — Married couples, — Males,	716	806
8	Adults, — Married couples, — Females,	716	806
9	Adults, — Other males,	28,640	28,369
10	Adults, — Other females,	18,074	19,532
11	Children under 15, — Of parents not able-bodied being inmates — Illegitimate,	477	470
12	Children under 15, — Of parents not able-bodied being inmates — Other children,	1,466	1,699
13	Children under 15, — Orphans, or other children relieved without parents,	6,926	6,464
	LUNATICS, INSANE PERSONS, AND IDIOTS.		
14	Adult males,	1,757	1,806
15	Adult females,	2,307	2,422
16	Children under 15,	103	109
17	Total number of males,	116,415	118,808
18	Do. females,	54,067	53,617
19	Do. children under 15,	34,711	38,350
20	Grand total,	205,193	210,779

No. 3.—CLASSIFICATION of PERSONS RELIEVED out of the WORKHOUSES during each of the half-years ended the 25th of March and the 29th of September, 1889, respectively, including persons relieved in Blind, and Deaf and Dumb institutions.

	Classes of persons relieved.	Number in the half-year ended 25th March, 1889.	Number in the half-year ended 29th Sept., 1889.
1	Blind persons maintained in institutions, . . Males, .	144	143
2	Blind persons maintained in institutions, Females,	231	236
3	Deaf and Dumb persons maintained in institutions, Males, .	235	238
4	Deaf and Dumb persons maintained in institutions, Females,	202	214
	Total, ...	812	831
	RELIEVED UNDER 10 VIC., C. 31, SEC. 1.		
5	Adult males permanently disabled by old age or infirmity,	9,612	9,730
6	Families of adult males under heading 5, ... Wives, ...	4,823	4,680
7	Families of adult males under heading 5, Children under 15, . .	2,063	1,998
8	Adult males relieved in cases of their own sickness or accident,	7,208	6,499
9	Families of adult males under heading 8, ... Wives, ...	4,727	4,169
10	Families of adult males under heading 8, Children under 15, . .	12,909	11,511
11	Adult women permanently disabled by old age or infirmity,	21,619	21,708
12	Children under 15, of women under heading 11, ... Legitimate, . .	424	494
13	Children under 15, of women under heading 11, Illegitimate, . .	47	57
14	Adult women relieved in cases of sickness or accident, .	3,737	3,474
15	Children under 15, of women under heading 14, ... Legitimate, . .	2,042	2,073
16	Children under 15, of women under heading 14, Illegitimate, . .	147	115
17	Able-bodied widows, having two or more legitimate children dependent on them, ...	3,980	3,978
18	Children under 15, dependent on widows under heading 17,	12,855	12,005
19	Lunatics, Insane persons, and Idiots, ... Males, ...	72	80
20	Lunatics, Insane persons, and Idiots, Females, ...	75	81
21	Lunatics, Insane persons, and Idiots, Children under 15, . .	37	34
	Total, ...	86,584	83,622
	PERSONS RELIEVED UNDER 10 VIC., C. 31, BUT NOT UNDER SEC. 1.		
22	Adult males, married or single, relieved on account of want of work, ...	-	-
23	Families of adult males under heading 22, ... Wives, ...	-	-
24	Families of adult males under heading 22, Children under 15, . .	-	-
25	Able-bodied women, Unmarried, ...	-	-
26	Able-bodied women, Widows not relievable under sec. 1, . .	-	-
27	Children of women under headings 25 and 26, ... Legitimate, . .	-	-
28	Children of women under headings 25 and 26, Illegitimate, . .	-	-
	Families relieved without husband or father.		
29	Husband or father in Gaol, . Wives, ...	-	-
30	Husband or father in Gaol, Children under 15, . .	-	-
31	Husband or father on service in Army or Navy, . . Wives, ...	-	-
32	Husband or father on service in Army or Navy, Children under 15, . .	-	-
33	Deserted by husband or father, Wives, ...	-	-
34	Deserted by husband or father, Children under 15, . .	-	-
35	Orphans and children relieved without either parent, .	-	-
36	Number of persons relieved provisionally, and not included in the foregoing, ...	3,935	3,905
	Total, ...	3,935	3,905
37	Number of persons relieved under 11 & 12 Vic., c. 47, sec. 4, and not included in the foregoing, ...	321	314
38	Orphans or Deserted children out at nurse under 39 and 40 Vic., cap. 38, ...	2,955	2,952
	Grand total (Nos. 5 to 38 inclusive), .	93,795	90,793

No. 4.—Summary of returns from Clerks of unions showing for each Province and for all Ireland the number of persons admitted to the workhouses during the year ended the 29th of September, 1889, distinguishing the number admitted in sickness; also the number of births and deaths in the workhouses during the year.

Provinces.	Number of persons admitted during the year. Number admitted in sickness. Suffering under Fever or other dangerous contagious disease.	Suffering under other diseases.	Suffering from accidental injury.	Total number admitted in sickness.	Number admitted who were not sick.	Total number admitted during the year.	No. of births in the workhouses during the year.	No. of deaths in the workhouses during the year.
Ulster, . .	787	0,203	683	9,763	60,067	69,430	561	2,917
Munster, . .	1,468	15,791	1,229	18,488	89,155	107,643	436	3,260
Leinster, . .	942	18,002	907	20,001	100,991	120,902	549	3,227
Connaught, . .	255	3,212	383	3,850	24,569	28,419	104	836
Total, Ireland,	3,452	45,308	3,202	52,102	274,382	326,481	1,753	9,720

No. 5.—Summary of returns showing for each Province and for all Ireland the number of sick persons who received medical treatment in the workhouse hospitals and fever hospitals during the year ended the 29th of September, 1889.

Provinces.	Under treatment at the commencement of the year. Fever or other dangerous contagious disease.	Other diseases.	Accidentally injured.	Total.	New cases. Fever or other dangerous contagious disease.	Other diseases.	Accidentally injured.	Total.	Total cases treated in hospitals during the year. Fever or other dangerous contagious disease.	Other diseases.	Accidentally injured.	Total.
Ulster, . .	110	2,720	110	2,940	1,180	14,156	840	16,182	1,290	16,883	950	19,129
Munster, . .	149	5,187	90	5,426	1,815	23,407	1,327	26,549	1,967	28,594	426	30,977
Leinster, . .	115	6,227	130	6,472	1,445	29,438	1,088	31,971	1,560	35,665	1,218	38,445
Connaught, . .	66	1,605	87	1,810	457	5,008	427	5,892	511	6,613	484	7,508
Total, Ireland,	428	15,115	396	16,469	4,900	72,099	3,682	80,687	5,334	87,744	4,078	97,156

No. 6.—Statement (in pursuance of sec. 20 of 12 & 13 Vic., c. 104,) relative to the audit of union accounts:—(in continuation of statement in seventeenth annual report. Appendix D., No. 6).

I. *Date up to which the accounts of unions have been audited.*

The accounts of all the unions have been audited up to the 29th of September, 1880.

II. *Sums disallowed or found due on audit of the accounts of unions in Ireland, up to the 29th of September, 1880, and whether recovered or in course of recovery from the persons debited.*

Union.	Half-year ended	Date of Audit.	Amount disallowed or found due.	Whether paid or in course of recovery.	Observations.—nature of sums disallowed, &c.
			£ s. d.		
Abbeyleix, .	30 September, .	16 Jan., 1880, .	7 2 0	Paid, ...	Fee for examination of a lunatic signed by only one Justice of the Peace.
Athy, . .	„	11, 12, 13, & 14 Feb., 1880.	3 10 0	Paid, ...	Overpayment to Master for temporary services during Clerk's illness.
Ballinasloe,	„	9 Nov., 1879, .	29 7 0	Paid, ...	Overpayment by Vice-Guardians on account of contract.
Ballymahon,	25 March, .	25 May, „ .	2 10 0	Paid, ...	Money expended on clothing for a pauper on her discharge from the workhouse. The pauper's own clothes had been destroyed by fire and their cost should have been paid by the Company with whom the workhouse buildings were insured.
Ballymena, .	„	12 Feb., 1879, .	6 0 0	In course of recovery, .	Illegal payment to a member of the Board of Guardians.
Ballyshannon, .	„	16 Aug., 1880, .	3 10 0	Not paid, . . .	Balance of bill for printing. Not enforced on subsequent explanation.
Baltinglass, .	„	12 & 13 Sept., 1879	0 10 0	Paid, . . .	Overpayment to Clerk under Labourers Acts.
„ . .	29 September, .	28 Feb., 1880, .	0 0 0	Paid, ...	Amount paid as travelling expenses to an engineer employed in connection with the building of labourers' cottages, in violation of the terms of his appointment.
Banbridge, .	„	17 Dec., 1880, .	6 6 7	Not paid, ...	Difference between cost of ordinary diet and officer's rations which had been allowed to an inmate of the workhouse. Surcharged

No. 6.—STATEMENT (in pursuance of sec. 20 of 12 & 13 Vic., c. 104,) relative to the AUDIT OF UNION ACCOUNTS:—(in continuation of statement in seventeenth annual report. Appendix D., No. 6)—*continued.*

II. Sums disallowed or found due on audit of the accounts of unions in Ireland, up to the 29th of September, 1859, and whether recovered or in course of recovery from the persons debited—*continued.*

Unions.	Half-year ended	Date of Audit	Amount disallowed or found due.	Whether paid or in course of recovery	Observations—nature of sums disallowed, &c.
			£ s. d.		
[illegible],	29 September,	5 Mar., 1860,	23 15 9	Not yet paid,	Balance of medical officer's superannuation allowance paid to his widow, probate, &c. having been taken out.
Cavan,	"	24 Feb., "	2 14 0	Not yet paid,	Illegal out-door relief
Clogheen,	"	4 Jan., "	1 1 6	In course of recovery,	Do.
Clonakilty,	"	9 Nov., 1859,	0 2 6	Not paid,	Out-door relief illegally afforded through misapprehension. Not enforced on subsequent explanation
Cootehill,	25 March,	4 Sept., "	2 12 8	Paid,	Illegal out-door relief. Surcharged to Guardian who authorized it.
"	29 September,	5 Feb., 1860,	4 17 0	Paid,	Do.
"	"	"	1 0 0	Part paid. Balance in course of recovery	Do.
"	"		1 2 0	In course of recovery,	Do.
Cork,	25 March,	23 July, 1859,	111 15 0	Portion paid,	Apparent overpayments to engineer for labourers' cottages. Balance not enforced on subsequent explanation
"	29 September,	3 Feb., 1860,	0 2 0	Will be enforced,	Illegal out-door relief
Delvin,	"	9 Dec., 1859,	0 10 0	Paid,	Overpayment in connection with labourers' cottages. Surcharged to Clerk
Drogheda,	"	15 Jan., 1860,	2 10 0	In course of recovery,	Illegal out-door relief. Surcharged to relieving officer
Dublin, South,	25 March,	15 June, 1860,	157 6 11	£131 15s. 2d. already paid,	Amount fraudulently appropriated by a late relieving officer. Sum charged to him and to his sureties.
Dunfanaghy,	"	20 July, "	0 4 1	Not paid,	Balance of solicitor's costs not taxed. Not enforced, a reduction having been made.
Fermoy,	29 September,	2 Jan., 1860,	0 7 0	Not paid,	Overpayment by relieving officer. Not enforced on subsequent explanation.
"	"		3 2 4	In course of recovery,	Unauthorized abatement in rent of labourers' cottage overdue.
Granard,	"	13 Dec., 1859,	2 0 0	Paid,	Money in lieu of clothes given to discharged pauper. Surcharged to Master
Kells,	"	8 Dec., "	5 0 0	Paid,	Cost of sending a person for medical treatment to a place which was not a hospital within the meaning of the law.
Killarney,	25 March,	20 July, "	3 0 0	Not paid,	Illegal out-door relief. Not enforced on subsequent explanation

Union	Half-year ended	Date	£	s.	d.	Result	Nature of Sum
"	"	"	4	10	0	In course of recovery,	Duplicate payment to contractor.
"	"	"	5	2	0	In course of recovery,	Overpayment to temporary medical officer.
"	29 September,	4, 5, and 6 Dec., 1889,	2	18	5	In course of recovery,	Illegal out-door relief.
"	"	"	40	0	0	Not enforced,	Payment to temporary Clerk whose appointment had not been sanctioned. Sanction subsequently obtained.
Kilrush,	25 March,	8 Aug., 1889,	1	10	2	Not paid,	Illegal out-door relief. Not enforced on subsequent explanation.
"	29 September,	10 Feb., 1890,	11	0	0	Not paid,	Do. Do.
Lurgan,	"	"	1	5	2	Not paid,	Unauthorised out-door relief. Surcharge not enforced on subsequent explanation.
Limerick,	25 March,	10 Aug., 1889,	0	10	0	Not paid,	Illegal outdoor relief. Not enforced on explanation.
"	29 September,	12 Feb., 1890,	1	10	6	In course of recovery,	Illegal out-door relief.
"	"	"	0	15	0	In course of recovery,	Do.
Lismore,	29 September,	11 March, "	30	0	0	Not yet paid,	Payment on account to Guardians' solicitor, his costs not having been taxed. Surcharged to Guardians who signed cheque.
"	"	"	0	13	6	Not yet paid,	Illegal expenditure for a political purpose.
Longford,	"	30 Dec., 1889,	17	0	0	Not paid,	Payment to building contractor without certificate of engineer. Surcharge not enforced—certificate subsequently obtained.
Loughrea,	"	15 Nov., "	0	6	0	Paid,	Illegal out-door relief.
"	"	"	1	0	0	Paid,	Do.
Macroom,	25 March,	30 May, "	5	0	0	Paid,	Overpayment to solicitor for law costs.
"	29 September,	19 Nov., "	0	4	0	Paid,	Illegal out-door relief.
Mallow,	25 March,	8 July, "	0	8	0	Paid,	Do.
"	"	"	8	3	8	Not enforced,	Expenditure for sanitary improvements on private property.
"	29 September,	1 Jan., 1890,	0	6	0	In course of recovery,	Illegal out-door relief.
"	"	"	8	17	0	Not paid,	Do. Not enforced on subsequent explanation.
Manorhamilton,	25 March,	18 July, 1889,	0	10	0	Paid,	Overpayment to paymaster. Surcharged to Clerk.
"	29 September,	22 Jan., 1890,	135	0	0	Matter pending,	Payments to contractors for building labourers' cottages without certification of Clerk of works. Surcharges will not be enforced if the certificates are obtained.
Mullingar,	"	18 Dec., 1889,	0	10	0	Paid,	Illegal and unauthorised out-door relief. Surcharged to relieving officer.
"	"	"	0	10	0	Will be enforced,	Illegal out-door relief. Surcharged to Guardian who authorised it.
"	"	"	4	4	0	Not paid,	Irregular out-door relief. Not enforced on subsequent explanation.
Navan,	29 March,	1 June, "	5	14	0	Not enforced,	Illegal out-door relief. Surcharged to relieving officer, who was subsequently dismissed by Sealed Order.
"	29 September,	7 Dec., "	0	1	0	Paid,	Illegal out-door relief. Surcharged to the chairman of the Board of Guardians who authorised it.
Nenagh,	25 March,	11 May, "	0	10	0	Paid,	Overcharge for out-door relief. Surcharged to relieving officer.
Newcastle,	"	13 May, "	4	9	0	Not paid,	Illegal out-door relief. Not enforced on subsequent explanation.
Parsonstown,	"	24 July, "	0	5	0	Paid,	Illegal out-door relief. Surcharged to Guardian who authorised it.
Portumna,	29 September,	11 Jan., 1890,	47	10	0	In course of recovery,	Illegal out-door relief.
"	"	"	10	0	0	Not paid,	Illegal out-door relief. Surcharge not enforced as the amount was not distributed.
"	"	"	2	10	0	Paid,	Illegal out-door relief.

No. 6.—STATEMENT (in pursuance of sec. 20 of 12 and 13 Vic., c. 104) relative to the AUDIT of UNION ACCOUNTS:—(in continuation of statement in seventeenth annual report, Appendix D., No. 6)—continued.

II. Sums disallowed or found due on audit of the accounts of unions in Ireland, up to the 29th of September, 1859, and whether recovered or in course of recovery from the persons debited—*continued.*

Unions.	Half-year ended	Date of audit.	Amount disallowed or found due.	Whether paid or in course of recovery.	Observations:—Nature of Sums disallowed, &c.
			£ s. d.		
Rathdrum,	25 March,	29 & 30 July, 1860,	1 0 0	Paid,	Duplicate payment to a medical officer for the conveyance of a lunatic.
Scariff,	29 September,	3 Feb., 1860,	1 10 0	In course of recovery,	Illegal out-door relief.
Shillelagh,	25 March,	31 July & 1 Aug., 1860	0 6 4	Paid,	Duplicate payment to a former relieving officer. Debited to Clerk.
Skibbereen,	"	27 May, "	3 0 0	Paid,	Illegal out-door relief.
"	29 September,	14 Nov., "	3 3 0	Debtors absconded,	The amount disallowed consists of two sums illegally expended on out-door relief.
"	"		0 5 0	Paid,	Illegal out-door relief. Surcharged to relieving officer.
Strabane,	25 March,	20 June, "	3 7 0	Not paid,	Unauthorized out-door relief. Surcharged to relieving officer but not enforced, authority having been subsequently obtained.
Tipperary,	"	10 July, "	5 0 0	Paid,	Illegal out-door relief.
"	"	"	8 16 0	Part paid, balance in course of recovery.	Do.
"	29 September,	10 Dec., "	5 10 0	In course of recovery,	Do.

No. 7.—Union Officers' Superannuation.—Statement of allowances under the Superannuation Acts in force during any portion of the year ended the 29th of September, 1889; showing also the cases in which the allowances terminated during the year. (In continuation of statement in seventeenth annual report, Appendix D, No. 7.)

Date of Consent of Local Government Board.	Union.	Name of Officer.	Office.	Age, Years.	Period of service as a Union Officer.	Cause of retirement.	Annual Salary.	Annual Superannuation allowance.	If terminated, date of termination.
							£ s. d.	£ s. d.	
17 June, 1870	Abbeyleix	Margaret Bingham	Fever Hospital Nurse	58	12	Permanent infirmity of body	18 0 0	10 0 0	
2 Mar. 1881	Do.	Thomas [illegible]	Medical Officer of Workhouse	67	24	Old age	85 0 0	40 0 0	
10 June, 1879	Antrim	John Reid	Master Tailor	70	24	Old age and infirmity of body.	40 10 8	26 0 0	
20 Aug. 1880	Do.	Martha M'Cullagh	Infirmary Nurse	60	14½	Infirmity of body	25 0 0	20 0 0	
6 Aug. 1879	Do.	Graham [illegible]	Shoemaker	77[illegible]	44[illegible]	Permanent infirmity of body	30 8 0	20 0 0	
8 Feb. 1880	Ardee	Henry Hyland	Master	63[illegible]	22	Old age and infirmity	100 18 0	55 0 0	
6 Aug. 1880	Do.	Ellen Fortune	Midwife of Dispensary District	73	[illegible]	Permanent infirmity of body	26 8 0	9 0 0	
16 July, 1869	Armagh	Eleanor Willis	Schoolmistress	39	16½	Infirmity of mind	22 8 0	10 0 0	
3 Feb. 1880	Do.	Joseph [illegible]	Medical Officer of Dispensary District	64	30½	Old age and infirmity	150 8 0	80 0 0	
19 April, 1879	Athlone	Michael B. Cassidy	Relieving Officer	64	24½	Infirmity of body	50 0 0	30 0 0	
18 Oct. 1878	Do.	Elizabeth Cowley	Schoolmistress	60	29½	Do.	54 0 7	25 0 8	
26 Dec. 1882	Athy	James Cooper	Collecting Officer	61½	25	Permanent infirmity of mind.	30 0 0	20 10 9	
21 Dec. 1888	Do.	William [illegible]	Medical Officer of Dispensary District	[illegible]	10[illegible]	Old age	120 0 0	80 0 0	
4 April, 1880	Do.	Kate Ryan	Cook and Laundress	55	10[illegible]	Permanent infirmity of body.	24 0 0	6 0 2	
16 Nov. 1874	Bailieborough	John M. [illegible]	Medical Officer of Dispensary District	78	[illegible]	Old age	90 0 0	30 0 0	6 Sept. 1880
30 April, 1870	Do.	Patrick Lynch	Collector	63	13½	Infirmity of body	30 18 10	19 0 0	

No. 7.—Union Officers' Superannuation.—Statement of allowances under the Superannuation Acts in force during any portion of the year ended the 29th of September, 1889, showing also the cases in which the allowances terminated during the year (in continuation of statement in seventeenth annual report, Appendix D, No. 7)—continued.

Date of Consent of Local Government Board.	Union.	Name of Officer.	Office.	Age. Years.	Period of service as a Union Officer.	Cause of retirement.	*Annual Salary. £ s. d.	Annual Superannuation allowance. £ s. d.	If terminated, date of termination.
8 May, 1881	Ballina . .	John P. Nolan .	Relieving Officer .	66	30½	Permanent infirmity of body and mind.	56 0 0	18 13 4	24 June, 1889.
6 Oct. 1883	Do. . . .	Charles Edwards .	Do.	60$\frac{1}{12}$	36	Permanent infirmity of body.	30 0 0	14 0 0	
18 May, 1886	Do. . . .	Richard O'Loughlin	Dispensary Porter .	66	30$\frac{1}{12}$	Do.	14 0 0	6 0 0	
[illegible] Aug. 1886	Do. . . .	Mary J. Forsyth .	Matron.	60½	[illegible]	Do.	[illegible] 0 0	10 0 0	
10 Aug. 1880	Ballinasloe . .	Edward Sharpe .	Relieving Officer . .	71	30½	Old age	56 8 0	18 13 0	28 Nov., 1888.
9 Aug. 1881	Do. . . .	William Seavy	Porter	62	16½	Permanent infirmity of body.	56 0 0	30 8 0	
18 Jan. 1886	Do. . . .	Edmund F. Sharkey	Medical Officer of Dispensary District.	70	30$\frac{1}{12}$	Old age .	234 18 0	76 3 0	
21 Oct. 1886	Do. . .	Maria Hennan,	Matron, . . .	66½	25½	Permanent infirmity of body.	45 0 0	26 16 0	
26 June, 1868	Ballinrobe .	John Maher .	Schoolmaster . . .	63	18	Infirmity of body . .	26 0 0	14 0 0	
8 Aug. 1870	Do. . . .	Mark Walsh . .	Dispensary Porter . .	76	27	Old age	6 0 0	4 0 0	
26 Sept. 1886	Ballycastle . .	Geo. M. O'Connor .	Medical Officer of Dispensary District.	71$\frac{1}{12}$	65½	Permanent infirmity of body.	165 7 0	56 10 0	
22 July, 1868	Ballyshannon . .	Sabina Mulroy . .	Matron	60$\frac{11}{12}$	25$\frac{1}{12}$	Old age	25 0 0	16 0 0	
10 July, 1867	Ballymoney . .	James Sultan . .	Porter	76$\frac{11}{12}$	25$\frac{1}{12}$	Do.	20 0 0	10 0 0	22 Oct., 1888.
21 Dec. 1881	Ballyshannon . .	Mary Daly .	Fever Hospital Nurse .	60	27½	Old age and permanent [illegible]	15 0 0	10 0 0	

[illegible]	Do.	Bridget M'Mahon	Nurse	[illegible]	[illegible]	Old age and infirmity of body	[illegible]	0	0	[illegible]	14	0	
[illegible] Dec. [illegible]	[illegible]	Emily L. Whelan	Fever Hospital Nurse	[illegible]	[illegible]	Infirmity of body	[illegible]	0	4	18	0	0	
[illegible] April, [illegible]	Do.	Wm. E. Adrian	Medical Officer of Workhouse and of Dispensary District	70	[illegible]	Old age and infirmity of body	[illegible]	0	0	[illegible]	17	0	[illegible] Sept., [illegible]
7 Jan. [illegible]	Do.	[illegible] Doyle	Midwife of Dispensary District	[illegible]	[illegible]	Old age	[illegible]	0	0	0	12	4	
[illegible] Aug. [illegible]	Do.	William [illegible]	Medical Officer of Dispensary District	[illegible]	[illegible]	Do.	[illegible]	17	[illegible]	[illegible]	11	4	
[illegible] Feb. [illegible]	[illegible]	Mary [illegible]	Schoolmistress	[illegible]	[illegible]	Infirmity of body	[illegible]	0	0	0	0	0	
[illegible] April, [illegible]	Do.	Thomas Allen	Master	[illegible]	[illegible]	Old age	[illegible]	10	0	[illegible]	0	0	
[illegible] Sept. [illegible]	Do.	Mary [illegible]	Fever Hospital Nurse	[illegible]	[illegible]	Permanent infirmity of body.	[illegible]	[illegible]	[illegible]	[illegible]	0	0	
[illegible] Aug. [illegible]	Do.	Geo. B. [illegible]	Medical Officer of Dispensary District.	[illegible]	[illegible]	Do.	[illegible]	0	0	[illegible]	0	0	
[illegible] Mar. [illegible]	Do.	John [illegible]	Wardmaster,	[illegible]	[illegible]	Permanent infirmity of mind and body	[illegible]	0	0	11	0	0	
[illegible] July, [illegible]	[illegible]	Fergus Osborne	Relieving Officer	[illegible]	[illegible]	Infirmity of mind and body	[illegible]	0	0	[illegible]	0	0	
11 Dec. [illegible]	[illegible]	James Fitzgerald	Do.	[illegible]	[illegible]	Old age	[illegible]	0	0	[illegible]	0	0	
[illegible] May, [illegible]	[illegible]	Mary Ryan,	Matron,	[illegible]	[illegible]	Do.	[illegible]	14	0	[illegible]	7	0	
[illegible] Jan. [illegible]	[illegible]	Wm. [illegible]	Porter	[illegible]	[illegible]	Infirmity of body	[illegible]	[illegible]	0	[illegible]	0	0	
[illegible] Jan. [illegible]	[illegible]	David M'[illegible]	Master	[illegible]	[illegible]	Do.	[illegible]	0	0	[illegible]	0	0	
[illegible] Dec. [illegible]	Do.	[illegible]	Relieving Officer	[illegible]	[illegible]	Do.	[illegible]	0	0	[illegible]	0	0	
7 June, [illegible]	Do.	John [illegible]	Collector	[illegible]	[illegible]	Infirmity of mind and body	[illegible]	0	0	[illegible]	0	0	1 Dec., [illegible]
[illegible] Sept. [illegible]	Do.	James Crawford	Apothecary of Dispensary District.	[illegible]	[illegible]	Permanent infirmity of body	[illegible]	0	0	[illegible]	0	0	
[illegible] April, [illegible]	Do.	Ann Thompson	Hospital Nurse	[illegible]	[illegible]	Old age	[illegible]	0	0	[illegible]	0	0	
7 Mar. [illegible]	Do.	Martha [illegible]	Midwife of Dispensary District.	[illegible]	[illegible]	Permanent infirmity of body	[illegible]	0	0	[illegible]	0	0	
[illegible] Dec. [illegible]	Do.	William [illegible]	Night Lunatic Keeper,	[illegible]	[illegible]	Do.	[illegible]	[illegible]	0	[illegible]	[illegible]	0	
[illegible] Dec. [illegible]	Do.	Catherine Wilkinson,	Fever Hospital Nurse,	[illegible]	[illegible]	Old age and permanent infirmity of body	[illegible]	[illegible]	0	[illegible]	0	0	
[illegible] Aug. [illegible]	Do.	William F. [illegible]	Clerk,	[illegible]	[illegible]	Permanent infirmity of body	[illegible]	0	0	[illegible]	0	0	

No. 7.—Union Officers' Superannuation.—Statement of allowances under the Superannuation Acts in force during any portion of the year ended the 29th of September, 1889; showing also the cases in which the allowances terminated during the year. (In continuation of statement in seventeenth annual report, Appendix D, No. 7)—continued.

Date of Consent of Local Government Board.	Union.	Name of Officer.	Office.	Age. Years.	Period of service as a Union Officer.	Cause of retirement.	* Annual Salary.	Annual Superannuation allowance.	If discontinued, date of termination.
							£ s. d.	£ s. d.	
10 Dec. 1866	[illegible]	Alicia M'Nally	Matron	60	15 7/12	Permanent infirmity of mind and body	22 0 0	10 0 0	
10 Jan. 1867	Do.	Catherine M'Closkey	Infirmary Nurse	66⅜	17¾	Permanent infirmity of body	41 0 0	11 0 0	
25 Mar. 1868	Do.	Cornelius Donnelly	Porter	73	12¾	Do.	60 15 4	10 0 0	
6 Feb. 1870	Borrisokane	Margaret Harris	Caretaker of Dispensary	77	30	Ceased to hold the office	8 0 0	6 0 0	
23 Oct. 1873	Do.	Hannah Smith	Matron	61	20½	Infirmity of body	31 0 0	60 5 0	
28 May, 1874	Boyle	Ellen Walsh	Do.	60	22	Do.	56 0 0	25 0 0	
4 Nov. 1880	Cahersiveen	Daniel A. O'Connell	Clerk	52	33 7/12	Permanent infirmity of body	45 0 0	30 13 4	
26 Jan. 1883	Do.	Ellen Dwyer	Fever Hospital Nurse	50	5¾	Permanent infirmity of mind	30 0 0	0 0 0	
8 April, 1886	Do.	Catherine Sullivan	Assistant Nurse in Fever Hospital	60¾	30¼	Infirmity of body	60 0 0	4 10 0	
11 Sep. 1889	Do.	Catherine Clifford	Fever Hospital Nurse	67	7	Permanent infirmity of	70 0 0	4 17 0	

14 Sept. 18[illegible]	Do. . .	Kate [illegible] .	Infirmary Nurse . .	[illegible]	[illegible]	Permanent infirmity of body.	[illegible]
[illegible] Jan. 187[illegible]	Carrick-on-Suir .	Christina Osborne .	Fever Hospital Nurse .	[illegible]	[illegible]	Infirmity of body . .	[illegible]
7 Feb. 18[illegible]	Do. . . .	John R. [illegible] .	Medical Officer of Dispensary District	[illegible]	[illegible]	Old age	[illegible]
4 May, 18[illegible]	[illegible] . . .	M. A. [illegible] .	Matron . . .	[illegible]	[illegible]	Permanent infirmity of body	[illegible]
[illegible] June, 1871	Castlebar . .	Mary [illegible] . .	Do.	[illegible]	[illegible]	Infirmity of mind and body	[illegible]
[illegible] Oct. 18[illegible]	Do. . . .	[illegible] Thompson .	Schoolmistress . .	[illegible]	[illegible]	Infirmity of body .	[illegible]
[illegible] Sept. 18[illegible]	Castlederg .	Margaret [illegible] .	Infirmary Nurse. . .	[illegible]	[illegible]	Do. .	[illegible]
[illegible] Feb. 18[illegible]	Do. . .	James Chisholm .	Porter	[illegible]	[illegible]	Old age and infirmity of body	[illegible]
[illegible] June, 18[illegible]	Castlerea . . .	Prudence Galbraith	Matron . . .	[illegible]	[illegible]	Infirmity of body	[illegible]
[illegible] Dec. 18[illegible]	Do. . . .	John [illegible] .	Relieving Officer . .	[illegible]	[illegible]	Do . .	[illegible]
[illegible] Dec. 18[illegible]	Do. . . .	Wm. [illegible] .	Medical Officer of Dispensary District.	[illegible]	[illegible]	Old age . .	[illegible]
[illegible] Mar 18[illegible]	Do. . . .	Stephen M'Dermott	Relieving Officer .	[illegible]	[illegible]	Infirmity of body . .	[illegible]
[illegible] June, 18[illegible],	Do. . . .	Michael O'[illegible]	Medical Officer of Workhouse and of Dispensary District.	[illegible]	[illegible]	Permanent infirmity of body.	[illegible]
[illegible] Nov 18[illegible]	Castletown . .	Philip A. Armstrong	Medical Officer of Dispensary District.	[illegible]	[illegible]	Old age . . .	[illegible]
[illegible] May, 18[illegible]	Do. .	[illegible] M'[illegible] .	Collector . .	[illegible]	[illegible]	Do. . . .	[illegible]
[illegible] Jan. 18[illegible]	Cavan	[illegible] [illegible] . .	Clerk	[illegible]	[illegible]	Old age and infirmity .	[illegible]
[illegible] Dec. 18[illegible]	Celbridge . .	Richard Graham .	Relieving Officer . .	[illegible]	[illegible]	Old age and infirmity of body	[illegible]
[illegible] Mar 18[illegible]	Do. . . .	Mary A. [illegible]	Midwife of Dispensary District.	[illegible]	[illegible]	Permanent infirmity of body	[illegible]
[illegible] Sept. 18[illegible]	Do. .	Edward M'[illegible] .	Porter	[illegible]	[illegible]	Do. . . .	[illegible]
[illegible] Nov. 18[illegible]	Do. . .	Patrick J. M'[illegible] .	Medical Officer of Dispensary District	[illegible]	[illegible]	Do . .	[illegible]
[illegible] Nov 18[illegible]	Claremorris .	Ellen J. [illegible] .	Schoolmistress . .	[illegible]	[illegible]	Do. .	[illegible]
[illegible] Oct. 18[illegible]	Clogheen	Joseph [illegible] .	Relieving Officer . .	[illegible]	[illegible]	Old age	[illegible]
[illegible] Jan. 18[illegible]	Clonakilty . .	Henry W. [illegible]	Medical Officer of Dispensary District	[illegible]	[illegible]	Permanent infirmity of body	[illegible]

No. 7.—Union Officers Superannuation.—Statement of allowances under the Superannuation Acts in force during any portion of the year ended the 29th of September, 1880; showing also the cases in which the allowances terminated during the year. (In continuation of statement in seventeenth annual report, Appendix D, No. 7)—continued.

Date of Consent of Local Government Board.	Union.	Name of Officer.	Office.	Age. Years.	Period of service as a Union Officer.	Cause of retirement.	*Annual Salary.	Annual Superannuation allowance.	If terminated, date of termination.
							£ s. d.	£ s. d.	
30 Nov. 1870	Clones . . .	James Fitzgerald	Medical Officer of Dispensary District.	60	24½	Infirmity of body . .	125 0 0	83 6 8	
26 Aug. 1880	Do. . . .	George Little . .	Master	66	21½	Do. .	60 0 0	36 0 0	
6 Nov. 1861	Clonmel . .	Susan Murphy .	Matron . . .	67	24½	Permanent infirmity of body.	60 0 0	36 0 0	
20 Nov. 1860	Do. . . .	Martha Ladley .	Fever Hospital Nurse .	70½	27½	Do. . . .	40 0 0	30 0 0	
30 Jan. 1865	Coleraine . .	Richard L. M'Intire	Medical Officer of Dispensary District.	69½	34½	Old age . . .	171½ 0 11	60 0 0	
8 July, 1870	Cookstown . .	Catherine Crawford.	Fever Hospital Nurse .	56	37½	Infirmity of body . .	0 0 0	20 0 0	
6 Jun 1865	Do. . . .	Robert Henry . .	Medical Officer of Dispensary District.	73	30 7/12	Old age	141 1 0	87 7 10	
4 Mar 1866	Do. . . .	Henry Gunn .	Do.	64½	38½	Old age and infirmity of body	172 10 0	115 6 4	
[illegible]	[illegible]	[illegible]	Matron	[illegible]	[illegible]	Permanent infirmity of	[illegible]	[illegible]	

7 Dec. 1891.	Do.	Ellen Corbett	Fever Hospital Nurse	[illegible]	[illegible]	Permanent infirmity of body	[illegible]	[illegible]	[illegible]	[illegible]	[illegible]	[illegible]
24 Mar 1887.	Do.	Mary A. Steele	Matron	[illegible]	[illegible]	Do.	[illegible]	[illegible]	[illegible]	[illegible]	[illegible]	[illegible]
8 Mar [illegible]	Do.	Ellen O'Leary	Female Searcher,	[illegible]	[illegible]	Old age	[illegible]	[illegible]	[illegible]	[illegible]	[illegible]	[illegible]
21 Feb. [illegible]	Carrowkeel	Michael M'Keown	Medical Officer of Dispensary District	[illegible]	[illegible]	Do.	[illegible]	[illegible]	[illegible]	[illegible]	[illegible]	[illegible]
7 July, 1876	Ossory	John Worrall	Do.	[illegible]	[illegible]	Infirmity of body	[illegible]	[illegible]	[illegible]	[illegible]	[illegible]	[illegible]
21 Sept. 1888	Do.	Catherine Griffin	Night Nurse	[illegible]	[illegible]	Permanent infirmity of mind and body.	[illegible]	[illegible]	[illegible]	[illegible]	[illegible]	[illegible]
7 Apr. 1883	Dalvin	William Leary	Porter	[illegible]	[illegible]	Permanent infirmity of body	[illegible]	[illegible]	[illegible]	7	[illegible]	[illegible]
27 Sept. 1889	Dingle	Mary Gray	Matron	[illegible]	[illegible]	Infirmity of body	[illegible]	[illegible]	[illegible]	[illegible]	[illegible]	[illegible]
4 Oct. 1889	Do.	Peter Kennedy	Clerk	[illegible]	[illegible]	Old age	347	[illegible]	[illegible]	[illegible]	[illegible]	[illegible]
28 Dec. 1870	Do.	Henry Webb	Apothecary of Workhouse and of Dispensary District.	[illegible]	[illegible]	Infirmity of body	[illegible]	[illegible]	[illegible]	[illegible]	[illegible]	[illegible]
10 May, 1886	Do.	Bridget Garvey	Schoolmistress	[illegible]	[illegible]	Permanent infirmity of mind and body.	[illegible]	[illegible]	[illegible]	[illegible]	[illegible]	[illegible]
6 Feb. 1889	Do.	Mary Moriarty,	Infirmary Nurse,	[illegible]	[illegible]	Old age	[illegible]	[illegible]	[illegible]	[illegible]	[illegible]	[illegible]
17 Sept. [illegible]	Do.	John W. [illegible],	Medical Officer of Dispensary District.	[illegible]	[illegible]	Do.	[illegible]	[illegible]	[illegible]	[illegible]	[illegible]	[illegible]
29 Sept. 1886	*Dunganstown (See note).	John Tuck	Master	[illegible]	[illegible]	Dissolution of Union	[illegible]	[illegible]	[illegible]	[illegible]	[illegible]	[illegible]
– –	Do.	Annie Johnson	Matron	[illegible]	[illegible]	Do.	[illegible]	[illegible]	[illegible]	[illegible]	[illegible]	[illegible]
– –	Do.	Richard R. D. Duckworth.	Medical Officer of Workhouse.	[illegible]	[illegible]	Do.	[illegible]	[illegible]	[illegible]	7	[illegible]	[illegible]
– –	Do.	Margaret Burgin	Schoolmistress	[illegible]	[illegible]	Do.	[illegible]	[illegible]	[illegible]	[illegible]	[illegible]	[illegible]
– –	Do.	Patrick Cubitt	Porter	[illegible]	[illegible]	Do.	[illegible]	[illegible]	[illegible]	51	19	4
– –	Do.	Ellen Dunne	Infirmary Nurse	[illegible]	[illegible]	Do.	[illegible]	[illegible]	[illegible]	[illegible]	[illegible]	[illegible]
– –	Do.	Margaret Loughnane	Wardswoman	[illegible]	[illegible]	Do.	[illegible]	[illegible]	[illegible]	[illegible]	[illegible]	[illegible]

No. 7.—Union Officers' Superannuation.—*Statement* of allowances under the Superannuation Acts in force during any portion of the year ended the 29th of September, 1889; showing also the cases in which the allowances terminated during the year. (In continuation of statement in seventeenth annual report, Appendix D, No 7)—*continued.*

Date of Sanction of Local Government Board.	Union.	Name of Officer.	Office.	Age, Years.	Period of service as a Union Officer.	Cause of retirement.	*Annual Salary	Annual Superannuation allowance.	If terminated, date of termination.
							£ s. d.	£ s. d.	
[illegible] Sept [illegible]	*Donaghmore (the late)	Margaret Dunne	Wardswoman . . .	3[illegible]	[illegible]	Dissolution of Union,	[illegible] 14 0	0 [illegible] 8	
" "	Do. .	Robert Pearson	Collector	[illegible]	[illegible]	Do. . .	60 10 0	57 4 0	
" "	Do.	Robert Locke .	Relieving Officer . .	6[illegible]	[illegible]	Do. . .	90 0 0	18 0 0	
17 Feb. [illegible]	Downpatrick .	Robert G. Shell .	Medical Officer of Dispensary District	[illegible]	[illegible]	Old age and infirmity of body	1[illegible] 10 0	[illegible] 0 0	23 July, 18[illegible]
16 Feb. 1884	Drogheda . .	Patrick M'Gain .	Relieving Officer . .	6[illegible]	[illegible]	Permanent infirmity of body	[illegible] 10 0	21 10 4	
6 Oct. [illegible]	Do. . . .	Ellen Farrelly .	Matron	6[illegible]	[illegible]	Do . . .	[illegible] 0 0	[illegible] 0 0	
4 Sept. [illegible]	Do. . . .	John Warren . .	Porter	[illegible]	[illegible]	Do. . . .	6[illegible] 17 2	[illegible] 1 0	

.	John M. [illegible]	Medical Officer of Dispensary District.	[illegible]	[illegible]	Do.	[illegible]	[illegible]	11	120	[illegible]	7	
.	Patrick Hughes	Night Watchman	72	13	Do.	37	10	0	13	10	0	
.	Mary A. A[illegible]	Schoolmistress	[illegible]	[illegible]	Old age and infirmity of body	[illegible]	10	0	[illegible]	13	0	
	William [illegible]	Baker	[illegible]	[illegible]	Permanent infirmity of body	[illegible]	[illegible]	0	[illegible]	[illegible]	[illegible]	
.	Peter Byrne	Assistant Master	[illegible]	44½	Do.	[illegible]	0	0	[illegible]	0	0	
.	Margaret Maher	Workhouse Superintendent	[illegible]	[illegible]	Do.	[illegible]	3	10	[illegible]	[illegible]	[illegible]	
	Michael M'[illegible]	Relieving Officer	[illegible]	[illegible]	Do.	150	0	0	[illegible]	0	0	
.	[illegible] Waddick	Assistant Matron and Workmistress.	[illegible]	[illegible]	Permanent infirmity of mind	[illegible]	[illegible]	[illegible]	[illegible]	0	0	
	Edward M'Evoy	Gate Porter	63	[illegible]	Infirmity of body	[illegible]	10	0	[illegible]	0	0	
.	Henry Cody	Medical Officer of Dispensary District.	71	27	Old age	[illegible]	0	0	[illegible]	0	0	
	Richard Rice	Male Lunatic Keeper	[illegible]	[illegible]	Old age and infirmity	[illegible]	0	0	[illegible]	0	0	
.	Peter [illegible]	Medical Officer of Workhouse.	[illegible]	30	Do.	[illegible]	0	0	100	0	0	
.	Rosanna Kennedy	Matron	[illegible]	[illegible]	Old age and permanent infirmity of body	[illegible]	0	0	[illegible]	0	0	
.	Henry J. [illegible]	Apothecary	[illegible]	[illegible]	Permanent infirmity of body	[illegible]	0	0	120	0	0	16 Sep. [illegible]
	George W. Owens	Medical Officer of Workhouse	[illegible]	[illegible]	Permanent infirmity of mind and body	[illegible]	0	0	[illegible]	0	[illegible]	
.	Patrick Lamb	Master Carpenter	[illegible]	[illegible]	Old age	[illegible]	0	0	[illegible]	[illegible]	[illegible]	
	John Carr	Roman Catholic Chaplain	[illegible]	[illegible]	Do.	[illegible]	[illegible]	[illegible]	100	0	0	
.	Samuel Campbell	Relieving Officer	[illegible]	17	Permanent infirmity of body	100	0	0	[illegible]	[illegible]	[illegible]	
	Ellen Anderson	Assistant Matron	[illegible]	[illegible]	Infirmity of mind	[illegible]	0	0	[illegible]	[illegible]	[illegible]	

No. 7.—Union Officers' Superannuation.—Statement of allowances under the Superannuation Acts in force during any portion of the year ended the 30th of September, 1889, showing also the cases in which the allowances terminated during the year. (In continuation of statement in seventeenth annual report, Appendix D, No. 7)—continued.

Date of Consent of Local Government Board.	Union.	Name of Officer.	Office.	Age. Years	Period of service as a Union Officer	Cause of retirement.	*Annual Salary.	Annual Superannuation allowance.	If terminated, date of termination.
							£ s. d.	£ s. d.	
18 Dec. [illegible]	Dublin, South, . .	John Horney .	Car Driver . .	63	36 [illegible]	Permanent infirmity of body.	48 0 0	24 0 0	
16 Aug [illegible]	Do. . . .	W. B Jennings .	Medical Officer of Workhouse	60	25 [illegible]	Do. . . .	150 0 0	93 10 0	
7 July, [illegible]	[illegible] . .	John Browne .	Medical Officer of Dispensary District.	[illegible]	[illegible]	Old age	[illegible] 0 10	[illegible] 0 0	
13 May, [illegible]	Do. . .	Anne Courtney	Midwife of Dispensary District.	72	24 [illegible]	Do. .	20 10 0	10 0 0	
7 March, [illegible]	Dunfanaghy . .	John W. [illegible] .	Relieving Officer .	75 [illegible]	[illegible]	Old age and permanent infirmity of body.	30 0 0	17 10 0	
17 Oct [illegible]	Dungannon . .	Rose O'Neill . .	Infirmary Nurse . .	60 [illegible]	[illegible]	Permanent infirmity of body	60 0 7	30 0 0	
27 Feb. [illegible]	Dungarvan . .	Ambrose [illegible] .	Medical Officer of Workhouse.	67	38	Do. . . .	120 0 0	60 0 0	
9 June, [illegible]	Do. . . .	James [illegible] .	Porter	[illegible]	17	Do. . . .	[illegible] 0 0	[illegible] 0 0	
10 Apr. [illegible]	Do. . .	James G. Fitzgerald	Clerk	66	30 [illegible]	Do. . . .	160 12 0	66 0 0	
7 Mar. [illegible]	[illegible] . .	[illegible] .	Medical Officer of Dispensary District.	[illegible]	[illegible]	Do. . . .	[illegible] 0 0	[illegible] 0 0	

14 Jan. [illegible]	Do.	Mary A. Flynn	Infirmary Nurse	[illegible]	[illegible]	Do.	[illegible]	[illegible]	7	[illegible]	0	0
30 Mar [illegible]	Do.	Thomas Ruals	Tailor	[illegible]	[illegible]	Old age	[illegible]	4	0	[illegible]	0	0
10 July, [illegible]	Do.	Patrick Hogan	Relieving Officer	70	[illegible]	Permanent infirmity of body.	[illegible]	0	0	[illegible]	[illegible]	4
4 May, [illegible]	Do.	William Waters	Medical Officer of Dispensary District.	[illegible]	[illegible]	Do.	[illegible]	[illegible]	0	70	0	0
9 Aug. [illegible]	Do.	Julia Ryan	Fever Hospital Nurse	[illegible]	[illegible]	Old age	[illegible]	14	[illegible]	[illegible]	[illegible]	4
19 Oct. [illegible]	Ennis	R. J. M'Namara	Schoolmistress	[illegible]	15	Infirmity of body	24	0	0	10	[illegible]	[illegible]
10 Aug. [illegible]	Do.	Honora Fay	Matron	[illegible]	30	Do.	[illegible]	0	[illegible]	[illegible]	[illegible]	[illegible]
14 Nov [illegible]	Do.	Patrick M. Cullinan	Medical Officer of Workhouse.	[illegible]	[illegible]	Old age	110	0	0	[illegible]	[illegible]	[illegible]
14 Nov. [illegible]	Do.	Mary A. Griffin	Infirmary Nurse	[illegible]	30	Permanent infirmity of body.	[illegible]	10	0	10	[illegible]	[illegible]
20 Oct. [illegible]	Enniscorthy	Margaret Mavis	Schoolmistress	[illegible]	[illegible]	Infirmity of body	[illegible]	[illegible]	0	[illegible]	0	[illegible]
26 July, [illegible]	Do.	George Maguire	Master	[illegible]	[illegible]	Old age and infirmity	[illegible]	[illegible]	0	[illegible]	[illegible]	[illegible]
30 Jan. [illegible]	Do.	Edward Leane	Shoemaker	[illegible]	[illegible]	Permanent infirmity of body	[illegible]	0	0	[illegible]	0	0
11 Sept. [illegible]	Ennistimon	Alexander Flood	Medical Officer of Dispensary District.	[illegible]	[illegible]	Infirmity of body	[illegible]	[illegible]	0	[illegible]	0	0
9 Feb. [illegible]	Do.	Margaret Blair	Fever Hospital Nurse	[illegible]	[illegible]	Permanent infirmity of body	[illegible]	0	0	[illegible]	0	0
26 Oct. [illegible]	Do.	Jane Scarlett	Matron	[illegible]	[illegible]	Do.	[illegible]	0	[illegible]	[illegible]	[illegible]	[illegible]
14 April, [illegible]	Do.	Edward Baget	Medical Officer of Workhouse.	[illegible]	[illegible]	Do.	100	0	0	[illegible]	[illegible]	4
12 Aug. [illegible]	Ennistymon	William Ryan	Medical Officer of Dispensary District.	[illegible]	[illegible]	Infirmity of body	100	0	0	[illegible]	0	0
18 April, [illegible]	Fermoy	Ellen Crawford	Hospital Nurse	[illegible]	[illegible]	Do.	[illegible]	0	0	[illegible]	0	[illegible]
1 Aug [illegible]	Do.	Kate M'Carthy	Matron	[illegible]	[illegible]	Permanent infirmity of body	[illegible]	0	[illegible]	[illegible]	[illegible]	[illegible]
16 June, [illegible]	Do.	Cornelius Thompson	Gate Porter	[illegible]	[illegible]	Do.	[illegible]	[illegible]	0	7	0	[illegible]
[illegible]	Galway	Nicholas Colahan	Medical Officer of Workhouse	[illegible]	11	Infirmity of body	[illegible]	[illegible]		[illegible]	0	0

No. 7.—UNION OFFICERS' SUPERANNUATION.—Statement of allowances under the Superannuation Acts in force during any portion of the year ended the 30th of September, 1880; showing also the cases in which the allowances terminated during the year. (In continuation of statement in seventeenth annual report, Appendix D, No. 7)—*continued.*

Date of Consent of Local Government Board.	Union.	Name of Officer.	Office.	Age. Years.	Period of service as a Union Officer.	Cause of retirement.	*Annual Salary.	Annual Superannuation Allowance.	If terminated, date of termination.
							£ s. d.	£ s. d.	
1 April, 1864	Galway . .	Honoria Kean . .	Fever Hospital Nurse .	60	20¼	Permanent infirmity of body.	30 0 0	15 0 0	[illegible]
19 Mar. 1867	Do. . . .	John F. Lynch	Master . . .	57	19½	Old age and permanent infirmity of body	170 0 0	66 0 0	
20 Feb. 1868	Glennamaddy . .	Ellen Mooney . .	Hospital Nurse .	60	10½	Infirmity of body . .	24 0 0	10 0 6	
30 July, 1869	Do. . .	Michael Kearney	Relieving Officer .	50	30	Do. . . .	30 0 0	10 0 0	
30 May, 1868	Glenties . . .	Luke Walsh .	Medical Officer of Dispensary District.	48	30$\frac{1}{12}$	Permanent infirmity of body	115 0 0	60 0 0	
22 Jan. 1871	Glin . . .	John Riordan . .	Assistant Medical Officer of Workhouse	66	20½	Infirmity and old age	30 0 0	20 0 2	
31 Dec. 1868	Do. . . .	Daniel O'Connor	Schoolmaster . . .	80	22	Old age . .	47 2 0	25 10 11	

21 Dec. 1860	Granard	Thomas W[illegible]	Medical Officer of Dispensary District.	60 $\frac{[illegible]}{[illegible]}$	15	Permanent infirmity of body	141	[illegible]	10	[illegible]	[illegible]	0
20 Feb. 1864	Do.	Margaret M'Mahon	Schoolmistress	60	24$\frac{1}{2}$	Do.	46	0	7	75	0	0
11 Sep. 1869	Do.	James Burke	Schoolmaster	60	20$\frac{[illegible]}{[illegible]}$	Do.	20	14	0	30	0	0
7 April, 1876	Drumcondra	Charles Humphreys	Relieving Officer	62	30	Infirmity of body	80	0	0	13	10	0
10 July, 1871	Kanturk	Kate Clifford	Matron	66	22$\frac{1}{2}$	Do.	30	0	0	20	0	0	26 June, 1880
20 April, 1880	Do.	Thomas R. Dagg	Master	60	22$\frac{[illegible]}{[illegible]}$	Permanent infirmity of body	142	0	0	70	0	0
21 Nov 1880	Do.	Mary Aylward	Midwife of Dispensary District.	46$\frac{1}{2}$	20$\frac{1}{2}$	Do	46	10	0	13	0	0
8 Sep. 1880	Do.	William H. O'Keeffe	Schoolmaster	47$\frac{1}{2}$	26$\frac{[illegible]}{[illegible]}$	Do.	100	10	10	30	0	0
26 Aug 1870	Kells	Ralph M'Dermott	Medical Officer of Dispensary District.	60	21$\frac{[illegible]}{[illegible]}$	Infirmity of body.	120	0	0	80	0	0
12 Dec. 1864	Do.	Edward Brady	Relieving Officer	13	21	Old age and permanent infirmity of body.	30	0	0	21	10	4
24 Nov. 1868	Do.	Patrick M'Donnell	Tailor	60$\frac{[illegible]}{[illegible]}$	46$\frac{1}{2}$	Permanent infirmity of body.	46	16	0	30	0	0
6 April, 1882	Kenmare	Adrian Taylor	Medical Officer of Dispensary District.	64	22	Infirmity of body	120	0	0	40	0	0
20 Aug. 1867	Do.	Julia Murphy	Infirmary Nurse	50	21	Permanent infirmity of body.	46	0	0	60	0	0
1 June, 1881	Killala	Richard Walsh	Dispensary Porter	66	22	Old age	6	0	0	8	0	0	8 May, 1882
19 Aug. 1881	Do.	John F. Kirkwood	Collector	50	30	Permanent infirmity of body	45	10	0	27	0	0
17 Dec. 1862	Do.	William Hogan	Master	70	20$\frac{1}{2}$	Old age	61	0	0	30	13	0
11 Nov 1878	Killarney	Bridget Lambert	Matron	52	27	Infirmity of body	100	0	0	60	0	0
21 April, 1880	Do.	John O'Halloran	Medical Officer of Dispensary District	50	60	Do	100	5	10	60	0	0
5 Oct. 1860	Do.	Robert Tutas	Do.	76	30	Old age and infirmity	100	0	0	66	0	0	20 May 1866
6 April, 1875	Kilcommon	Margaret Walsh	Matron	67	30	Infirmity of body	54	0	0	35	0	0
[illegible] Feb. [illegible]	Kilmallock	Thomas [illegible]	Relieving Officer	[illegible]	12$\frac{1}{2}$	Infirmity of mind and body	65	0	0	10	0	0
8 April, 1870	Do.	Edmund Walsh	Do	78	17	Infirmity of body	20	0	0	10	0	0

No. 7.—Union Officials' Superannuation.—Statement of allowances under the Superannuation Acts in force during any portion of the year ended the 29th of September, 1889; showing also the cases in which the allowances terminated during the year. (In continuation of statement in seventeenth annual report, Appendix D, No. 7)—continued.

Date of Sanction of Local Government Board.	Union.	Name of Officer.	Office.	Age, Years.	Period of service as a Union Officer.	Cause of retirement.	Annual Salary.	Annual Superannuation Allowance.	If terminated, date of termination.
							£ s. d.	£ s. d.	
27 Dec. 1881	Kilmallock . .	Catherine Meade .	Fever Hospital Nurse	[illegible]	36½	Infirmity of body.	18 0 0	9 15 [illegible]	Nov. 1888.
17 Nov. 1882	Do. . . .	Richard Quigley	Clerk . . .	57	21¾	Permanent infirmity of body.	120 0 0	130 0 0	
14 Jan. 1881	Do. . . .	Ellen Byrne .	Infirmary Nurse . .	65	38	Old age	85 0 0	61 0 0	
8 May, 1880	Do. . . .	James Nelson	Master	50½	30½	Permanent infirmity of body.	254 0 0	170 0 0	
8 May, 1883	Do. . . .	Annie Nelson .	Matron . . .	80¾	12½	Do. . . .	104 0 0	80 0 0	
21 Mar. 1886	Do. . . .	Jane Cruinston .	Midwife of Dispensary District.	60	16½	Permanent infirmity of body and mind.	90 0 0	[illegible]	
25 Nov. 1884	Do. . . .	Mary O'Neill . .	Assistant Schoolmistress .	49¾	18¾	Permanent infirmity of body	70 0 0	35 0 0	
10 Nov. 1884	Do . . .	Daniel Riordan .	Medical Officer of Dispensary District	68	31½	Old age	120 0 0	80 0 0	30 May 1889
10 Feb. 1884	Do. . . .	John Lenihan .	Carpenter . . .	85	20¾	Old age and infirmity .	60 0 0	34 14 0	

Date	Union	Name	Office	Age	Service	Cause	£	s.	d.	£	s.
6 Nov. [illegible]	Limerick . . .	Julia Scully . .	Hospital Accountant .	[illegible]	[illegible]	Infirmity of body . .	[illegible]	0	0	10	0
8 Nov. [illegible]	Do. . . .	Johanna Flynn .	Wardmistress . . .	60	[illegible]	Do. . . .	[illegible]	0	0	20	0
6 Aug. [illegible]	Do. . .	John [illegible] .	Collector . . .	65	34	Infirmity of mind and body.	[illegible]	[illegible]	7	[illegible]	0
[illegible] Mar. [illegible]	Do. . . .	John [illegible] . .	Male Lunatic Keeper .	[illegible]	[illegible]	Infirmity of body . .	60	0	11	[illegible]	0
[illegible] April, [illegible]	Do. . . .	Ellen [illegible] . .	Wardsmaid . . .	60	[illegible]	Do. . . .	31	0	0	[illegible]	0
18 Nov. [illegible]	Do. .	Honorah Dundon .	Hospital Nurse . .	46	[illegible]	Permanent infirmity of body	[illegible]	0	0	[illegible]	0
30 May, [illegible]	Do. . . .	Jonathan Elmes	Medical Officer of Dispensary District.	60	[illegible]	Old age	[illegible]	18	0	73	0
3 Nov. [illegible]	Do. . . .	Marcus Going . .	Do. . . .	64	[illegible]	Do. . . .	216	0	0	70	0
23 April, [illegible]	Lismore . . .	Sarah C. Murray .	Matron	60	20	Infirmity of mind . .	[illegible]	0	0	[illegible]	0
[illegible] Aug. [illegible]	Do. . . .	Ellen M. O'Keeffe .	Infirmary Nurse . .	60	19	Permanent infirmity of body	41	0	0	[illegible]	0
30 Aug. [illegible]	Lisnaskea . .	James Haire . .	Clerk	51	[illegible]	Infirmity of mind and body	[illegible]	0	0	[illegible]	0
16 June, [illegible]	Do. . .	Maxwell Beatty .	Sub-administrator . . .	45	[illegible]	Infirmity of body . .	[illegible]	0	0	9	0
6 Jan. [illegible]	Listowel .	Garrett Fitzmaurice	Relieving Officer . .	40	17	Do. . . .	[illegible]	0	0	[illegible]	0
23 Apr. [illegible]	Do. . . .	John M'Carthy .	Clerk	[illegible]	[illegible]	Permanent infirmity of mind and body	274	3	0	130	0
16 July, 1870	Londonderry . .	Ellen Cochrane .	Matron	60	60	Infirmity of body . .	[illegible]	0	0	20	0
16 Mar. [illegible]	Do. . .	Thomas Corbett .	Medical Officer of Dispensary District.	60	[illegible]	Old age and infirmity .	[illegible]	0	0	[illegible]	0
11 April, [illegible]	Loughrea . .	James Stanton .	Porter	65	[illegible]	Infirmity of body . .	15	0	0	[illegible]	[illegible]
6 Mar. [illegible]	Do. . . .	Susan Foley . .	Hospital Nurse . .	[illegible]	[illegible]	Old age	[illegible]	0	0	[illegible]	0
6 Jan. 1870	Lurgan . . .	Susan Anderson .	Matron	60	[illegible]	Do.	40	0	0	[illegible]	0
22 June, [illegible]	Do. . . .	George Riddell .	Relieving Officer . .	[illegible]	[illegible]	Do.	[illegible]	0	0	[illegible]	0
30 Dec. [illegible]	Do. . .	Emmanuel J Harman	Medical Officer of Dispensary [illegible].	67	[illegible]	Permanent infirmity of body	136	0	0	[illegible]	10
30 Oct. 1870	Macroom . . .	Thomas Godfrey .	Do. . . .	71	[illegible]	Old age	[illegible]	3	11	[illegible]	0

No. 7.—Union Officers' Superannuation.—Statement of allowances under the Superannuation Acts in force during any portion of the year ended the 29th of September, 1889; showing also the cases in which the allowances terminated during the year. (In continuation of statement in seventeenth annual report, Appendix D, No. 7)—continued.

Date of Consent of Local Government Board.	Union.	Name of Officer.	Office.	Age. Years.	Period of service as a Union Officer.	Cause of retirement.	*Annual Salary.	Annual Superannuation Allowance.	If terminated, date of termination.
							£ s. d.	£ s. d.	
11 Oct. 1880	Macroom.	Thomas F. Hurley	Clerk	54	30	Permanent infirmity of body	166 0 0	116 0 0	
4 May, 1883	Do.	Catherine Harrington	Caretaker of Dispensary	60	$27\frac{7}{12}$	Do.	9 0 0	6 0 0	30 May, 1889
27 Feb. 1880	Mallow	Parsons Barry	Medical Officer of Dispensary District	69	33[illegible]	Infirmity of body	175 0 0	100 0 0	
27 June, 1888	Do.	[illegible] Leary	[illegible] Tailor	70	[illegible]	Old age	58 [illegible]	19 0 0	6 Dec. 1888
1 April, 1882	Do.	Mary Connell	Caretaker of Dispensary	70	30½	Permanent infirmity of body	7 4 0	5 0 0	
1 April, 1887	Do.	Elizabeth Walstead	Infirmary Nurse	71½	27½	Old age	36 0 0	20 4 0	
8 Sept. 1870	Mitchelstown	Thomas Davis	Medical Officer of Workhouse	58	35½	Infirmity of body	100 0 0	65 13 4	
6 Aug. 1880	Do.	Catherine Burke	Fever Hospital Nurse	63	30	Old age	36 0 0	20 0 0	12 Apr. 1889
9 April, 1880	Do.	Thomas M. Nash	Medical Officer of Dispensary District	66	33	Infirmity of body	177 0 0	80 0 0	
6 Dec. 1878	Midleton	Catherine Curry	Infirmary Nurse	66	28½	Old age and infirmity of body	30 0 0	16 0 0	
1 June, 1881	Do.	William Ahearn	Baker	65	36	Permanent infirmity of mind	32 0 0	24 10 4	
9 Feb. 1880	Do.	Patrick Burke	Master	69½	39½	Old age	111 0 0	70 0 0	
26 May, 1888	Do.	Margaret Scanlan	Wardsmistress	70½	24½	Old age and permanent infirmity of body	31 0 0	20 14 0	
18 Oct. 1888	Do.	Thomas Sandiford	Medical Officer of Dispensary District	75½	29½	Old age	138 1 0	94 8 0	

9 Oct. 1877	Do.	Catherine Walsh	Matron	60	16½	Infirmity of body	40	0	0	20	0	0	
7 Jan. 1879	Mitchelstown	James Fitzgibbon	Shoemaker	66	27	Old age and infirmity	30	17	9	16	0	0	
18 Aug. 1871	Mohill	Patrick Mulholland	Relieving Officer	60	60	Old age	[illegible]	0	0	[illegible]	0	0	
14 Mar. 1868	Do.	Michael Blake	Tailor	75[illegible]	30[illegible]	Old age and infirmity of body.	[illegible]	0	0	15	10	0	
24 Mar. 1878	Monaghan	John Douglas	Relieving Officer	64	64	Infirmity of body	40	0	0	20	0	0	
6 Aug. 1879	Do.	Margaret Rakin	Matron	61	28[illegible]	Do.	35	0	0	18	0	0	
6 April, 1871	Mountmellick	Margaret Dimond	Do.	54	29[illegible]	Infirmity of mind and body	30	0	0	18	0	0	
1 Sept. 1881	Do.	Joseph Clarke	Medical Officer of Workhouse and of Dispensary District.	69[illegible]	40	Old age and permanent infirmity of body.	200	0	0	100	0	0	
26 April, 1880	Do.	Robert Goodbody	Clerk	[illegible]	20[illegible]	Permanent infirmity of body	270	0	0	140	0	0	
5 July, 1880	Do.	Sarah Conroy	Fever Hospital Nurse	49[illegible]	20[illegible]	Do.	64	18	10	30	0	0	
18 July, 1872	Mullingar	John H. Pilkington	Relieving Officer	60	24	Infirmity of body	65	0	0	40	0	0	
24 Mar. 1879	Do.	Francis Kerr	Do.	66	27	Do.	60	0	0	40	0	0	
6 Sept. 1878	Do.	Marianne Russell	Schoolmistress	60	17	Do.	40	10	0	30	0	0	
1 Feb. 1880	Do.	Henry Jackson	Master Tailor	50[illegible]	20[illegible]	Permanent infirmity of body	35	0	0	27	0	0	
7 Jan. 1880	Do.	Honoria Meara	Laundress	60	60	Old age and permanent infirmity of body	30	0	0	20	0	0	
10 April, 1880	Do.	Richard English	Master	60	22[illegible]	Old age	119	15	7	40	18	0	
" "	Do.	Anne English	Matron	60[illegible]	20[illegible]	Permanent infirmity of body.	40	10	7	20	18	0	
6 Aug. 1885	Do.	Anne M'Ternan	Midwife of Dispensary District and Dispensary Caretaker	63	10	Do.	30	0	0	20	0	0	
27 Aug. 1880	Do.	Maria Connell	Infirmary Nurse	60	17[illegible]	Do.	40	0	0	20	0	0	8 Apr. 188[illegible]
21 April, 1878	Naas	Elizabeth Gunning	Do.	61	10[illegible]	Infirmity of body	64	0	0	30	0	0	
20 May, 1878	Do.	Patrick Ransom	Schoolmaster	62	6[illegible]	Do.	35	0	0	30	0	0	30 Dec. 1880

No. 7.—Union Officers' Superannuation.—Statement of allowances under the Superannuation Acts in force during any portion of the year ended the 29th of September, 1889; showing also the cases in which the allowances terminated during the year. (In continuation of statement in seventeenth annual report, Appendix D, No. 5)—continued.

Date of Consent of Local Government Board.	Union.	Name of Officer.	Office.	Age. Years.	Period of service as a Union Officer.	Cause of retirement.	*Annual Salary. £ s. d.	Annual Superannuation Allowance. £ s. d.	If terminated, date of termination.
19 June, 1880	Naas . .	Margaret Murtagh .	Midwife . . .	64	34	Old age and permanent infirmity of body	30 0 0	5 0 0	
10 Feb. 1888	Do. .	Robert S. Hayes .	Medical Officer of Dispensary District.	74	39	Old age	210 0 0	60 0 0	Dec., 1888
10 Feb. 1887	Do. . . .	Anne Hovery .	Assistant Schoolmistress .	37	9	Abolition of office . .	26 0 0	8 15 0	
21 Mar., 1885	Navan . . .	Thomas Morgan .	Porter	40	10	Permanent infirmity of body.	40 0 0	10 0 0	
19 Sept. 1872	Nenagh . . .	Mary M'Glynn .	Schoolmistress . . .	48	13	Infirmity of body . .	35 0 0	10 0 0	
11 Sept. 1879	Do. . . .	Margaret Carroll .	Infirmary Nurse . .	50	20	Permanent infirmity .	35 0 0	25 0 0	
21 Mar. 1889	Do. . . .	James Going .	Master . .	60	30	Permanent infirmity of body.	150 0 0	80 0 0	
10 July, 1880	Do. . . .	Francis Cahalan .	Medical Officer of Dispensary District.	60	34	Old age and permanent infirmity of body.	125 0 0	67 0 0	
14 Nov. 1887	Do. . .	Daniel Connell .	Collector	70	30	Old age	94 15 5	55 0 0	
20 Nov. 1888	Newcastle . .	George Bohner .	Medical Officer of Dispensary District.	77	41	Do.	110 10 0	73 10 0	
23 Sept. 1878	New Ross . .	Thomas Rossiter .	Do. . . .	60	30	Do.	150 0 0	44 10 0	
10 May, 1887	Do. . . .	Martin Wyse .	Porter	70	30	Permanent infirmity of body	48 0 0	12 0 0	

							£	s.	d.	£	s.	d.	
20 Jan. 1864	Do.	James Aitkin	Medical Officer of Workhouse	60	34$\frac{1}{2}$	Do.	104	0	0	68	10	6	
11 Apr. 1880	Do.	Richard Ridgeway	Medical Officer of Dispensary District	70	40	Do.	120	0	0	80	0	0	
21 Dec. 1877	Omagh	William S. Love	Do.	62	20	Infirmity of body	140	0	0	100	0	0	
7 July, 1866	Do.	Anne Boothe	Fever Hospital Nurse	41$\frac{1}{2}$	11$\frac{7}{12}$	Permanent infirmity of body	64	0	0	15	0	0	
4 Dec. 1873	Oughterard	Matthew Ness	Relieving Officer	64	23	Old age and infirmity of body	30	0	0	17	0	0	
12 Feb. 1867	Do.	Daniel Walsh	Do.	64	10$\frac{1}{2}$	Old age and infirmity	17	10	0	6	13	4	
11 May, 1850	Parsonstown	Thomas Clogue	Dispensary Porter	60	10	Infirmity of body	10	0	0	6	10	0	26 Apr., 1880
16 Aug. 1867	Do.	Thomas Daly	Master	60$\frac{1}{2}$	20$\frac{1}{2}$	Old age and permanent infirmity of body	130	0	0	86	17	4	
15 Feb. 1880	Do.	Michael Sheehy	Tailor	76	14$\frac{1}{2}$	Do.	40	10	0	10	10	0	
7 Sept. 1871	Rathdown	Bernard M'Cabe	Master Shoemaker	60	20	Old age and infirmity	30	0	0	18	0	0	
9 June, 1880	Do.	Sarah Buckley	Matron	62	20	Old age	61	0	0	30	0	11	
20 Dec. 1864	Do.	Catherine Greene	Midwife of Dispensary District	79	30	Do.	36	0	0	18	0	0	
24 Feb. 1865	Do.	Laurence Plunkett	Tailor	75	30$\frac{1}{2}$	Do.	30	0	0	20	0	0	6 Feb. 1882
4 Dec. 1866	Do.	Bridget Lewis	Midwife of Dispensary District	60	22	Do.	12	6	6	6	0	0	
20 May, 1867	Do.	Anne Smyth	Caretaker of Dispensary	60	25	Do.	9	0	0	6	0	0	
29 Oct. 1867	Do.	James F. Pollock	Medical Officer of Dispensary District	67	30	Permanent infirmity of body	130	13	4	70	0	0	
10 Dec. 1865	Do.	Catherine Mulligan	Midwife of Dispensary District	60	24$\frac{1}{2}$	Old age and permanent infirmity of body	30	0	0	11	0	0	
20 Mar. 1880	Do.	Sarah Miller	Do.	66	20$\frac{1}{2}$	Old age	22	6	8	11	3	4	
21 April, 1861	Roscommon	Ellen Curran	Fever Hospital Nurse	70	30	Do.	20	0	0	20	0	0	
10 Sept. 1880	Rathkeale	John Fitzgibbon	Apothecary of Dispensary District	70$\frac{1}{2}$	44$\frac{5}{12}$	Do.	70	0	0	60	0	0	
26 April, 1861	Roscommon	Thomas Ryan	Relieving Officer and Collector	61	30	Do.	30	0	0	20	0	0	
10 Nov. 1881	Do.	Isabel O'Keeffe	Schoolmistress	46	20$\frac{1}{2}$	Permanent infirmity of [illegible]	60	10	0	30	0	0	

No. 7.—UNION OFFICERS' SUPERANNUATION.—Statement of allowances under the Superannuation Acts in force during any portion of the year ended the 29th of September, 1889; showing also the cases in which the allowances terminated during the year. (In continuation of statement in seventeenth annual report, Appendix D, No. 7)—*continued*.

Date of Consent of Local Government Board.	Union.	Name of Officer.	Office.	Age. Years.	Period of service as a Union Officer.	Cause of retirement.	*Annual Salary.	Annual Superannuation Allowance.	If terminated, date of termination.
							£ s. d.	£ s. d.	
20 Jan. 1879	Roscrea	James Gray	Clerk	63½	37	Old age	120 10 0	77 0 0	
18 April, 1887	Do.	William R. Hayes	Master	65½	38	Do.	147 11 6	78 7 8	
" "	Do.	Margaret M'Kinstry	Matron	62½	30	Do.	67 11 6	40 0 0	
1 Oct., 1887	Scariff	James M'Namara	Porter	70½	21½	Do.	30 0 0	10 0 4	
18 May, 1888	Shillelagh	Ellen Dowse	Matron	64	24	Infirmity	20 0 0	6 0 0	
10 Sept. 1879	Do.	John W. Boakey	Medical Officer of Workhouse and of Dispensary District.	66	27	Infirmity of body	133 0 0	104 10 1	
26 Aug. 1880	Skibbereen	James G. Somerville	Medical Officer of Dispensary District.	71	30	Old age	140 10 6	90 0 0	
20 July, 1884	Do.	Honora Attridge	Matron	67½	23½	Do.	40 0 0	40 0 0	
5 Mar. 1884	Do.	John I. Donovan	Medical Officer of Dispensary District.	36½	4½	Infirmity of mind and body	136 10 0	30 0 0	
" "	Do.	Do.	Medical Officer of Workhouse.	60½	4½	Do.	90 0 0	18 10 0	
30 June, 1879	Skull	Ellen Holland	Hospital Nurse	80	27	Old age and infirmity	8 0 0	6 0 0	14 Aug. 1889.
30 Oct. 1878	Sligo	Bridget M'Manus	Assistant Hospital Nurse	48	11	Infirmity of body	27 1 7	9 13 10	
8 Apr. 1886	Do.	Matthew Feeney	Relieving Officer	90	40½	Old age	40 0 0	26 10 4	
8 Sept. 1871	Strabane	John O. Gregory	Do.	60	24	Old age and infirmity	36 0 0	20 0 0	

6 April, 1867	Do.	Margaret Mathews	Schoolmistress	54	20½	Do.	36 11 0	24 8 0	
30 Nov. 1876	Stranorlar	Henry A. Waller	Medical Officer of Dispensary District.	60	27½	Infirmity of body	100 0 0	60 0 0	
24 July, 1876	Do.	Ellen Doherty	Fever Hospital Nurse	60	18½	Do.	20 0 0	9 10 4	
30 May, 1882	Do.	James Love	Medical Officer of Workhouse and of Dispensary District	87	12	Permanent infirmity of body.	100 0 0	50 0 0	
19 Apr. 1883	Do.	Hannah Lafferty	Porter	70	13½	Do.	25 0 0	7 0 0	
6 May, 1880	Do.	Bridget Gourley	Matron	60	20½	Do.	40 17 0	15 0 0	
17 May, 1864	Strokestown	James Gray	Relieving Officer	70	23½	Old age	30 0 0	20 0 0	
24 July, 1872	Swineford	Catherine Fitzpatrick	Schoolmistress	50	10	Infirmity of body	24 0 0	10 0 0	
16 Nov 1869	Do.	Philip C. Phillips	Medical Officer of Dispensary District.	75	20½	Old age	100 0 0	66 10 0	
18 Nov 1863	Do.	Anne Carroll	Matron	80½	22½	Old age and permanent infirmity of body.	40 0 0	26 0 0	
5 Oct. 1856	Thomastown	Myles Sterling	Medical Officer of Workhouse and of Dispensary District.	[illegible]	34½	Old age	154 13 7	96 0 0	26 July, 1880.
8 June, 1879	Thurles	Honoria Walsh	Matron	60	17¾	Infirmity of body	60 0 0	30 0 0	
10 Dec. 1866 10 Jan. 1874	Do.	Thomas Cullen	Porter	[illegible]	23½	Old age and permanent infirmity of body	45 7 11	26 19 4 5 0 11	16 May, 1880
7 April, 1870	Tipperary	Michael Reardon	Master	40	20	Infirmity of body	90 0 0	46 10 4	
11 July, 1867	Do.	Matthew J. Kennedy	Medical Officer of Dispensary District.	54	20½	Permanent infirmity of body	124 0 0	67 0 0	4 June, 1880.
10 Jan. 1860	Do.	Edmund Quillinan	Porter	60½	13½	Do.	30 0 0	15 0 0	
6 Aug. 1846	Tobercurry	Patrick F. M'Ginis	Medical Officer of Dispensary District.	40¾	[illegible]	Do.	130 10 0	40 0 0	
4 Dec. 1872	Tralee	Robert Fitzmaurice	Do.	45	21	Infirmity of body	120 0 0	64 0 0	
30 May, 1878	Do.	Margaret Walsh	Wardmistress	60	20	Permanent infirmity	30 0 0	15 0 0	
1 Nov 1870	Do.	[illegible] Murphy	Fever Hospital Nurse	60	20	Old age and infirmity of body	36 0 0	20 0 0	
10 Dec. 1856	Do.	Thomas Tangney	Tailor	64½	[illegible]	Do.	32 0 0	21 0 0	

No. 7.– UNION OFFICERS' SUPERANNUATION.—Statement of allowances under the Superannuation Acts in force during any portion of the year ended the 29th of September, 1889; showing also the cases in which the allowances terminated during the year. (In continuation of statement in seventeenth annual report, Appendix D, No. 7)—continued.

Date of Consent of Local Government Board	Union.	Name of Officer	Office	Age. Years.	Period of service as a Union Officer.	Cause of retirement.	*Annual Salary.	Annual Superannuation Allowance.	If terminated, date of termination.
							£ s. d.	£ s. d.	
1 Oct. 1879	Trim	Peter Byrne	Relieving Officer	[illegible]	[illegible]	Old age and infirmity	[illegible] 0 0	[illegible] 0 0	
[illegible] June 188[illegible]	Do.	Bridget Moore	Matron	[illegible]	[illegible]	Permanent infirmity of body.	[illegible] 4 0	[illegible] 0 0	
27 Oct. 188[illegible]	Do.	John Moore	Schoolmaster	[illegible]	[illegible]	Do.	[illegible] 0 0	[illegible] 0 0	
[illegible] Mar. 18[illegible]	Do.	Mary A. Mulvany	Midwife of Dispensary District.	[illegible]	[illegible]	Do.	[illegible] 0 0	[illegible] 0 0	
[illegible] May. 1879	Tuam	Digby French	Medical Officer of Dispensary District.	72	[illegible]	Old age	1[illegible] 0 0	100 0 0	
19 Aug. 18[illegible]	Do.	Martin Kerrigan	Porter	70	[illegible]	Permanent infirmity of body.	[illegible] 0 0	[illegible] 4 0	
13 Mar. 18[illegible]	Tulla	Joanna Baker	Matron	[illegible]	[illegible]	Do.	[illegible] 10 0	[illegible] 0 0	
26 June, 1879	Waterford	James Rooney	Relieving Officer	[illegible]	16	Infirmity of body	90 0 0	[illegible] 0 0	
21 Dec. 18[illegible]	Do.	Robert J. Burkitt	Medical Officer of Workhouse.	77[illegible]	[illegible]	Old age	1[illegible] 0 0	[illegible] 10 4	
[illegible] Feb. 18[illegible]	Do.	Mary R. O'Connell	Schoolmistress	[illegible]	27	Permanent infirmity of body	1[illegible] 0 0	[illegible] 0 0	
27 June, 18[illegible]	Westport	Ellen H. A. Wilson	Matron	[illegible]	19	Infirmity of body	[illegible] 10 0	[illegible] 0 0	
9 Oct. 1876	Do.	James Davis	Medical Officer of Workhouse and of Dispensary District.	79	[illegible]	Old age	[illegible] 5 10	144 16 11	
1 Mar. 18[illegible]	Do.	James Walsh	Master	[illegible]	[illegible]	Do.	[illegible] 0 0	[illegible] 0 0	
[illegible] Sept. 18[illegible]	Youghal	Henry O. Gorde	Medical Officer of Dispensary District.	[illegible]	[illegible]	Infirmity of body	[illegible] 0 0	[illegible] 0 0	
7 Feb. 18[illegible]	Do.	Johanna Coleman	Caretaker of Dispensary	72	18	Permanent infirmity of body.	17 0 0	0 13 6	
[illegible] Feb. 18[illegible]	Do.	John Ahern	Porter	[illegible]	[illegible]	Old age and permanent infirmity of body.	[illegible] 0 0	[illegible] 0 0	

APPENDIX E.

TABULAR RETURNS IN CONNECTION WITH RELIEF UNDER THE MEDICAL CHARITIES ACT.

[NOTE.—In this series of tables, the unions are classed in the Counties and Provinces in which the chief or central place of each union is situate; but many of the unions comprise parts of more than one County or Province. The total population of the unions in the respective Counties and Provinces, as arranged in the summary of Table No. 2, does not, therefore, agree with the summaries of those Counties and Provinces in the census returns. An index of the dispensary districts is annexed (No. 6), showing the name of the union in which each district is situate, and referring to the table and page in which the particulars relating to each district are to be found.]

TABLE No. 1.

STATEMENT of ALTERATIONS in DISPENSARY DISTRICTS of unions in Ireland (arranged in Provinces and Counties) according to the Orders issued in pursuance of sec. 6 of 14 and 15 Vic., cap. 68:—(*from the completion of table No. 1, appendix E, in the seventeenth annual Report, to 25th March*, 1890).

UNIONS.	DISPENSARY DISTRICTS.	No. of members of Committees of Management.	No. of medical officers authorised.	Number of apothecaries.	Number of midwives.	Date of Order.
1.	2.	3.	4.	5.	6.	7.
PROVINCE OF ULSTER.						
COUNTY OF ANTRIM.						
BALLYMENA, . .	Ballymena, . . .	20	–	–	–	29th April, 1889.
COUNTY OF DONEGAL.						
MILFORD, . . .	Fannett, . . .	–	–	–	1	23rd September, 1889.
COUNTY OF DOWN.						
DOWNPATRICK, .	Ballynahinch, .	19	–	–	–	30th May, 1889.
COUNTY OF TYRONE.						
DUNGANNON, . .	Benburb, . .	19	–	–	–	12th April, 1889.
Do., . . .	Coalisland, . .	23	–	–	–	Do.
PROVINCE OF MUNSTER.						
COUNTY OF CORK.						
CORK, ...	Cork, ...	–	–	–	2	16th April, 1889.
Do., ...	Do. . . .	–	–	–	1	23rd September, 1889.
Do., ...	Douglas, . . .	17	–	–	–	3rd May, 1889.
KANTURK, . . .	Newmarket, . .	–	–	*	–	7th October, 1889.
COUNTY OF LIMERICK.						
RATHKEALE, . .	Rathkeale, . . .	–	–	†	–	18th September, 1889.
COUNTY OF TIPPERARY.						
CLOGHEEN, . .	Caher, ...	–	–	–	1	24th July, 1889.
TIPPERARY, . .	Grean, ...	22	–	–	–	16th August, 1889.

* The Order in this case rescinds a previous Order authorising the appointment of Apothecary.

† The Order in this case provides that the person to be appointed Apothecary in pursuance of an already existing Order may be either an Apothecary or Pharmaceutical Chemist.

TABLE No. 1.—*continued.*

STATEMENT of ALTERATIONS in DISPENSARY DISTRICTS of unions in Ireland—(*continued.*)

Unions.	Dispensary Districts.	No. of members of Committee of Management.	No. of medical officers authorised.	Number of apothecaries.	Number of midwives.	Date of Order.
1.	2.	3.	4.	5.	6.	7.
PROVINCE OF LEINSTER.						
COUNTY OF CARLOW.						
CARLOW, . . .	Carlow, ...	–	–	1	–	10th July, 1889.
COUNTY OF DUBLIN.						
DUBLIN, SOUTH, .	Rathfarnham, .	–	–	1	–	23rd May, 1889.
COUNTY OF KILDARE.						
NAAS, ...	Blessington & Ballymore.	–	–	–	1	6th December, 1889.
COUNTY OF LOUTH.						
DUNDALK, . .	Carlingford, . .	17	–	–	–	2nd July, 1889.
Do., . .	Ravensdale, . .	16	–	–	–	Do.
COUNTY OF WESTMEATH.						
ATHLONE, . .	Bridewell, . .	–	–	–	1	24th December, 1889.

SUMMARY OF DISPENSARY DISTRICTS, BY PROVINCES, AS ALTERED BY THE FOREGOING TABLE UP TO THE 25TH MARCH, 1890.

Provinces.	Number of unions.	Number of dispensary districts.	Number of electoral divisions.	Population: 1881.	Area: in statute acres.	Poor Law Valuation, 20th Sept., 1889.	Number of medical officers authorised.	Number of apothecaries.	Number of midwives.
1.	2.	3.	4.	5.	6.	7.	8.	9.	10.
						£			
ULSTER, .	43	214	879	1,743,075	5,483,201	4,392,455	235	3	93
MUNSTER, .	50	206	1,032	1,331,115	6,067,723	3,444,485	293	20	61
LEINSTER, .	39	202	938	1,278,989	4,876,918	4,763,449	239	15	146
CONNAUGHT, .	28	98	595	821,657	4,392,006	1,365,846	114	3	27
Total, Ireland,	160	720	3,444	5,174,836	20,819,848	13,966,235	810	41	327

TABLE No. 2.—FINANCIAL and RELIEF RETURNS.—LIST, in pursuance of § 20 of the Medical Charities Act (14 & 15 Vic., c. 68), of all DISPENSARY DISTRICTS in the several UNIONS in Ireland (arranged in Provinces and Counties)—showing the NUMBER of DISPENSARIES in each, and the EXPENSES of each dispensary district for the year ended the 30th of September, 1889; with a RETURN,—for the year ended the 30th of September, 1889,—of the NUMBER of CASES of MEDICAL RELIEF afforded to patients at dispensaries and at their own homes, respectively; the number of TICKETS for medical relief cancelled by the Committees of Management, under § 9 of the Act; number of cases of VACCINATION; number of DANGEROUS LUNATICS certified; and number of days of attendance of Medical Officers in BRIDEWELLS or houses of correction.

NOTES ON TABLE, No 2.

Columns 1, 2, 5, 6 and 7, inclusive, are abstracted from the Orders of the Poor Law Commissioners, or of the Local Government Board.

Columns 8 and 9 to 17, inclusive, are abstracted from returns received from the Clerks of unions.

Columns 10 to 24, inclusive, are abstracted from returns received from the Medical Officers of dispensary districts.

Column 9.—In various instances in which rent does not appear in this table as part of the annual expenses, the dispensary of the district is held in a house which was used for a dispensary under the late system, or in a court-house, or other public building, the use of which is obtained by the Guardians for the purpose, or in a house granted by the proprietor, rent free, or at a nominal rent. In some cases also the dispensary is the property of the Guardians, having been built by means of a loan obtained under the Dispensary Houses (Ireland) Act, 1879.

Columns 5 and 11.—In some instances two dispensary districts, in the same or in different but adjoining unions, are attended by the same medical officer.

Unions.	Dispensary Districts.	Population in 1881.		No. of Officers appointed.			Expenses of Year ended 30th September, 1889												Medical Relief afforded in Year ended 30th September, 1889								
											Salaries (including payments for substitutes provided).			Vaccination Expenses.					Number of New Cases attended and registered during the year.								
				Medical Officers.	Apothecaries.	Midwives.					Medical Officers.	Apothecaries.	Midwives.						Dispensary.	Visiting.		Total.					

No. 2.—Dispensary Districts, with the Expenses, and Amount of Medical Relief afforded, in the several Unions—continued.

Unions.	Dispensary Districts.	Population in 1851.	No. of Dispensary Stations	No. of Officers appointed: Medical Officers	Apothecaries	Midwives	Expenses of Year ended 29th September, 1859: Medicines and Medical Appliances	Rent of Dispensary Buildings	Books, Forms, Stationery, Printing, and Advertising	Salaries (excluding payments for Vaccination): Medical Officers	Apothecaries	Midwives	Vaccination Expenses: Amount of Fees paid to Medical Officers	Other Expenses of Vaccination	Other Expenses	Total Expenditure for the Year ended 29th Sept. 1859	Medical Relief afforded in Year ended 29th September, 1859: Number of Tickets issued: Dispensary Tickets	Visiting Tickets	Total	21	22	23	24
1.	2.	3.	4.	5.	6.	7.	8.	9.	10.	11.	12.	13.	14.	15.	16.	17.	18.	19.	20.	21.	22.	23.	24.
PROVINCE OF ULSTER—continued.							£ s. d.	£ s. d.	£ s. d.	£ s. d.	£ s. d.	£ s. d.	£ s. d.	£ s. d.	£ s. d.	£ s. d.							
County of Antrim—con.																							
Lisburn,	1. Annahilt,	[illegible]	[illegible]	[illegible]	–	–	[illegible]	[illegible]	[illegible]	[illegible]	–	–	[illegible]	[illegible]	[illegible]	[illegible]	[illegible]	[illegible]	[illegible]	–	[illegible]	–	–
	2. Ballylesson,	[illegible]	[illegible]	[illegible]	–	–	[illegible]	[illegible]	[illegible]	[illegible]	–	–	[illegible]	[illegible]	[illegible]	[illegible]	[illegible]	[illegible]	[illegible]	–	[illegible]	[illegible]	–
	3. Dunmurry,	[illegible]	[illegible]	[illegible]	–	–	[illegible]	[illegible]	[illegible]	[illegible]	–	–	[illegible]	[illegible]	[illegible]	[illegible]	[illegible]	[illegible]	[illegible]	–	[illegible]	–	–
	4. Glenavy,	[illegible]	[illegible]	[illegible]	–	–	[illegible]	[illegible]	[illegible]	[illegible]	–	–	[illegible]	[illegible]	[illegible]	[illegible]	[illegible]	[illegible]	[illegible]	–	[illegible]	–	–
	5. Hillsborough,	[illegible]	[illegible]	[illegible]	–	–	[illegible]	[illegible]	[illegible]	[illegible]	–	–	[illegible]	[illegible]	[illegible]	[illegible]	[illegible]	[illegible]	[illegible]	–	[illegible]	[illegible]	–
	6. [illegible],	[illegible]	[illegible]	[illegible]	–	–	[illegible]	[illegible]	[illegible]	[illegible]	–	–	[illegible]	[illegible]	[illegible]	[illegible]	[illegible]	[illegible]	[illegible]	–	[illegible]	–	–
	7. Lisburn,	[illegible]	[illegible]	[illegible]	–	–	[illegible]	[illegible]	[illegible]	[illegible]	–	–	[illegible]	[illegible]	[illegible]	[illegible]	[illegible]	[illegible]	[illegible]	–	[illegible]	[illegible]	–
	8. [illegible],	[illegible]	[illegible]	[illegible]	–	–	[illegible]	[illegible]	[illegible]	[illegible]	–	–	[illegible]	[illegible]	[illegible]	[illegible]	[illegible]	[illegible]	[illegible]	[illegible]	[illegible]	[illegible]	–
		66,640	11	[illegible]	–	–	[illegible]	[illegible]	[illegible]	[illegible]	–	–	[illegible]	[illegible]	[illegible]	[illegible]	[illegible]	[illegible]	[illegible]	[illegible]	[illegible]	[illegible]	–
County of Armagh.																							
Armagh,	1. Armagh,	[illegible]	[illegible]	[illegible]	–	[illegible]	[illegible]	[illegible]	[illegible]	[illegible]	–	[illegible]	[illegible]	[illegible]	[illegible]	[illegible]	[illegible]	[illegible]	[illegible]	[illegible]	[illegible]	[illegible]	–
	2. Blackwatertown,	[illegible]	[illegible]	[illegible]	–	[illegible]	[illegible]	[illegible]	[illegible]	[illegible]	–	[illegible]	[illegible]	[illegible]	[illegible]	[illegible]	[illegible]	[illegible]	[illegible]	–	[illegible]	–	–
	3. Collone,	[illegible]	[illegible]	[illegible]	–	–	[illegible]	[illegible]	[illegible]	[illegible]	–	–	[illegible]	–	[illegible]	[illegible]	[illegible]	[illegible]	[illegible]	–	[illegible]	–	–
	4. Keady,	[illegible]	[illegible]	[illegible]	–	–	[illegible]	[illegible]	[illegible]	[illegible]	–	–	[illegible]	[illegible]	[illegible]	[illegible]	[illegible]	[illegible]	[illegible]	–	[illegible]	[illegible]	–
	5. Loughgall,	[illegible]	[illegible]	[illegible]	–	[illegible]	[illegible]	[illegible]	[illegible]	[illegible]	–	[illegible]	[illegible]	[illegible]	[illegible]	[illegible]	[illegible]	[illegible]	[illegible]	–	[illegible]	–	–
	6. Markethill,	[illegible]	[illegible]	[illegible]	–	[illegible]	[illegible]	[illegible]	[illegible]	[illegible]	–	[illegible]	[illegible]	[illegible]	[illegible]	[illegible]	[illegible]	[illegible]	[illegible]	–	[illegible]	–	–

Expenses of Year ended [illegible] September, [illegible].										Medical Relief afforded in Year ended [illegible] September, [illegible].						
Medicines and Medical Appliances.	Rent of Dispensary Buildings.	Books, Forms, Stationery, Printing and Advertising.	Salaries [illegible]: Medical Officers.	Apothecaries.	Midwives.	Vaccination Expenses: [illegible]	[illegible]	Other Expenses [illegible]	Total Expenditure for each Dispensary District for Year ended [illegible] Sept., [illegible]	Number of New Cases attended and registered during the year: [illegible]	[illegible]	Total.	[illegible]	[illegible]	[illegible]	[illegible]
8.	9.	10.	11.	12.	13.	14.	15.	16.	17.	18.	19.	20.	21.	22.	23.	24.
£ s. d.	£ s. d.	£ s. d.	£ s. d.	£ s. d.	£ s. d.	£ s. d.	£ s. d.	£ s. d.	£ s. d.							
[illegible]	[illegible]	[illegible]	[illegible]	—	[illegible]	[illegible]	—	—	[illegible]	[illegible]	[illegible]	[illegible]	—	[illegible]	[illegible]	—
[illegible]	[illegible]	[illegible]	[illegible]	—	—	[illegible]	[illegible]	[illegible]	[illegible]	[illegible]	[illegible]	[illegible]	—	[illegible]	—	—
[illegible]	[illegible]	[illegible]	[illegible]	—	[illegible]	[illegible]	[illegible]	[illegible]	[illegible]	[illegible]	[illegible]	[illegible]	—	[illegible]	[illegible]	—
[illegible]	[illegible]	[illegible]	[illegible]	—	[illegible]	[illegible]	[illegible]	[illegible]	[illegible]	[illegible]	[illegible]	[illegible]	—	[illegible]	—	—
—	[illegible]	—	[illegible]	—	—	[illegible]	—	[illegible]	[illegible]	[illegible]	[illegible]	[illegible]	—	[illegible]	[illegible]	—
[illegible]	[illegible]	[illegible]	[illegible]	—	[illegible]	[illegible]	[illegible]	[illegible]	[illegible]	1,366	[illegible]	[illegible]	—	[illegible]	[illegible]	—
[illegible]	[illegible]	[illegible]	[illegible]	—	—	[illegible]	—	[illegible]	[illegible]	[illegible]	[illegible]	[illegible]	—	[illegible]	[illegible]	—
—	[illegible]	[illegible]	[illegible]	—	—	[illegible]	—	[illegible]	[illegible]	[illegible]	[illegible]	[illegible]	—	[illegible]	[illegible]	—
[illegible]	[illegible]	[illegible]	[illegible]	—	—	[illegible]	—	[illegible]	[illegible]	[illegible]	[illegible]	[illegible]	—	[illegible]	[illegible]	—
[illegible]	[illegible]	[illegible]	[illegible]	—	[illegible]	[illegible]	[illegible]	—	[illegible]	[illegible]	[illegible]	[illegible]	[illegible]	[illegible]	[illegible]	—
[illegible]	[illegible]	[illegible]	[illegible]	—	—	[illegible]	[illegible]	[illegible]	[illegible]	[illegible]	[illegible]	[illegible]	—	[illegible]	—	—
[illegible]	[illegible]	[illegible]	[illegible]	—	—	[illegible]	[illegible]	[illegible]	[illegible]	[illegible]	[illegible]	[illegible]	—	[illegible]	—	—
[illegible]	[illegible]	[illegible]	[illegible]	—	[illegible]	[illegible]	[illegible]	[illegible]	[illegible]	[illegible]	[illegible]	[illegible]	—	[illegible]	—	—
[illegible]	[illegible]	[illegible]	[illegible]	—	[illegible]	—	—	—	[illegible]	[illegible]	[illegible]	[illegible]	—	[illegible]	[illegible]	—
[illegible]	[illegible]	[illegible]	[illegible]	—	[illegible]	[illegible]	[illegible]	[illegible]	[illegible]	[illegible]	[illegible]	[illegible]	[illegible]	[illegible]	[illegible]	—
[illegible]	[illegible]	[illegible]	[illegible]	—	[illegible]	[illegible]	[illegible]	[illegible]	[illegible]	1,311	[illegible]	[illegible]	[illegible]	[illegible]	[illegible]	—

No. 3.—Dispensary Districts, with the Expenses, and Amount of Medical Relief afforded, in the several Unions.—continued.

Unions.	Dispensary Districts.	Population in 1851.	[illegible]	No. of officers authorized: Medical Officers.	Apothecaries.	Midwives.	Expenditure Year ended 29th September, 1856: Medicines and Medical Appliances.	Rent of Dispensary Buildings.	Books, Forms, Printing, Stationery and Advertising.	Salaries: Medical Officers.	Apothecaries.	Midwives.	Vaccination Expenses: [illegible]	[illegible]	[illegible]	Total Expenditure for each Dispensary District for Year ended 29th Sept., 1857	Medical Relief afforded in Year ended 30th September, 1856: Number of New Cases attended and registered during the year: Dispensary Tickets.	Visiting Tickets.	Total.	[illegible]	[illegible]	[illegible]	[illegible]
1.	2.	3.	4.	5.	6.	7.	8.	9.	10.	11.	12.	13.	14.	15.	16.	17.	18.	19.	20.	21.	22.	23.	24.
							£ s. d.	£ s. d.	£ s. d.	£ s. d.	£ s. d.	£ s. d.	£ s. d.	£ s. d.	£ s. d.	£ s. d.							
PROVINCE OF ULSTER—continued. County of Down—con.																							
Newry,	1. Donaghmore,	[illegible]	[illegible]	[illegible]	-	-	[illegible]	[illegible]	[illegible]	[illegible]	-	-	[illegible]	[illegible]	-	[illegible]	[illegible]	[illegible]	[illegible]	-	[illegible]	-	-
	2. Forkhill,	[illegible]	[illegible]	[illegible]	-	-	[illegible]	[illegible]	[illegible]	[illegible]	-	-	[illegible]	-	[illegible]	[illegible]	[illegible]	[illegible]	[illegible]	[illegible]	[illegible]	[illegible]	-
	3. Meigh,	[illegible]	[illegible]	[illegible]	-	-	[illegible]	[illegible]	[illegible]	[illegible]	-	-	[illegible]	-	[illegible]	[illegible]	[illegible]	[illegible]	[illegible]	-	[illegible]	-	-
	4. Mountnorris,	[illegible]	[illegible]	[illegible]	-	-	[illegible]	[illegible]	[illegible]	[illegible]	-	-	[illegible]	-	[illegible]	[illegible]	[illegible]	[illegible]	[illegible]	-	[illegible]	-	-
	5. Mullaghglass,	[illegible]	[illegible]	[illegible]	-	[illegible]	[illegible]	[illegible]	[illegible]	[illegible]	-	[illegible]	[illegible]	-	[illegible]	[illegible]	[illegible]	[illegible]	[illegible]	[illegible]	[illegible]	[illegible]	-
	6. Newry,	[illegible]	[illegible]	[illegible]	-	[illegible]	[illegible]	[illegible]	[illegible]	[illegible]	-	[illegible]	[illegible]	-	[illegible]	[illegible]	[illegible]	[illegible]	[illegible]	-	[illegible]	[illegible]	[illegible]
	7. Poyntzpass,	[illegible]	[illegible]	[illegible]	-	-	[illegible]	[illegible]	[illegible]	[illegible]	-	-	[illegible]	-	-	[illegible]	[illegible]	[illegible]	[illegible]	-	[illegible]	[illegible]	-
	8. Rathfriland,	[illegible]	[illegible]	[illegible]	-	-	[illegible]	[illegible]	[illegible]	[illegible]	-	-	[illegible]	-	[illegible]	[illegible]	[illegible]	[illegible]	[illegible]	-	[illegible]	[illegible]	-
	9. Warrenpoint,	[illegible]	[illegible]	[illegible]	-	[illegible]	[illegible]	[illegible]	[illegible]	[illegible]	-	[illegible]	[illegible]	-	-	[illegible]	[illegible]	[illegible]	[illegible]	-	[illegible]	[illegible]	-
		[illegible]	[illegible]	[illegible]	-	[illegible]	[illegible]	[illegible]	[illegible]	[illegible]	-	[illegible]	[illegible]	[illegible]	[illegible]	[illegible]	[illegible]	[illegible]	[illegible]	[illegible]	[illegible]	[illegible]	[illegible]
Newtownards,	1. Comber,	[illegible]	[illegible]	[illegible]	-	-	[illegible]	[illegible]	[illegible]	[illegible]	-	-	[illegible]	-	[illegible]	[illegible]	[illegible]	[illegible]	[illegible]	-	[illegible]	-	-

No. 2.—Dispensary Districts, with the Expenses, and Amount of Medical Relief afforded, in the several Unions—*continued.*

Unions.	Dispensary Districts.	Population 1861.	4	5	6	7	8	9	10	11	12	13	14	15	16	17	18	19	20	21	22	23	24
1.	2.	3.	4	5	6	7.	8.	9.	10	11	12.	13.	14	15	16.	17	18.	19	20.	21	22.	23	24
PROVINCE OF ULSTER—continued.							£ s. d.	£ s. d.	£ s. d.	£ s. d.	£ s. d.		£ s. d.	£ s. d.	£ s. d.	£ s. d.							
Co. of Londonderry—con.																							
Magherafelt.	1. Bellaghy,	10,687	[illegible]	[illegible]	–	–	[illegible]	[illegible]	[illegible]	[illegible]	–	–	[illegible]	[illegible]	[illegible]	[illegible]	[illegible]	[illegible]	[illegible]	[illegible]	[illegible]	[illegible]	–
	2. [illegible],	6,301	[illegible]	[illegible]	–	–	[illegible]	[illegible]	[illegible]	[illegible]	–	–	[illegible]	–	[illegible]	[illegible]	[illegible]	[illegible]	[illegible]	–	[illegible]	[illegible]	–
	3. Maghera,	[illegible]	[illegible]	[illegible]	–	–	[illegible]	[illegible]	[illegible]	[illegible]	–	–	[illegible]	[illegible]	[illegible]	[illegible]	[illegible]	[illegible]	[illegible]	–	[illegible]	[illegible]	–
	4. [illegible],	[illegible]	[illegible]	[illegible]	–	–	[illegible]	[illegible]	[illegible]	[illegible]	–	–	[illegible]	[illegible]	[illegible]	[illegible]	[illegible]	[illegible]	[illegible]	–	[illegible]	[illegible]	–
	5. [illegible],	9,210	[illegible]	[illegible]	–	–	[illegible]	[illegible]	[illegible]	[illegible]	–	–	[illegible]	[illegible]	[illegible]	[illegible]	[illegible]	[illegible]	[illegible]	1	[illegible]	[illegible]	–
		[illegible]	6	[illegible]	–	–	[illegible]	[illegible]	[illegible]	[illegible]	–	–	[illegible]	[illegible]	[illegible]	[illegible]	[illegible]	[illegible]	[illegible]	[illegible]	[illegible]	[illegible]	–
County of Monaghan.																							
Carrickmacross.	1. Carrickmacross,	[illegible]	1	[illegible]	–	[illegible]	[illegible]	[illegible]	–	[illegible]	–	[illegible]	[illegible]	[illegible]	[illegible]	[illegible]	[illegible]	[illegible]	[illegible]	–	[illegible]	[illegible]	–
	2. [illegible],	[illegible]	1	[illegible]	–	[illegible]	[illegible]	[illegible]	–	[illegible]	–	[illegible]	[illegible]	[illegible]	[illegible]	[illegible]	[illegible]	[illegible]	[illegible]	[illegible]	[illegible]	–	–
	3. [illegible],	[illegible]	1	[illegible]	–	[illegible]	[illegible]	[illegible]	–	[illegible]	–	[illegible]	[illegible]	[illegible]	[illegible]	[illegible]	[illegible]	[illegible]	[illegible]	–	[illegible]	–	–
		[illegible]	3	3	–	[illegible]	[illegible]	[illegible]	–	[illegible]	–	[illegible]	[illegible]	[illegible]	[illegible]	[illegible]	[illegible]	[illegible]	[illegible]	1	[illegible]	[illegible]	–
Castleblayney.	1. Ballybay,	[illegible]	1	[illegible]	–	[illegible]	[illegible]	[illegible]	[illegible]	[illegible]	–	[illegible]	[illegible]	–	[illegible]	[illegible]	[illegible]	[illegible]	[illegible]	–	[illegible]	[illegible]	–
	2. Castleblayney,	[illegible]	1	[illegible]	–	[illegible]	[illegible]	[illegible]	[illegible]	[illegible]	[illegible]	[illegible]	[illegible]	–	[illegible]	[illegible]	[illegible]	[illegible]	[illegible]	–	[illegible]	[illegible]	–
	3. [illegible],	[illegible]	1	[illegible]	–	[illegible]	[illegible]	[illegible]	[illegible]	[illegible]	–	[illegible]	[illegible]	–	[illegible]	[illegible]	[illegible]	[illegible]	[illegible]	–	[illegible]	[illegible]	–
	4. [illegible],	[illegible]	1	1	–	–	[illegible]	[illegible]	–	[illegible]	–	–	[illegible]	–	[illegible]	[illegible]	[illegible]	[illegible]	[illegible]	1	[illegible]	[illegible]	–
		[illegible]	4	4	–	3	[illegible]	[illegible]	[illegible]	[illegible]	–	[illegible]	[illegible]	–	[illegible]	[illegible]	[illegible]	[illegible]	[illegible]	1	[illegible]	[illegible]	–
Clones.	1. Clones,	[illegible]	[illegible]	[illegible]	–	–	[illegible]	[illegible]	–	[illegible]	–	–	[illegible]	[illegible]	[illegible]	[illegible]	[illegible]	[illegible]	[illegible]	–	[illegible]	[illegible]	–
	2. Newtownbutler,	[illegible]	[illegible]	[illegible]	–	–	[illegible]	[illegible]	–	[illegible]	–	–	[illegible]	[illegible]	[illegible]	[illegible]	[illegible]	[illegible]	[illegible]	–	[illegible]	[illegible]	–
	3. [illegible],	[illegible]	[illegible]	[illegible]	–	–	[illegible]	[illegible]	–	[illegible]	–	–	[illegible]	[illegible]	[illegible]	–	[illegible]	[illegible]	[illegible]	–	[illegible]	[illegible]	–

Union	Dispensary District	[illegible]	Remaining columns
[illegible],	1. [illegible]	[illegible]	[illegible]
	2. [illegible]	[illegible]	[illegible]
	3. [illegible]	[illegible]	[illegible]
	4. [illegible]	[illegible]	[illegible]
	5. [illegible]	[illegible]	[illegible]
		[illegible]	[illegible]
COUNTY OF TYRONE.			
Castlederg,	1. Castlederg, and Killeter,	[illegible]	[illegible]
	2. Drumquin,	3,200	[illegible]
		[illegible]	[illegible]
Clogher,	1. Aughnacloy,	4,780	[illegible]
	2. Ballygawley,	[illegible]	[illegible]
	3. Clogher,	[illegible]	[illegible]
	4. Fivemiletown,	[illegible]	[illegible]
		[illegible]	[illegible]
Cookstown,	1. Coagh,	4,081	[illegible]
	2. Cookstown,	[illegible]	[illegible]
	3. Pomeroy,	[illegible]	[illegible]
	4. Stewartstown,	[illegible]	[illegible]
		[illegible]	[illegible]
Dungannon,	1. Ballygawley,	[illegible]	[illegible]
	2. [illegible]	[illegible]	[illegible]
	3. [illegible]	[illegible]	[illegible]
	4. Coal Island,	[illegible]	[illegible]
	5. Dungannon,	[illegible]	[illegible]
		[illegible]	[illegible]
Gortin,	1. Gortin,	-	[illegible]
	2. Plumb Bridge,	-	[illegible]
		-	[illegible]

[illegible]

† See note at foot of pages [illegible] and [illegible]. The particulars given above respecting the dispensary districts of this union are for the half year ended the [illegible] of March; those for the following half year are included in Omagh and [illegible] unions, respectively: see page [illegible].

No. 2.—Dispensary Districts, with the Expenses, and Amount of Medical Relief afforded, in the several Unions—*continued.*

Unions.	Dispensary Districts.	Population in 1851.	[illegible]	No. of Officers: [illegible]	No. of Officers: Apothecaries.	No. of Officers: [illegible]	Medicines and Medical Appliances.	Rent of Dispensary Buildings.	Books, Forms, Stationery, Printing, and Advertising.	Salaries: Medical Officers.	Salaries: Apothecaries.	Salaries: Midwives.	Vaccination Expenses: [illegible]	Vaccination Expenses: [illegible]	[illegible]	Total Expenditure [illegible]	Number of [illegible]: [illegible]	Number of [illegible]: [illegible]	Number of [illegible]: [illegible]	[illegible]	[illegible]	[illegible]	[illegible]
1.	2.	3.	4.	5.	6.	7.	8.	9.	10.	11.	12.	13.	14.	15.	16.	17.	18.	19.	20.	21.	22.	23.	24.
PROVINCE OF ULSTER—*continued.*							£ s. d.	£ s. d.	£ s. d.	£ s. d.	£ s. d.	£ s. d.	£ s. d.	£ s. d.	£ s. d.	£ s. d.							
County of Tyrone—*con.*																							
Omagh,	1. Dromore,	[illegible]	[illegible]	[illegible]	-	-	[illegible]	[illegible]	[illegible]	[illegible]	-	-	[illegible]	[illegible]	[illegible]	[illegible]	[illegible]	[illegible]	[illegible]	-	[illegible]	[illegible]	-
	2. Drumquin,	[illegible]	[illegible]	[illegible]	-	-	[illegible]	[illegible]	[illegible]	[illegible]	-	-	[illegible]	-	[illegible]	[illegible]	[illegible]	[illegible]	[illegible]	-	[illegible]	[illegible]	-
	3. Fintona,	[illegible]	[illegible]	[illegible]	-	[illegible]	[illegible]	[illegible]	[illegible]	[illegible]	-	[illegible]	[illegible]	[illegible]	[illegible]	[illegible]	[illegible]	[illegible]	[illegible]	-	[illegible]	[illegible]	-
	4. Gortin,	[illegible]	[illegible]	[illegible]	-	[illegible]			-	[illegible]	-	-	-	-	[illegible]	[illegible]	[illegible]	[illegible]	[illegible]	-	[illegible]	-	
	5. Omagh,	[illegible]	[illegible]	[illegible]	-	[illegible]	[illegible]	[illegible]	[illegible]	[illegible]	-	[illegible]	[illegible]	[illegible]	[illegible]	[illegible]	[illegible]	[illegible]	[illegible]	[illegible]	[illegible]	[illegible]	-
	6. Newtownstewart,	[illegible]	[illegible]	[illegible]	-	[illegible]	[illegible]	[illegible]	[illegible]	[illegible]	-	-	[illegible]	-	[illegible]	[illegible]	[illegible]	[illegible]	[illegible]	-	[illegible]	[illegible]	-
		[illegible]	[illegible]	[illegible]	-	[illegible]	[illegible]	[illegible]	[illegible]	[illegible]	-	[illegible]	[illegible]	[illegible]	[illegible]	[illegible]	[illegible]	[illegible]	[illegible]	[illegible]	[illegible]	[illegible]	-
Strabane,	1. Castle Finn,	[illegible]	[illegible]	[illegible]	-	[illegible]	[illegible]	[illegible]	[illegible]	[illegible]	-	[illegible]	[illegible]	[illegible]	[illegible]	[illegible]	[illegible]	[illegible]	[illegible]	-	[illegible]	[illegible]	-
	2. Donoughmore,	[illegible]	[illegible]	[illegible]	-	[illegible]	[illegible]	[illegible]	[illegible]	[illegible]	-	[illegible]	[illegible]	-	[illegible]	[illegible]	[illegible]	[illegible]	[illegible]	-	[illegible]	[illegible]	-
	3. [illegible]	[illegible]	[illegible]	[illegible]	-	[illegible]	[illegible]	[illegible]	[illegible]	[illegible]	-	[illegible]	[illegible]	[illegible]	[illegible]	[illegible]	[illegible]	[illegible]	[illegible]	-	[illegible]	[illegible]	-
	4. [illegible]	[illegible]	[illegible]	[illegible]	-	-	-	-	[illegible]	[illegible]	-	[illegible]	-	-	[illegible]	[illegible]	[illegible]	[illegible]	[illegible]	-	[illegible]	-	-
	5. [illegible]	[illegible]	[illegible]	[illegible]	-	[illegible]	[illegible]	[illegible]	[illegible]	[illegible]	-	[illegible]	[illegible]	-	-	[illegible]	[illegible]	[illegible]	[illegible]	-	[illegible]	[illegible]	-
	6. Strabane,	[illegible]	[illegible]	[illegible]	-	[illegible]	[illegible]	-	[illegible]	[illegible]	-	[illegible]	[illegible]	[illegible]	[illegible]	[illegible]	[illegible]	[illegible]	[illegible]	-	[illegible]	[illegible]	-

* See note on page [illegible].

† [illegible]

No. 2.—Dispensary Districts, with the Expenses, and Amount of Medical Relief afforded, in the several Unions—continued.

Union.	Dispensary District.	Population in 18[illegible].	[illegible]	No. of Officers [illegible]			Expenditure for Year ended 29th September, 18[illegible]. Medicines and Medical Appliances.	Rent of Dispensary Buildings.	Books, Forms, Stationery, Printing and Advertising.	Salaries: Medical Officers.	Salaries: Apothecaries.	Salaries: Midwives.	Vaccination Expenses.		[illegible]	Total Expenditure for Year ended [illegible]	Medical Relief afforded in Year ended 29th September, 18[illegible]. Number of new Cases [illegible] during the year: Dispensary Tickets.	Visiting Tickets.	Total.	[illegible]	[illegible]	[illegible]	[illegible]
				Med. Officers.	Apothecaries.	Midwives.																	
1.	2.	3.	4.	5.	6.	7.	8.	9.	10.	11.	12.	13.	14.	15.	16.	17.	18.	19.	20.	21.	22.	23.	[illegible]
							£ s. d.	£ s. d.	£ s. d.	£ s. d.	£ s. d.	£ s. d.	£ s. d.	£ s. d.	£ s. d.	£ s. d.							
PROVINCE OF MUNSTER—continued. County of Cork—con.																							
Bantry,	1. Bantry,	[illegible]	1	1	—	—	[illegible]	[illegible]	[illegible]	[illegible]	—	—	[illegible]	—	[illegible]	[illegible]	[illegible]	[illegible]	[illegible]	—	[illegible]	[illegible]	[illegible]
	2. Durrus and Kilcrohane,	[illegible]	[illegible]	1	—	—	[illegible]	[illegible]	[illegible]	[illegible]	—	—	[illegible]	—	[illegible]	[illegible]	[illegible]	[illegible]	[illegible]	1	[illegible]	—	—
	3. Glengarriff,	[illegible]	[illegible]	1	—	—	[illegible]	[illegible]	[illegible]	[illegible]	—	—	[illegible]	—	[illegible]	[illegible]	[illegible]	[illegible]	[illegible]		[illegible]		—
	4. Kealkill,	[illegible]	1	1	—	—	[illegible]	[illegible]	[illegible]	[illegible]	—	—	[illegible]	—	—	[illegible]	[illegible]	[illegible]	[illegible]	—	[illegible]	—	—
		[illegible]	[illegible]	4	—	—	[illegible]	[illegible]	[illegible]	[illegible]	—	—	[illegible]	—	[illegible]	[illegible]	[illegible]	[illegible]	[illegible]	1	[illegible]	[illegible]	[illegible]
Castletown,	1. Castletown,	[illegible]	[illegible]	1	—	[illegible]	[illegible]	[illegible]	—	[illegible]	—	[illegible]	[illegible]	[illegible]	[illegible]	[illegible]	[illegible]	[illegible]	[illegible]	—	[illegible]	[illegible]	—
	2. Kilcatherine,	[illegible]	[illegible]	1	—	[illegible]	[illegible]	[illegible]	[illegible]	[illegible]	—	[illegible]	[illegible]	[illegible]	[illegible]	[illegible]	[illegible]	[illegible]	[illegible]	—	[illegible]	—	—
		[illegible]	[illegible]	2	—	[illegible]	[illegible]	[illegible]	[illegible]	[illegible]		[illegible]	[illegible]	[illegible]	[illegible]	[illegible]	[illegible]	[illegible]	[illegible]	—	[illegible]	[illegible]	
Clonakilty,	1. Clonakilty,	[illegible]	1	1	—	—	[illegible]	[illegible]	—	[illegible]	—	—	[illegible]	[illegible]	[illegible]	[illegible]	[illegible]	[illegible]	[illegible]	—	[illegible]	[illegible]	—
	2. Rosscarbery,	[illegible]	[illegible]	[illegible]	—	—	[illegible]	[illegible]	—	[illegible]	—	—	[illegible]	[illegible]	[illegible]	[illegible]	[illegible]	[illegible]	[illegible]	—	[illegible]	[illegible]	—
	3. Timoleague,	[illegible]	1	[illegible]	—	—	[illegible]	—	—	[illegible]	—	—	[illegible]	—	[illegible]	[illegible]	[illegible]	[illegible]	[illegible]	—	[illegible]	[illegible]	—
		[illegible]	[illegible]	[illegible]	—	—	[illegible]	[illegible]	—	[illegible]	—	—	[illegible]	[illegible]	[illegible]	[illegible]	[illegible]	[illegible]	[illegible]	—	[illegible]	[illegible]	—
Cork,	1. Ballincollig,	[illegible]	[illegible]	[illegible]	—	—	[illegible]	[illegible]	[illegible]	[illegible]	—	—	[illegible]	—	[illegible]	[illegible]	[illegible]	[illegible]	[illegible]	—	[illegible]	[illegible]	—
	2. Ballygarvan,	[illegible]	[illegible]	[illegible]	—	—	[illegible]	[illegible]	[illegible]	[illegible]	—	—	[illegible]	—	[illegible]	[illegible]	[illegible]	[illegible]	[illegible]	—	[illegible]	—	—
	3. [illegible]	[illegible]	[illegible]	[illegible]	[illegible]	[illegible]	[illegible]	[illegible]	[illegible]	[illegible]	[illegible]	[illegible]	[illegible]	[illegible]	[illegible]	[illegible]	[illegible]	[illegible]	[illegible]	[illegible]	[illegible]	[illegible]	[illegible]
	4. Carrigaline,	[illegible]	[illegible]	[illegible]	[illegible]	[illegible]	[illegible]	[illegible]	[illegible]	[illegible]	[illegible]	[illegible]	[illegible]	[illegible]	[illegible]	[illegible]	[illegible]	[illegible]	[illegible]	[illegible]	[illegible]	[illegible]	[illegible]
	5. [illegible]	[illegible]	[illegible]	[illegible]	[illegible]	[illegible]	[illegible]	[illegible]	[illegible]	[illegible]	[illegible]	[illegible]	[illegible]	[illegible]	[illegible]	[illegible]	[illegible]	[illegible]	[illegible]	[illegible]	[illegible]	[illegible]	[illegible]
	6. Cork,	[illegible]	[illegible]	[illegible]	[illegible]	[illegible]	[illegible]	[illegible]	[illegible]	[illegible]	[illegible]	[illegible]	[illegible]	[illegible]	[illegible]	[illegible]	[illegible]	[illegible]	[illegible]	[illegible]	[illegible]	[illegible]	[illegible]
	7. Douglas,	[illegible]	[illegible]	[illegible]	[illegible]	[illegible]	[illegible]	[illegible]	[illegible]	[illegible]	[illegible]	[illegible]	[illegible]	[illegible]	[illegible]	[illegible]	[illegible]	[illegible]	[illegible]	[illegible]	[illegible]	[illegible]	[illegible]
	8. [illegible]	[illegible]	[illegible]	[illegible]	[illegible]	[illegible]	[illegible]	[illegible]	[illegible]	[illegible]	[illegible]	[illegible]	[illegible]	[illegible]	[illegible]	[illegible]	[illegible]	[illegible]	[illegible]	[illegible]	[illegible]	[illegible]	[illegible]
	9. [illegible]	[illegible]	[illegible]	[illegible]	[illegible]	[illegible]	[illegible]	[illegible]	[illegible]	[illegible]	[illegible]	[illegible]	[illegible]	[illegible]	[illegible]	[illegible]	[illegible]	[illegible]	[illegible]	[illegible]	[illegible]	[illegible]	[illegible]
	10. [illegible]	[illegible]	[illegible]	[illegible]	[illegible]	[illegible]	[illegible]	[illegible]	[illegible]	[illegible]	[illegible]	[illegible]	[illegible]	[illegible]	[illegible]	[illegible]	[illegible]	[illegible]	[illegible]	[illegible]	[illegible]	[illegible]	[illegible]

No. 2.—Dispensary Districts, with the Expenses, and Amount of Medical Relief afforded, in the several Unions—continued.

Unions.	Dispensary Districts.	Population in 1861.	[illegible]	No. of Officers employed. Medical Officers.	Apothecaries.	Midwives.	Expenses of Year ended 29th September, 1862. Medicines and Medical Appliances.	Rent of Dispensary Buildings.	Books, Forms, Stationery, Printing, and Advertising.	Salaries (including payments for temporary service). Medical Officers.	Apothecaries.	Midwives.	Vaccination Expenses. [illegible]	[illegible]	All other Expenses [illegible]	Total Expenditure for each Dispensary District, for Year ended 29th Sept., 1862.	Medical Relief afforded in Year ended 29th September, 1862. Number of New Cases attended and registered during the year. Dispensary Tickets.	Visiting Tickets.	Total.	[illegible]	[illegible]	[illegible]	[illegible]
1.	2.	3.	4.	5.	6.	7.	8.	9.	10.	11.	12.	13.	14.	15.	16.	17.	18.	19.	20.	21.	22.	23.	24.
							£ s. d.	£ s. d.	£ s. d.	£ s. d.	£ s. d.	£ s. d.	£ s. d.	£ s. d.	£ s. d.	£ s. d.							
PROVINCE OF MUNSTER—continued.																							
County of Cork—con.																							
Midleton,	1. Aghada,	[illegible]	1	1	–	–	[illegible]	[illegible]	[illegible]	[illegible]	–	–	–	[illegible]	[illegible]	[illegible]	[illegible]	[illegible]	[illegible]	–	[illegible]	–	–
	2. Castlemartyr,	[illegible]	1	1	–	–	[illegible]	[illegible]	[illegible]	[illegible]	–	–	[illegible]	[illegible]	[illegible]	[illegible]	[illegible]	[illegible]	[illegible]	–	[illegible]	–	–
	3. Cloyne,	[illegible]	1	1	–	–	[illegible]	[illegible]	[illegible]	[illegible]	–	–	–	[illegible]	[illegible]	[illegible]	[illegible]	[illegible]	[illegible]	–	[illegible]	[illegible]	–
	4. Midleton,	[illegible]	2	2	–	–	[illegible]	[illegible]	[illegible]	[illegible]	–	–	[illegible]	[illegible]	[illegible]	[illegible]	[illegible]	[illegible]	1,[illegible]	–	[illegible]	[illegible]	–
	5. [illegible] East,	[illegible]	1	1	–	–	[illegible]	–	[illegible]	[illegible]	–	–	[illegible]	[illegible]	[illegible]	[illegible]	[illegible]	[illegible]	[illegible]	–	[illegible]		–
		[illegible]	6	6	–	–	[illegible]	[illegible]	[illegible]	[illegible]	–	–	[illegible]	[illegible]	[illegible]	[illegible]	[illegible]	[illegible]	[illegible]	–	[illegible]	[illegible]	–
Millstreet,	1. Cullen,	[illegible]	[illegible]	1	–	–	[illegible]	[illegible]	[illegible]	[illegible]	–	–	[illegible]	–	[illegible]	[illegible]	[illegible]	[illegible]	[illegible]	–	[illegible]	[illegible]	–
	2. Millstreet,	[illegible]	1	1	–	–	[illegible]	[illegible]	–	[illegible]	–	–	[illegible]	–	[illegible]	[illegible]	[illegible]	[illegible]	[illegible]	–	[illegible]	[illegible]	–

Union	Dispensary District	Population
[illegible]	[illegible]	[illegible]
[illegible]	[illegible]	[illegible]
County of Kerry.		
Cahersiveen,	1. Cahir, 2. Derrynane, 3. Dromid, 4. Glenbeigh, 5. Valentia	[illegible]
Dingle,	1. Annascaul, 2. Castlegregory, 3. Dingle, 4. Ventry	[illegible]
Kenmare,	1. Kenmare, 2. Kilgarvan, 3. Sneem, 4. Tuosist	[illegible]
Killarney,	[illegible]	[illegible]
Listowel,	1. Ballybunion, 2. Ballyheigue, 3. Ballylongford, 4. Listowel	[illegible]

§ Office of Midwife vacant. ‡ One Midwife acts for both districts. ‖ A Midwife has not been appointed.

[continued.

Unions.	Dispensary Districts.	Population in 1851.	4	5	6	7	Medicines and Medical Appliances	Rent of Dispensary Buildings	Books, Forms, Stationery, Printing, and Advertising	Salaries: Medical Officers	Salaries: Apothecaries	Salaries: Midwives	Vaccination Fees: 14	Vaccination Fees: 15	16	17	18	19	Total	21	22	23	24
1.	2.	3.	4.	5.	6.	7.	8.	9.	10.	11.	12.	13.	14.	15.	16.	17	18.	19.	20.	21.	22.	23.	24.
PROVINCE OF MUNSTER—continued.							£ s. d.	£ s. d.	£ s. d.	£ s. d.	£ s. d.	£ s. d.	£ s. d.	£ s. d.	£ s. d.	£ s. d.							
COUNTY OF KERRY—con.																							
Tralee,	1. Ardfert,	[illegible]	[illegible]	[illegible]	-	-	[illegible]	[illegible]	[illegible]	[illegible]	-	-	[illegible]	[illegible]	[illegible]	[illegible]	[illegible]	[illegible]	[illegible]	-	[illegible]	[illegible]	-
	2. Brosna,	[illegible]	[illegible]	[illegible]		-	[illegible]	[illegible]	[illegible]	[illegible]	-	-	[illegible]	[illegible]	[illegible]	[illegible]	[illegible]	[illegible]	[illegible]	-	[illegible]	1	-
	3. Castle Island,	[illegible]	[illegible]	[illegible]	-	-	[illegible]	[illegible]	[illegible]	[illegible]	-	-	[illegible]	-	[illegible]	[illegible]	[illegible]	[illegible]	[illegible]		[illegible]	1	-
	4. Castlemaine,	[illegible]	[illegible]	[illegible]	-	-	[illegible]	[illegible]	[illegible]	[illegible]	-	-	[illegible]	[illegible]	[illegible]	[illegible]	[illegible]	[illegible]	[illegible]		[illegible]	[illegible]	-
	5. Killorglin,	[illegible]	[illegible]	[illegible]	-	-	[illegible]	[illegible]	[illegible]	[illegible]	-	-	[illegible]	[illegible]	[illegible]	[illegible]	[illegible]	[illegible]	[illegible]	-	[illegible]	-	-
	6. Tralee,	[illegible]	[illegible]	[illegible]	[illegible]	-	[illegible]	[illegible]	[illegible]	[illegible]	[illegible]	-	[illegible]	[illegible]	[illegible]	[illegible]	[illegible]	[illegible]	[illegible]	7	[illegible]	[illegible]	[illegible]
		[illegible]	[illegible]	[illegible]	[illegible]	-	[illegible]	[illegible]	[illegible]	[illegible]	[illegible]	-	[illegible]	[illegible]	[illegible]	[illegible]	[illegible]	[illegible]	[illegible]	7	[illegible]	[illegible]	[illegible]
COUNTY OF LIMERICK.																							
Croom,	1. Adare,	[illegible]	[illegible]	[illegible]	-	-	[illegible]	[illegible]	[illegible]	[illegible]	-	-	[illegible]	[illegible]	[illegible]	[illegible]	[illegible]	[illegible]	[illegible]	-	[illegible]	[illegible]	-
	2. Castletown,	[illegible]	[illegible]	[illegible]	-	-	[illegible]	[illegible]	[illegible]	[illegible]	-	-	[illegible]	[illegible]	[illegible]	[illegible]	[illegible]	[illegible]	[illegible]	-	[illegible]	[illegible]	-
	3. Croom,	[illegible]	[illegible]	[illegible]	[illegible]	-	[illegible]	[illegible]	[illegible]	[illegible]	[illegible]	-	[illegible]	[illegible]	[illegible]	[illegible]	[illegible]	[illegible]	[illegible]	-	[illegible]	[illegible]	-
		[illegible]	[illegible]	[illegible]	[illegible]	-	[illegible]	[illegible]	[illegible]	[illegible]	[illegible]	-	[illegible]	[illegible]	[illegible]	[illegible]	[illegible]	[illegible]	[illegible]	-	[illegible]	[illegible]	-
Glin,	1. Shanagolden,	[illegible]	[illegible]	[illegible]	-	-	[illegible]	[illegible]	-	[illegible]	-	-	[illegible]	[illegible]	[illegible]	[illegible]	[illegible]	[illegible]	[illegible]	-	[illegible]	1	-
	2. Tarbert,	[illegible]	[illegible]	[illegible]	-	-	[illegible]	[illegible]	-	[illegible]	-	-	[illegible]	[illegible]	[illegible]	[illegible]	[illegible]	[illegible]	[illegible]	1	[illegible]	[illegible]	-
		[illegible]	[illegible]	[illegible]	-	-	[illegible]	[illegible]	-	[illegible]	-	-	[illegible]	[illegible]	[illegible]	[illegible]	[illegible]	[illegible]	[illegible]	1	[illegible]	[illegible]	-

* Office of apothecary vacant.

† A midwife has not been appointed.

No. 2.—Dispensary Districts, with the Expenses, and Amount of Medical Relief afforded, in the several Unions—continued.

Unions.	Dispensary Districts.	Population in 1861.	4.	5.	6.	7.	8.	9.	10.	11.	12.	13.	14.	15.	16.	17.	18.	19.	20.	21.	22.	23.	24.
1.	2.	3.	4.	5.	6.	7.	8.	9.	10.	11.	12.	13.	14.	15.	16.	17.	18.	19.	20.	21.	22.	23.	24.
PROVINCE OF MUNSTER—continued.							£ s. d.	£ s. d.	£ s. d.	£ s. d.	£ s. d.	£ s. d.	£ s. d.	£ s. d.	£ s. d.	£ s. d.							
County of Tipperary—con. Clogheen,	1. Ardfinnan,	[illegible]	[illegible]	[illegible]	–	–	–	[illegible]	–	[illegible]	–	–	[illegible]	[illegible]	[illegible]	[illegible]	[illegible]	[illegible]	[illegible]	–	[illegible]	–	–
	2. Cahir,	[illegible]	1	1	–	1	10 8 11	[illegible]	[illegible]	[illegible]	–	–	[illegible]	[illegible]	[illegible]	[illegible]	[illegible]	[illegible]	[illegible]	–	[illegible]	[illegible]	–
	3. Clogheen,	[illegible]	[illegible]	[illegible]	–	[illegible]	[illegible]	[illegible]	–	[illegible]	–	–	[illegible]	[illegible]	[illegible]	[illegible]	341	[illegible]	[illegible]	–	[illegible]	–	–
		[illegible]	[illegible]	[illegible]	–	[illegible]	[illegible]	[illegible]	[illegible]	[illegible]		–	[illegible]	[illegible]	[illegible]	[illegible]	[illegible]	[illegible]	[illegible]	–	[illegible]	[illegible]	–
Clonmel,	1. Ballymacarbry,	2,816	1	[illegible]	–	–	[illegible]	[illegible]	–	[illegible]	–	–	[illegible]	[illegible]	[illegible]	[illegible]	[illegible]	[illegible]	[illegible]	–	[illegible]	–	–
	2. Clonmel and St. Mary's,	[illegible]	1	[illegible]	[illegible]	–	[illegible]	–	[illegible]	[illegible]	[illegible]	[illegible]	–	[illegible]	[illegible]	[illegible]	[illegible]	[illegible]	[illegible]	1	[illegible]	[illegible]	–
	3. Kilsheelan,	[illegible]	[illegible]	[illegible]	–	–	[illegible]	[illegible]	–	[illegible]	–	–	[illegible]	[illegible]	[illegible]	[illegible]	[illegible]	[illegible]	[illegible]	–	[illegible]	[illegible]	–
	4. [illegible],	[illegible]	[illegible]	[illegible]	–	[illegible]	[illegible]	[illegible]		[illegible]	–	[illegible]	[illegible]	[illegible]	[illegible]	[illegible]	[illegible]	[illegible]	[illegible]	–	[illegible]	–	–
	5. Marlfield,	[illegible]	[illegible]	[illegible]	–	1	[illegible]	[illegible]		[illegible]		[illegible]	[illegible]	[illegible]	[illegible]	[illegible]	[illegible]	[illegible]	[illegible]	–	81	–	–
		[illegible]	[illegible]	[illegible]	1	[illegible]	[illegible]	[illegible]	[illegible]	[illegible]	[illegible]	[illegible]	[illegible]	[illegible]	[illegible]	[illegible]	[illegible]	[illegible]	[illegible]	1	[illegible]	[illegible]	–

* A Midwife has not been appointed. † Office of Midwife vacant. ‡ Office of Apothecary vacant. § Office of one Midwife vacant.

No. 2.—Dispensary Districts, with the Expenses, and Amount of Medical Relief afforded, in the several Unions—*continued.*

Unions.	Dispensary Districts.	Population in 1861.	4	5	6	7	8	9	10	11	12	13	14	15	16	17	18	19	20	21	22	23	24
1.	2.	3.	4.	5.	6.	7.	8.	9.	10.	11.	12.	13.	14.	15.	16.	17.	18.	19.	20.	21.	22.	23.	24.
PROVINCE OF LEINSTER.							£ s. d.	£ s. d.	£ s. d.	£ s. d.	£ s. d.	£ s. d.	£ s. d.	£ s. d.	£ s. d.	£ s. d.							
County of Carlow.																							
Carlow, . .	1 Bagenalstown,	[illegible]	[illegible]	[illegible]	[illegible]	[illegible]	[illegible]	[illegible]	[illegible]	[illegible]	[illegible]	[illegible]	[illegible]	[illegible]	[illegible]	[illegible]	[illegible]	[illegible]	[illegible]	[illegible]	[illegible]	[illegible]	[illegible]
	2 Ballickmoyler and Newtown,	[illegible]	[illegible]	[illegible]	[illegible]	[illegible]	[illegible]	[illegible]	[illegible]	[illegible]	[illegible]	[illegible]	[illegible]	[illegible]	[illegible]	[illegible]	[illegible]	[illegible]	[illegible]	[illegible]	[illegible]	[illegible]	[illegible]
	3 Borris, .	[illegible]	[illegible]	[illegible]	[illegible]	[illegible]	[illegible]	[illegible]	[illegible]	[illegible]	[illegible]	[illegible]	[illegible]	[illegible]	[illegible]	[illegible]	[illegible]	[illegible]	[illegible]	[illegible]	[illegible]	[illegible]	[illegible]
	4 Carlow,	[illegible]	[illegible]	[illegible]	[illegible]	[illegible]	[illegible]	[illegible]	[illegible]	[illegible]	[illegible]	[illegible]	[illegible]	[illegible]	[illegible]	[illegible]	[illegible]	[illegible]	[illegible]	[illegible]	[illegible]	[illegible]	[illegible]
	5 Fenagh and Myshall, .	[illegible]	[illegible]	[illegible]	[illegible]	[illegible]	[illegible]	[illegible]	[illegible]	[illegible]	[illegible]	[illegible]	[illegible]	[illegible]	[illegible]	[illegible]	[illegible]	[illegible]	[illegible]	[illegible]	[illegible]	[illegible]	[illegible]
	6 Leighlinbridge,	[illegible]	[illegible]	[illegible]	[illegible]	[illegible]	[illegible]	[illegible]	[illegible]	[illegible]	[illegible]	[illegible]	[illegible]	[illegible]	[illegible]	[illegible]	[illegible]	[illegible]	[illegible]	[illegible]	[illegible]	[illegible]	[illegible]
	7 Tullow, . .	[illegible]	[illegible]	[illegible]	[illegible]	[illegible]	[illegible]	[illegible]	[illegible]	[illegible]	[illegible]	[illegible]	[illegible]	[illegible]	[illegible]	[illegible]	[illegible]	[illegible]	[illegible]	[illegible]	[illegible]	[illegible]	[illegible]
		[illegible]	[illegible]	[illegible]	[illegible]	[illegible]	[illegible]	[illegible]	[illegible]	[illegible]	[illegible]	[illegible]	[illegible]	[illegible]	[illegible]	[illegible]	[illegible]	[illegible]	[illegible]	[illegible]	[illegible]	[illegible]	[illegible]
County of Dublin.																							
Balrothery,	1 Balbriggan, .	[illegible]	[illegible]	[illegible]	[illegible]	[illegible]	[illegible]	[illegible]	[illegible]	[illegible]	[illegible]	[illegible]	[illegible]	[illegible]	[illegible]	[illegible]	[illegible]	[illegible]	[illegible]	[illegible]	[illegible]	[illegible]	[illegible]
	2 Holmpatrick,	[illegible]	[illegible]	[illegible]	[illegible]	[illegible]	[illegible]	[illegible]	[illegible]	[illegible]	[illegible]	[illegible]	[illegible]	[illegible]	[illegible]	[illegible]	[illegible]	[illegible]	[illegible]	[illegible]	[illegible]	[illegible]	[illegible]
	3 [illegible],	[illegible]	[illegible]	[illegible]	[illegible]	[illegible]	[illegible]	[illegible]	[illegible]	[illegible]	[illegible]	[illegible]	[illegible]	[illegible]	[illegible]	[illegible]	[illegible]	[illegible]	[illegible]	[illegible]	[illegible]	[illegible]	[illegible]
	4 Lusk, .	[illegible]	[illegible]	[illegible]	[illegible]	[illegible]	[illegible]	[illegible]	[illegible]	[illegible]	[illegible]	[illegible]	[illegible]	[illegible]	[illegible]	[illegible]	[illegible]	[illegible]	[illegible]	[illegible]	[illegible]	[illegible]	[illegible]
	5 Malahide, .	[illegible]	[illegible]	[illegible]	[illegible]	[illegible]	[illegible]	[illegible]	[illegible]	[illegible]	[illegible]	[illegible]	[illegible]	[illegible]	[illegible]	[illegible]	[illegible]	[illegible]	[illegible]	[illegible]	[illegible]	[illegible]	[illegible]
	6 Swords, .	[illegible]	[illegible]	[illegible]	[illegible]	[illegible]	[illegible]	[illegible]	[illegible]	[illegible]	[illegible]	[illegible]	[illegible]	[illegible]	[illegible]	[illegible]	[illegible]	[illegible]	[illegible]	[illegible]	[illegible]	[illegible]	[illegible]

Union	Electoral Division	Population	Other columns
Dublin, South	1. Clondalkin	[illegible]	[illegible]
	2. Donnybrook	[illegible]	[illegible]
	3. Palmerstown	[illegible]	[illegible]
	4. Rathfarnham	[illegible]	[illegible]
	5. Rathmines	[illegible]	[illegible]
	6. South City	[illegible]	[illegible]
	7. Tallaght	[illegible]	[illegible]
		[illegible]	[illegible]
Rathdown	1. [illegible] and Stillorgan	21,[illegible]	[illegible]
	2. Bray and Rathmichael	[illegible]	[illegible]
	3. Dalkey	[illegible]	[illegible]
	4. Dundrum and Glencullen	[illegible]	[illegible]
	5. Killiney	[illegible]	[illegible]
	6. Kingstown	[illegible]	[illegible]
	7. Powerscourt	[illegible]	[illegible]
		67,[illegible]	[illegible]
County of Kildare.			
Athy	1. Athy	[illegible]	[illegible]
	2. [illegible]	[illegible]	[illegible]
	3. Castledermot	[illegible]	[illegible]
	4. Fontstown	[illegible]	[illegible]
	5. Monasterevan	[illegible]	[illegible]
	6. [illegible]	4,[illegible]	[illegible]
		17,[illegible]	[illegible]
Celbridge	1. Celbridge	[illegible]	[illegible]
	2. Kilcock	[illegible]	[illegible]
	3. Lucan	[illegible]	[illegible]
	4. Maynooth	[illegible]	[illegible]
	5. Rathcoole	[illegible]	[illegible]
		[illegible]	[illegible]

No. 2.—Dispensary Districts, with the Expenses, and Amount of Medical Relief afforded in the several Unions—continued.

Union.	Dispensary Districts.	Population in 1861.	4	5	6	7	Medicines and Medical Appliances.	Rent of Dispensary Buildings.	Books, Forms, Stationery, and Advertising.	Salaries: Medical Officers.	Salaries: Apothecaries.	Salaries: Midwives.	Vaccination Expenses	Vaccination Expenses	Other expenses	Total Expenditure for each Dispensary District for Year ended 29th Sept.	Dispensary Tickets.	Visiting Tickets.	Total.	21	22	23	24
1.	2.	3.	4.	5.	6.	7.	8.	9.	10.	11.	12.	13.	14.	15.	16.	17.	18.	19.	20.	21.	22.	23.	24.
PROVINCE OF LEINSTER—continued.							£ s. d.	£ s. d.	£ s. d.	£ s. d.	£ s. d.	£ s. d.	£ s. d.	£ s. d.	£ s. d.	£ s. d.							
County of Kildare—con. Naas,	1. Blessington & Ballymore,	[illegible]	[illegible]	[illegible]	–	[illegible]	[illegible]	[illegible]	[illegible]	[illegible]	–	[illegible]	[illegible]	[illegible]	3 17 0	[illegible]	[illegible]	[illegible]	[illegible]	–	[illegible]	[illegible]	–
	2. Clane and Timahoe, North	[illegible]	[illegible]	[illegible]	–	[illegible]	[illegible]	[illegible]	[illegible]	[illegible]	–	[illegible]	–	[illegible]	–	[illegible]	[illegible]	[illegible]	[illegible]	–	[illegible]	[illegible]	–
	3. Kilcullen,	[illegible]	[illegible]	[illegible]	–	[illegible]	[illegible]	[illegible]	[illegible]	[illegible]	–	[illegible]	[illegible]	[illegible]	7 3 0	[illegible]	[illegible]	[illegible]	[illegible]	–	[illegible]	–	–
	4. Kildare,	[illegible]	[illegible]	[illegible]	–	[illegible]	[illegible]	[illegible]	[illegible]	[illegible]	–	[illegible]	[illegible]	[illegible]	–	[illegible]	[illegible]	[illegible]	[illegible]	–	[illegible]	–	–
	5. Naas-Oughterard,	[illegible]	[illegible]	[illegible]	–	[illegible]	[illegible]	[illegible]	[illegible]	[illegible]	–	[illegible]	[illegible]	[illegible]	[illegible]	[illegible]	[illegible]	[illegible]	[illegible]	–	[illegible]	[illegible]	–
	6. Newbridge,	[illegible]	[illegible]	[illegible]	–	[illegible]	[illegible]	[illegible]	[illegible]	[illegible]	–	[illegible]	[illegible]	[illegible]	–	[illegible]	[illegible]	[illegible]	[illegible]	–	[illegible]	–	–
	7. Rathmore,	[illegible]	[illegible]	[illegible]	–	[illegible]	[illegible]	[illegible]	[illegible]	[illegible]	–	[illegible]	[illegible]	[illegible]	–	[illegible]	[illegible]	[illegible]	[illegible]	–	[illegible]	–	–
	8. Robertstown and Kilmeague,	[illegible]	[illegible]	[illegible]	–	[illegible]	[illegible]	[illegible]	[illegible]	[illegible]	–	[illegible]	[illegible]	[illegible]	[illegible]	[illegible]	[illegible]	[illegible]	[illegible]	–	[illegible]	–	–
		[illegible]	[illegible]	[illegible]	–	[illegible]	[illegible]	[illegible]	[illegible]	[illegible]	–	[illegible]	[illegible]	[illegible]	34 4 0	[illegible]	[illegible]	[illegible]	[illegible]	–	[illegible]	[illegible]	–
County of Kilkenny. Callan,	1. Ballingarry,	[illegible]	[illegible]	[illegible]	–	–	[illegible]	[illegible]	[illegible]	[illegible]	–	–	[illegible]	–	–	[illegible]	[illegible]	[illegible]	[illegible]	[illegible]	[illegible]	–	–
	2. Callan,	[illegible]	[illegible]	[illegible]	–	–	[illegible]	[illegible]	[illegible]	[illegible]	–	–	[illegible]	–	[illegible]	[illegible]	[illegible]	[illegible]	[illegible]	–	[illegible]	[illegible]	–
	3. Kilmaganny,	[illegible]	[illegible]	[illegible]	–	[illegible]	[illegible]	[illegible]	[illegible]	[illegible]	–	[illegible]	[illegible]	–	[illegible]	[illegible]	[illegible]	[illegible]	[illegible]	–	[illegible]	[illegible]	–
	4. Mullinahone,	[illegible]	[illegible]	[illegible]	–	–	[illegible]	[illegible]	[illegible]	[illegible]	–	–	–	–	[illegible]	[illegible]	[illegible]	[illegible]	[illegible]	–	[illegible]	–	–
		[illegible]	[illegible]	[illegible]	–	[illegible]	[illegible]	[illegible]	[illegible]	[illegible]	–	[illegible]	[illegible]	–	[illegible]	[illegible]	[illegible]	[illegible]	[illegible]	[illegible]	[illegible]	[illegible]	–
Castlecomer,	1. Ballyragget,	[illegible]	[illegible]	[illegible]	–	–	[illegible]	[illegible]	[illegible]	[illegible]	–	–	[illegible]	–	–	[illegible]	[illegible]	[illegible]	[illegible]	–	[illegible]	–	–
	2. Castlecomer,	[illegible]	[illegible]	[illegible]	–	–	[illegible]	[illegible]	[illegible]	[illegible]	–	–	[illegible]	[illegible]	–	[illegible]	[illegible]	[illegible]	[illegible]	[illegible]	[illegible]	[illegible]	–
		[illegible]	[illegible]	[illegible]	–	–	[illegible]	[illegible]	[illegible]	[illegible]	–	–	[illegible]	[illegible]	–	[illegible]	[illegible]	[illegible]	[illegible]	[illegible]	[illegible]	[illegible]	–

No. 2.—Dispensary Districts, with the Expenses, and Amount of Medical Relief afforded, in the several Unions—continued.

Unions.	Dispensary Districts.	Population in 1851.	4	No. of officers: Med. Officers	Apothecaries	Midwives	Medicines and Medical Appliances	Rent of Dispensary Buildings	Books, Forms, Stationery, and Advertising	Salaries: Medical Officers	Apothecaries	Midwives	Vaccination Expenses	15	Other Expenses	Total Expenditure for each Dispensary District for Year ended 29th Sept. 1851	New cases: Dispensary	Visited at Homes	Total	21	22	23	24
1	2	3	4	5	6	7	8	9	10	11	12	13	14	15	16	17	18	19	20	21	22	23	24
							£ s. d.	£ s. d.	£ s. d.	£ s. d.	£ s. d.	£ s. d.	£ s. d.	£ s. d.	£ s. d.	£ s. d.							
PROVINCE OF LEINSTER—continued.																							
COUNTY OF LONGFORD.																							
BALLYMAHON	1. Abbeyshrule,	[illegible]	[illegible]	[illegible]	—	[illegible]	[illegible]	[illegible]	[illegible]	[illegible]	—	—	[illegible]	—	[illegible]	[illegible]	[illegible]	[illegible]	[illegible]	—	[illegible]	[illegible]	—
	2. Ballymahon,	[illegible]	[illegible]	[illegible]	—	[illegible]	[illegible]	[illegible]	—	[illegible]	—	—	[illegible]	—	[illegible]	[illegible]	[illegible]	[illegible]	[illegible]	—	[illegible]	[illegible]	—
	3. Ballymore,	[illegible]	[illegible]	[illegible]	—	—	[illegible]	[illegible]	—	[illegible]	—	—	[illegible]	—	[illegible]	[illegible]	[illegible]	[illegible]	[illegible]	—	[illegible]	[illegible]	—
		[illegible]	[illegible]	[illegible]	—	[illegible]	[illegible]	[illegible]	[illegible]	[illegible]	—	—	[illegible]	—	[illegible]	[illegible]	[illegible]	[illegible]	[illegible]	—	[illegible]	13	—
GRANARD,	1. Ballinalee,	[illegible]	[illegible]	[illegible]	—	—	[illegible]	[illegible]	[illegible]	[illegible]	—	—	[illegible]	[illegible]	[illegible]	[illegible]	[illegible]	[illegible]	[illegible]	—	[illegible]	—	—
	2. Coole,	[illegible]	[illegible]	[illegible]	—	—	—	[illegible]	[illegible]	[illegible]	—	—	[illegible]	—	[illegible]	[illegible]	[illegible]	[illegible]	[illegible]	—	[illegible]	—	—
	3. Finnea,	[illegible]	[illegible]	[illegible]	—	—	[illegible]	[illegible]	[illegible]	[illegible]	—	—	[illegible]	[illegible]	[illegible]	[illegible]	[illegible]	[illegible]	[illegible]	—	[illegible]	—	—
	4. Granard,	[illegible]	[illegible]	[illegible]	—	—	[illegible]	—	[illegible]	[illegible]	—	—	[illegible]	[illegible]	[illegible]	[illegible]	[illegible]	[illegible]	[illegible]	[illegible]	[illegible]	[illegible]	—
	5. [illegible],	[illegible]	[illegible]	[illegible]	—	—	[illegible]	[illegible]	[illegible]	[illegible]	—	—	[illegible]	[illegible]	[illegible]	[illegible]	[illegible]	[illegible]	[illegible]	—	[illegible]	—	—
	6. Street,	[illegible]	[illegible]	[illegible]	—	—	[illegible]	[illegible]	[illegible]	[illegible]	—	—	[illegible]	—	[illegible]	[illegible]	[illegible]	[illegible]	[illegible]	—	[illegible]	[illegible]	—
		[illegible]	7	[illegible]	—	[illegible]	[illegible]	[illegible]	[illegible]	[illegible]	—	—	[illegible]	[illegible]	[illegible]	[illegible]	[illegible]	[illegible]	[illegible]	[illegible]	[illegible]	[illegible]	—
LONGFORD,	1. Drumlish,	[illegible]	1	[illegible]	—	[illegible]	[illegible]	[illegible]	[illegible]	[illegible]	—	—	[illegible]	[illegible]	[illegible]	[illegible]	[illegible]	[illegible]	[illegible]	[illegible]	[illegible]	[illegible]	—
	2. Killashee,	[illegible]	1	[illegible]	—	[illegible]	—	[illegible]	[illegible]	[illegible]	—	—	[illegible]	—	[illegible]	[illegible]	[illegible]	[illegible]	[illegible]	—	[illegible]	[illegible]	—
	3. Longford,	[illegible]	[illegible]	[illegible]	—	[illegible]	[illegible]	[illegible]	[illegible]	[illegible]	—	[illegible]	[illegible]	[illegible]	[illegible]	[illegible]	[illegible]	[illegible]	[illegible]	—	[illegible]	[illegible]	—

No. 2.—Dispensary Districts, with the Expenses, and Amount of Medical Relief afforded, in the several Unions—*continued.*

Unions.	Dispensary Districts.	Population in 1851.	[illegible]	No. of Officers authorized.			Expenses of Year ended 29th September, 18[illegible].										Medical Relief afforded in Year ended 29th September, 18[illegible].							
1.	2.	3.	4.	5.	6.	7.	8.	9.	10.	11.	12.	13.	14.	15.	16.	17.	18.	19.	20.	21.	22.	23.	24.
PROVINCE OF LEINSTER—*continued.*							£ s. d.	£ s. d.	£ s. d.	£ s. d.	£ s. d.	£ s. d.	£ s. d.	£ s. d.	£ s. d.	£ s. d.							
County of Meath—*con.*																							
Trim,	1. Athboy,	[illegible]	[illegible]	[illegible]	–	1	[illegible]	[illegible]	[illegible]	[illegible]	–	[illegible]	[illegible]	[illegible]	[illegible]	[illegible]	[illegible]	[illegible]	[illegible]	[illegible]	[illegible]	–	–
	2. [illegible],	[illegible]	[illegible]	[illegible]	–	1	[illegible]	[illegible]	[illegible]	[illegible]	–	[illegible]	[illegible]	[illegible]	[illegible]	[illegible]	[illegible]	[illegible]	[illegible]	–	[illegible]	[illegible]	–
	3. Summerhill,	[illegible]	[illegible]	[illegible]	–	1	[illegible]	[illegible]	[illegible]	[illegible]	–	[illegible]	[illegible]	–	[illegible]	[illegible]	[illegible]	[illegible]	[illegible]	–	[illegible]	[illegible]	–
	4. Trim,	[illegible]	[illegible]	[illegible]	–	1	[illegible]	[illegible]	[illegible]	[illegible]	–	[illegible]	[illegible]	[illegible]	[illegible]	[illegible]	[illegible]	[illegible]	[illegible]	–	[illegible]	[illegible]	–
		[illegible]	[illegible]	[illegible]	–	4	[illegible]	[illegible]	[illegible]	[illegible]	–	[illegible]	[illegible]	[illegible]	[illegible]	[illegible]	[illegible]	[illegible]	[illegible]	[illegible]	[illegible]	[illegible]	–
Queen's County.																							
Abbeyleix,	1. Abbeyleix,	[illegible]	[illegible]	[illegible]	–	–	[illegible]	[illegible]	[illegible]	[illegible]	–	–	[illegible]	–	[illegible]	[illegible]	[illegible]	[illegible]	[illegible]	–	[illegible]	[illegible]	–
	2. Ballinakill,	[illegible]	[illegible]	[illegible]	–	[illegible]	[illegible]	[illegible]	[illegible]	[illegible]	–	[illegible]	[illegible]	–	[illegible]	[illegible]	[illegible]	[illegible]	[illegible]	–	[illegible]	–	–
	3. Ballyroan,	[illegible]	[illegible]	[illegible]	–	–	[illegible]	[illegible]	[illegible]	[illegible]	–	–	–	–	[illegible]	[illegible]	[illegible]	[illegible]	[illegible]	–	[illegible]	–	–
	4. Castletown,	[illegible]	[illegible]	[illegible]	–	[illegible]	[illegible]	[illegible]	[illegible]	[illegible]	–	–	[illegible]	–	[illegible]	[illegible]	[illegible]	[illegible]	[illegible]	–	[illegible]	–	–
	5. Durrow,	[illegible]	[illegible]	[illegible]	–	[illegible]	[illegible]	[illegible]	[illegible]	[illegible]	–	[illegible]	[illegible]	–	[illegible]	[illegible]	[illegible]	[illegible]	[illegible]	[illegible]	[illegible]	[illegible]	–
	6. Rathdowney,	[illegible]	[illegible]	[illegible]	–	[illegible]	[illegible]	–	[illegible]	[illegible]	–	[illegible]	[illegible]	–	[illegible]	[illegible]	[illegible]	[illegible]	[illegible]	[illegible]	[illegible]	[illegible]	–
		[illegible]	[illegible]	[illegible]	1	[illegible]	[illegible]	[illegible]	[illegible]	[illegible]	–	[illegible]	[illegible]	–	[illegible]	[illegible]	[illegible]	[illegible]	[illegible]	[illegible]	[illegible]	[illegible]	–

Union	Dispensary District	Figures
COUNTY OF WATERFORD.		
[illegible]	1. [illegible]	[illegible]
	2. [illegible]	[illegible]
	3. [illegible]	[illegible]
	4. [illegible]	[illegible]
	5. [illegible]	[illegible]
	Total	[illegible]
[illegible]	1. [illegible]	[illegible]
	2. [illegible]	[illegible]
	3. [illegible]	[illegible]
	Total	[illegible]
[illegible]	1. [illegible]	[illegible]
	2. [illegible]	[illegible]
	3. [illegible]	[illegible]
	4. [illegible]	[illegible]
	5. [illegible]	[illegible]
	6. [illegible]	[illegible]
	7. [illegible]	[illegible]
	Total	[illegible]
COUNTY OF WEXFORD.		
Enniscorthy	1. Clonroche	[illegible]
	2. Enniscorthy	[illegible]
	3. Ferns	[illegible]
	4. Killann	[illegible]
	5. Newtownbarry	[illegible]
	6. Oulart	[illegible]
	Total	[illegible]
Gorey	1. Camolin	[illegible]
	2. Coolgreany	[illegible]
	3. Gorey	[illegible]
	4. [illegible] and [illegible]	[illegible]
	Total	[illegible]

[illegible]

No. 2.—Dispensary Districts, with the Expenses, and Amount of Medical Relief afforded, in the several Unions—continued.

Union.	Dispensary Districts.	Population in 1861.	[illegible]	No. of [illegible]			Expenditure of Year ended 29th September, 1862.										Medical Relief afforded in Year ended 29th September, 1862.						
				[illegible]	[illegible]	[illegible]	Medicines and Medical Appliances.	Rent of Dispensary Buildings.	Books, Forms, Stationery, Printing and Advertising.	Salaries (including payments for temporary services).			Vaccination Expenses.		[illegible]	Total Expenditure [illegible] 29th Sept., 1862.	Number of New Cases attended and registered during the year.			[illegible]	[illegible]	[illegible]	[illegible]
										Medical Officers.	Apothecaries.	Midwives.	[illegible]	[illegible]			Dispensary Tickets.	Visiting Tickets.	Total.				
1.	2.	3.	4.	5.	6.	7.	8.	9.	10.	11.	12.	13.	14.	15.	16.	17.	18.	19.	20.	21.	22.	23.	24.
							£ s. d.	£ s. d.	£ s. d.	£ s. d.	£ s. d.	£ s. d.	£ s. d.	£ s. d.	£ s. d.	£ s. d.							
PROVINCE OF LEINSTER—continued.																							
County of Wexford—con.																							
New Ross,	1. Carrickbyrne,	[illegible]	[illegible]	[illegible]	—	[illegible]	[illegible]	[illegible]	[illegible]	[illegible]	—	[illegible]	[illegible]	—	[illegible]	[illegible]	[illegible]	[illegible]	[illegible]	—	[illegible]	—	—
	2. [illegible]	[illegible]	[illegible]	[illegible]	—	[illegible]	[illegible]	[illegible]	[illegible]	[illegible]	—	[illegible]	—	—	[illegible]	[illegible]	[illegible]	[illegible]	[illegible]	—	[illegible]	[illegible]	—
	3. Fethard,	[illegible]	[illegible]	[illegible]	—	[illegible]	[illegible]	[illegible]	[illegible]	[illegible]	—	[illegible]	[illegible]	[illegible]	[illegible]	[illegible]	[illegible]	[illegible]	[illegible]	—	[illegible]	[illegible]	—
	4. New Ross,	[illegible]	[illegible]	[illegible]	—	[illegible]	[illegible]	[illegible]	[illegible]	[illegible]	—	[illegible]	[illegible]	—	[illegible]	[illegible]	[illegible]	[illegible]	[illegible]	—	[illegible]	[illegible]	[illegible]
	5. Old Ross,	[illegible]	[illegible]	[illegible]	—	[illegible]	[illegible]	[illegible]	[illegible]	[illegible]	—	[illegible]	[illegible]	—	[illegible]	[illegible]	[illegible]	[illegible]	[illegible]	—	[illegible]	[illegible]	—
	6. St. Mullins,	[illegible]	[illegible]	[illegible]	—	[illegible]	[illegible]	[illegible]	[illegible]	[illegible]	—	[illegible]	[illegible]	[illegible]	[illegible]	[illegible]	[illegible]	[illegible]	[illegible]	—	[illegible]	[illegible]	—
	7. [illegible]	[illegible]	[illegible]	[illegible]	—	[illegible]	[illegible]	[illegible]	[illegible]	[illegible]	—	—	[illegible]	—	[illegible]	[illegible]	[illegible]	[illegible]	[illegible]	—	[illegible]	[illegible]	—
		[illegible]	[illegible]	[illegible]	—	7	[illegible]	[illegible]	[illegible]	[illegible]	—	[illegible]	[illegible]	[illegible]	[illegible]	[illegible]	[illegible]	[illegible]	[illegible]	—	[illegible]	[illegible]	[illegible]
Wexford,	1. [illegible]	[illegible]	[illegible]	[illegible]	—	[illegible]	[illegible]	[illegible]	[illegible]	[illegible]	—	[illegible]	[illegible]	—	[illegible]	[illegible]	[illegible]	[illegible]	[illegible]	—	[illegible]	—	—
	2. Bridgetown,	[illegible]	[illegible]	[illegible]	—	[illegible]	[illegible]	[illegible]	[illegible]	[illegible]	—	[illegible]	[illegible]	—	[illegible]	[illegible]	[illegible]	[illegible]	[illegible]	[illegible]	[illegible]	[illegible]	—
	3. [illegible]	[illegible]	[illegible]	[illegible]	—	[illegible]	[illegible]	[illegible]	[illegible]	[illegible]	—	[illegible]	[illegible]	—	[illegible]	[illegible]	[illegible]	[illegible]	[illegible]	—	[illegible]	—	—
	4. [illegible]	[illegible]	[illegible]	[illegible]	—	[illegible]	—	[illegible]	[illegible]	[illegible]	—	[illegible]	[illegible]	[illegible]	[illegible]	[illegible]	[illegible]	[illegible]	[illegible]	—	[illegible]	—	—
	5. [illegible] and [illegible],	[illegible]	[illegible]	[illegible]	—	[illegible]	[illegible]	[illegible]	[illegible]	[illegible]	—	[illegible]	[illegible]	—	[illegible]	[illegible]	[illegible]	[illegible]	[illegible]	—	[illegible]	[illegible]	—
	6. Wexford,	[illegible]	[illegible]	[illegible]	[illegible]	[illegible]	[illegible]	[illegible]	[illegible]	[illegible]	[illegible]	[illegible]	[illegible]	[illegible]	[illegible]	[illegible]	[illegible]	[illegible]	[illegible]	—	[illegible]	[illegible]	—
		[illegible]	[illegible]	[illegible]	[illegible]	7	[illegible]	[illegible]	[illegible]	[illegible]	[illegible]	[illegible]	[illegible]	[illegible]	[illegible]	[illegible]	[illegible]	[illegible]	[illegible]	[illegible]	[illegible]	[illegible]	—
County of Wicklow.																							
Baltinglass,	1. Baltinglass,	[illegible]	[illegible]	[illegible]	—	[illegible]	[illegible]	[illegible]	—	[illegible]	—	[illegible]	[illegible]	—	—	[illegible]	[illegible]	[illegible]	[illegible]	—	[illegible]	[illegible]	—
	2. Dunlavin,	[illegible]	[illegible]	[illegible]	—	[illegible]	[illegible]	[illegible]	—	[illegible]	—	—	[illegible]	—	—	[illegible]	[illegible]	[illegible]	[illegible]	—	[illegible]	[illegible]	—
	3. [illegible]	[illegible]	[illegible]	[illegible]	—	[illegible]	—	[illegible]	—	[illegible]	—	—	[illegible]	—	—	[illegible]	[illegible]	[illegible]	[illegible]	—	[illegible]	[illegible]	—
	4. [illegible]	[illegible]	[illegible]	[illegible]	—	[illegible]	[illegible]	[illegible]	—	[illegible]	—	—	[illegible]	—	[illegible]	[illegible]	[illegible]	[illegible]	[illegible]	—	[illegible]	[illegible]	—

Barony	Parish / Division		Remaining columns
[illegible]	1. [illegible]	[illegible]	[illegible]
	2. Arklow,	[illegible]	[illegible]
	3. Aughrim,	[illegible]	[illegible]
	4. [illegible]	[illegible]	[illegible]
	5. [illegible]	[illegible]	[illegible]
	6. [illegible]	[illegible]	[illegible]
	7. Rathdrum,	[illegible]	[illegible]
	8. Wicklow,	[illegible]	[illegible]
		33,4?6	[illegible]
[illegible]	1. [illegible] and [illegible],	4,700	[illegible]
	2. [illegible] and [illegible],	[illegible]	[illegible]
	3. [illegible],	[illegible]	[illegible]
		[illegible]	[illegible]
PROVINCE OF CONNAUGHT.			
County of Galway.			
Ballinasloe[?]	1. [illegible]	[illegible]	[illegible]
	2. Ballinasloe[?],	[illegible]	[illegible]
	3. [illegible]	[illegible]	[illegible]
	4. [illegible]	[illegible]	[illegible]
	5. [illegible]	[illegible]	[illegible]
	6. Lawrencetown[?]	[illegible]	[illegible]
		[illegible]	[illegible]
Clifden[?],	1. Clifden,	[illegible]	[illegible]
	2. [illegible]	[illegible]	[illegible]
	3. [illegible]	[illegible]	[illegible]
		[illegible]	[illegible]
Galway,	1. [illegible]	[illegible]	[illegible]
	2. Moycullen[?],	[illegible]	[illegible]
	3. Oughterard[?],	[illegible]	[illegible]
	4. Spiddal[?],	[illegible]	[illegible]
	5. [illegible]	[illegible]	[illegible]
		[illegible]	[illegible]

No. 2.—Dispensary Districts, with the Expenses, and Amount of Medical Relief afforded, in the several Unions — continued.

Union.	Dispensary Districts.	Population in 1851.	[illegible]	No. of Officers [illegible]			Expenses of Year ended 29th September, 1856.										Medical Relief afforded to Year ended 29th September, 1856.					
				[illegible]	[illegible]	[illegible]	Medicines and Medical Appliances.	Rent of Dispensary Buildings.	Books, Forms, Stationery, Printing, and Advertising.	Salaries (including payments [illegible]) Medical Officers.	Apothecaries.	Midwives.	Vaccination Expenses. [illegible]	[illegible]	[illegible]	Total Expenditure [illegible]	Number of New Cases [illegible] Dispensary.	Visiting [illegible].	Total.	[illegible]	[illegible]	[illegible]
1.	2.	3.	4.	5.	6.	7.	8.	9.	10.	11.	12.	13.	14.	15.	16.	17.	18.	19.	20.	21.	22.	23.
							£ s. d.	£ s. d.	£ s. d.	£ s. d.	£ s. d.	£ s. d.	£ s. d.	£ s. d.	£ s. d.	£ s. d.						
PROVINCE OF CONNAUGHT—continued. County of Galway—con.																						
[illegible]	1. [illegible],	[illegible]	1	[illegible]	–	–	–	8 0 0	–	[illegible]	–	–	7 0 0	[illegible]	[illegible]	[illegible]	[illegible]	[illegible]	[illegible]	–	[illegible]	1
	2. [illegible],	7,360	1	[illegible]	–	–	[illegible]	–	–	[illegible]	–	–	–	[illegible]	[illegible]	[illegible]	[illegible]	[illegible]	[illegible]	–	[illegible]	[illegible]
	3. Williamstown,	[illegible]	1	[illegible]	–	–	[illegible]	10 0 0	–	[illegible]	–	–	[illegible]	[illegible]	[illegible]	[illegible]	[illegible]	[illegible]	[illegible]	–	[illegible]	[illegible]
		[illegible]	3	[illegible]	–	–	[illegible]	[illegible]	–	[illegible]	–	–	[illegible]	[illegible]	[illegible]	[illegible]	713	[illegible]	[illegible]	–	[illegible]	7
Gort,	1. [illegible],	[illegible]	[illegible]	[illegible]	–	–	[illegible]	[illegible]	–	[illegible]	–	–	3 0 0	–	–	[illegible]	[illegible]	[illegible]	[illegible]	–	[illegible]	–
	2. Gort,	[illegible]	1	[illegible]	–	–	[illegible]	–	–	[illegible]	–	–	[illegible]	–	–	[illegible]	[illegible]	[illegible]	[illegible]	–	[illegible]	4
	3. [illegible],	[illegible]	[illegible]	[illegible]	–	–	[illegible]	[illegible]	–	[illegible]	–	–	[illegible]	–	–	[illegible]	[illegible]	[illegible]	[illegible]	–	[illegible]	–
		[illegible]	[illegible]	[illegible]	–	–	[illegible]	[illegible]	–	[illegible]	–	–	[illegible]	–	–	[illegible]	1,734	[illegible]	[illegible]	–	[illegible]	4
[illegible],	1. [illegible],	[illegible]	[illegible]	[illegible]	–	–	[illegible]	[illegible]	[illegible]	[illegible]	–	–	[illegible]	[illegible]	[illegible]	[illegible]	[illegible]	[illegible]	[illegible]	–	[illegible]	[illegible]
	2. [illegible],	[illegible]	[illegible]	[illegible]	–	–	[illegible]	[illegible]	[illegible]	[illegible]	–	–	[illegible]	[illegible]	[illegible]	[illegible]	[illegible]	[illegible]	[illegible]	–	[illegible]	–
	3. [illegible],	[illegible]	[illegible]	[illegible]	–	–	[illegible]	[illegible]	[illegible]	[illegible]	–	–	–	[illegible]	[illegible]	[illegible]	[illegible]	[illegible]	[illegible]	–	[illegible]	[illegible]
	4. [illegible],	[illegible]	3	[illegible]	–	–	[illegible]	[illegible]	[illegible]	[illegible]	–	–	[illegible]	[illegible]	[illegible]	[illegible]	[illegible]	[illegible]	[illegible]	–	[illegible]	–
		[illegible]	[illegible]	[illegible]	–	–	[illegible]	[illegible]	[illegible]	[illegible]	–	–	[illegible]	[illegible]	[illegible]	[illegible]	715	[illegible]	[illegible]	–	[illegible]	[illegible]

Union	Dispensary District	Returns
Oughterard,	1. [illegible],	[illegible]
	2. [illegible],	[illegible]
	3. Oughterard,	[illegible]
	Total	[illegible]
Portumna,	1. Eyrecourt,	[illegible]
	2. Portumna,	[illegible]
	Total	[illegible]
Tuam,	1. Abbey,	[illegible]
	2. Dunmore,	[illegible]
	3. Headford,	[illegible]
	4. Tuam,	[illegible]
	Total	[illegible]
County of Leitrim.		
Carrick-on-Shannon,	1. Aughrim,	[illegible]
	2. Drumshanbo,	[illegible]
	3. Jamestown,	[illegible]
	4. Leitrim,	[illegible]
	Total	[illegible]
Manorhamilton,	1. Drumahaire,	[illegible]
	2. [illegible],	[illegible]
	3. [illegible],	[illegible]
	4. Manorhamilton,	[illegible]
	Total	[illegible]
Mohill,	1. Carrigallen,	[illegible]
	2. Mohill,	[illegible]
	3. [illegible],	[illegible]
	4. [illegible],	[illegible]
	Total	[illegible]
County of Meath.		
[illegible],	1. [illegible],	[illegible]
	2. [illegible],	[illegible]
	Total	[illegible]

* Office of Midwife vacant.

† A Midwife has not been appointed.

Population in 1881.	[illegible]	No. of Officers [illegible]: Med. Officers	Apothecaries	Midwives	Medicines and Medical Appliances	Rent of Dispensary Buildings	Books, Forms, Stationery, Printing and Advertising	Salaries (including payments for temporary services): Medical Officers	Salaries: Apothecaries	Salaries: Midwives	Vaccination Expenses: [illegible]	Vaccination Expenses: [illegible]	[illegible]	Total Expenditure [illegible] for year ended [illegible] 1881	Number of New Cases attended and registered during the year: Dispensary Tickets	Visiting Tickets	Total	[illegible]	[illegible]	[illegible]	[illegible]
3.	4.	5.	6.	7.	8.	9.	10.	11.	12.	13.	14.	15.	16.	17.	18.	19.	20.	21.	22.	23.	24.
					£ s. d.	£ s. d.	£ s. d.	£ s. d.	£ s. d.	£ s. d.	£ s. d.	£ s. d.	£ s. d.	£ s. d.							
[illegible]	[illegible]	[illegible]	-	-	[illegible]	[illegible]	-	[illegible]	-	-	[illegible]	[illegible]	[illegible]	[illegible]	[illegible]	[illegible]	[illegible]	-	[illegible]	[illegible]	-
[illegible]	[illegible]	[illegible]	-	-	[illegible]	[illegible]	-	[illegible]	-	-	[illegible]	-	[illegible]	[illegible]	[illegible]	[illegible]	[illegible]	-	[illegible]	-	-
[illegible]	[illegible]	[illegible]	-	-	[illegible]	[illegible]	-	[illegible]	-	-	[illegible]	[illegible]	[illegible]	[illegible]	[illegible]	[illegible]	[illegible]	-	[illegible]	[illegible]	-
[illegible]	[illegible]	[illegible]	-	-	[illegible]	[illegible]	-	[illegible]	-	-	[illegible]	[illegible]	[illegible]	[illegible]	[illegible]	[illegible]	[illegible]	-	[illegible]	[illegible]	-
[illegible]	[illegible]	[illegible]	-	-	[illegible]	[illegible]	[illegible]	[illegible]	-	-	[illegible]	[illegible]	[illegible]	[illegible]	[illegible]	[illegible]	[illegible]	-	[illegible]	-	-
[illegible]	[illegible]	[illegible]	-	[illegible]	[illegible]	-	[illegible]	[illegible]	-	-	[illegible]	[illegible]	[illegible]	[illegible]	[illegible]	[illegible]	[illegible]	[illegible]	[illegible]	[illegible]	-
[illegible]	[illegible]	[illegible]	-	-	[illegible]	[illegible]	[illegible]	[illegible]	-	-	[illegible]	[illegible]	[illegible]	[illegible]	[illegible]	[illegible]	[illegible]	-	[illegible]	-	-
[illegible]	[illegible]	[illegible]	-	[illegible]	[illegible]	[illegible]	[illegible]	[illegible]	-	-	[illegible]	[illegible]	[illegible]	[illegible]	[illegible]	[illegible]	[illegible]	[illegible]	[illegible]	[illegible]	-
[illegible]	[illegible]	[illegible]	-	-	[illegible]	[illegible]	[illegible]	[illegible]	-	-	[illegible]	[illegible]	[illegible]	[illegible]	[illegible]	[illegible]	[illegible]	-	[illegible]	-	-
[illegible]	[illegible]	[illegible]	-	[illegible]	[illegible]	[illegible]	[illegible]	[illegible]	-	[illegible]	[illegible]	[illegible]	[illegible]	[illegible]	[illegible]	[illegible]	[illegible]	-	[illegible]	[illegible]	-
[illegible]	[illegible]	[illegible]	[illegible]	[illegible]	[illegible]	[illegible]	[illegible]	[illegible]	-	[illegible]	[illegible]	[illegible]	[illegible]	[illegible]	[illegible]	[illegible]	[illegible]	-	[illegible]	[illegible]	-

Union	Division	[illegible]
[illegible]	1. [illegible]	[illegible]
	2. [illegible]	[illegible]
	3. [illegible]	[illegible]
	4. [illegible]	[illegible]
	5. [illegible]	[illegible]
		[illegible]
Westport,	1. [illegible]	[illegible]
	2. [illegible]	[illegible]
	3. Louisburgh,	[illegible]
	4. Newport,	[illegible]
	5. Westport,	[illegible]
		[illegible]
County of Roscommon		
Boyle,	1. [illegible]	[illegible]
	2. [illegible]	[illegible]
	3. Boyle,	[illegible]
	4. [illegible]	[illegible]
	5. Keadue,	[illegible]
		[illegible]
Castlerea,	1. [illegible]	[illegible]
	2. Castleplunket,	[illegible]
	3. Castlerea,	[illegible]
	4. Frenchpark,	[illegible]
		[illegible]
Roscommon,	1. Athleague,	[illegible]
	2. [illegible]	[illegible]
	3. Roscommon,	[illegible]
		[illegible]

Union.	Dispensary District.	Population in 1881.	4.	No. of Officers authorised. Med. Officers.	Apothecaries.	Midwives.	Medicines and Medical Appliances.	Rent of Dispensary Buildings.	Books, Forms, Stationery, Printing, and Advertising.	Salaries: Medical Officers.	Apothecaries.	Midwives.	Vaccination Expenses		Other Expenses.	Total Expenditure for Year ended 29th Sept.
1.	2.	3.	4.	5.	6.	7.	8.	9.	10.	11.	12.	13.	14.	15.	16.	17.
							£ s. d.	£ s. d.	£ s. d.	£ s. d.	£ s. d.	£ s. d.	£ s. d.	£ s. d.	£ s. d.	£ s. d.
PROVINCE OF CONNAUGHT—continued. County of Roscommon—continued.																
Strokestown,	1. [illegible],	[illegible]	1	1	–	–	40 [illegible] [illegible]	[illegible] 0 0	–	[illegible] 0 0	–	–	[illegible]	[illegible]	[illegible]	[illegible]
	2. [illegible],	[illegible]	[illegible]	1	0	1	[illegible]	[illegible] 0 0	–	[illegible] 0 0	–	–	[illegible]	[illegible]	[illegible]	[illegible]
	3. Strokestown,	6,414	1	2	–	–	47 5 0	8 0 0	–	[illegible] 0 0	–	–	–	7 17 [illegible]	6 10 6	142 1 3
		21,724	4	[illegible]	–	1	157 [illegible] [illegible]	30 0 0	–	[illegible] 0 0	–	–	[illegible] 0 0	[illegible] 7 [illegible]	31 17 4	[illegible] [illegible] 0
County of Sligo.																
Dromore West,	1. Easkey,	11,760	6	[illegible]	–	[illegible]	[illegible] 9 4	10 0 0	–	[illegible] 0 0	–	–	–	[illegible]	[illegible]	[illegible] [illegible] 1
	2. Skreen,	6,041	1	1	–	[illegible]	41 10 [illegible]	6 0 0	–	[illegible] 0 0	–	–	–	[illegible]	7 3 [illegible]	[illegible] [illegible] 0

Expenditure of Year ended 29th September, 188[illegible].

SUMMARY OF FOREGOING TABLE, No. 2.

Provinces.	Population (Census 1851).*	[illegible]	[illegible]	[illegible]	[illegible]	[illegible]	[illegible]	Medicines and Medical Appliances.	Rent of Dispensary Buildings.	Books, Forms, Stationery, Printing and Advertising.	Salaries: Medical Officers.	Salaries: Apothecaries.	Salaries: Midwives.	Vaccination Fees	Vaccination Fees	[illegible]	Total Expenses of Dispensary Districts.	Dispensary Tickets.	Visiting Tickets.	Total.	[illegible]	[illegible]	[illegible]	[illegible]
1	2	3	4	5	6	7	8	9	10	11	12	13	14	15	16	17	18	19	20	21	22	23	24	25
								£ s. d.	£ s. d.	£ s. d.	£ s. d.	£ s. d.	£ s. d.	£ s. d.	£ s. d.	£ s. d.	£ s. d.							
Ulster,	[illegible]	[illegible]	[illegible]	[illegible]	[illegible]	[illegible]	[illegible]	[illegible]	[illegible]	[illegible]	[illegible]	[illegible]	[illegible]	[illegible]	[illegible]	[illegible]	[illegible]	[illegible]	[illegible]	[illegible]	[illegible]	[illegible]	[illegible]	[illegible]
Munster,	[illegible]	[illegible]	[illegible]	[illegible]	[illegible]	[illegible]	[illegible]	[illegible]	[illegible]	[illegible]	[illegible]	[illegible]	[illegible]	[illegible]	[illegible]	[illegible]	[illegible]	[illegible]	[illegible]	[illegible]	[illegible]	[illegible]	[illegible]	[illegible]
Leinster,	[illegible]	[illegible]	[illegible]	[illegible]	[illegible]	[illegible]	[illegible]	[illegible]	[illegible]	[illegible]	[illegible]	[illegible]	[illegible]	[illegible]	[illegible]	[illegible]	[illegible]	[illegible]	[illegible]	[illegible]	[illegible]	[illegible]	[illegible]	[illegible]
Connaught,	[illegible]	[illegible]	[illegible]	[illegible]	[illegible]	[illegible]	[illegible]	[illegible]	[illegible]	[illegible]	[illegible]	[illegible]	[illegible]	[illegible]	[illegible]	[illegible]	[illegible]	[illegible]	[illegible]	[illegible]	[illegible]	[illegible]	[illegible]	[illegible]
Total, Ireland,	[illegible]	[illegible]	[illegible]	[illegible]	[illegible]	[illegible]	[illegible]	[illegible]	[illegible]	[illegible]	[illegible]	[illegible]	[illegible]	[illegible]	[illegible]	[illegible]	[illegible]	[illegible]	[illegible]	[illegible]	[illegible]	[illegible]	[illegible]	[illegible]

* The population of each of the Provinces [illegible]

† [illegible]

No. 3.—General Summary of previous tables, in Provinces:—containing, 1. dispensary districts formed under § 6 of the Medical Charities Act, 14 & of dispensaries, officers, &c.:—2. Financial Statement; showing the 1888, to 29th September, 1889:—and 3. Relief Return; showing the homes, respectively; the number of cases in which tickets for medical vaccination performed; number of cases of dangerous lunatics certified; year ended the 30th of September, 1889.

Heads of Particulars in foregoing Tables.	Ulster.		Munster.	
1.	2.	3.	4.	5.
Statistics of Unions and Districts:				
Population of Unions, in Provinces,—1881,	. .	1,743,075	. .	1,331,115
Area of Unions and Dispensary Districts, in statute acres,	. .	5,488,201	. .	6,067,722
Poor Law Valuation of Unions, in Provinces,—1889,	. .	£4,392,455	. .	£3,444,4[illegible]
Number of Unions,	. .	*44	. .	50
" Electoral Divisions,	. .	879	. .	1,031
" Dispensary Districts,	. .	214	. .	206
" Dispensaries or Dispensary Stations therein,	. .	310	. .	347
" Medical Officers authorized to be appointed for Dispensary Districts,	. .	235	. .	232
" Apothecaries,	. .	3	. .	21
" Midwives,	. .	93	. .	61
Expenditure in Year ended 29th September, 1889:—	£		£	
Medicines and Medical Appliances,	7,516	. .	7,391	. .
Rent of Dispensary Buildings,	2,847	. .	2,879	. .
Books, Forms, Stationery, Printing, and Advertising,	324	. .	301	. .
Salaries of Medical Officers, including payments for temporary services,	24,742	. .	25,706	. .
" Apothecaries, do. do. do.	412	. .	822	. .
" Midwives, do. do. do.	1,870	. .	748	. .
Vaccination Expenses,	8,350	. .	2,781	. .
Fuel, Attendance, and Incidental Expenses,	2,700	. .	5,047	. .
Total Expenditure in year ended 29th September, 1889,	. .	£42,760	. .	£48,10[illegible]
Relief Returns, and Duties of Medical Officers for year ended 30th September, 1889:—				
Number of cases attended on Dispensary Tickets,	107,070	. .	99,254	. .
" " on Visiting Tickets,	56,380	. .	41,740	. .
Total new cases in the year,	. .	163,350	. .	141,0[illegible]
Number of cases in which Tickets for Medical Relief were cancelled in the year,	. .	87	. .	42
Number of cases of Vaccination, including cases of Re-vaccination, in the year,	. .	31,076	. .	23,27[illegible]
Number of cases of dangerous Lunatics certified in the year,	. .	500	. .	[illegible]
Number of days of attendance at bridewells, or houses of correction during the year,	. .	28	. .	1[illegible]

* This number includes Gortin union, respecting which see note at foot of pages 103 and 104.

Statistical Statement; showing the number of unions, electoral divisions, and
15 Vic., c. 68; the total and average population, area, and valuation; number
expenditure under the Medical Charities Act for the year from 30th September,
number of cases of medical relief afforded at the dispensaries and at the patients'
relief have been cancelled by the dispensary committees; the number of cases of
number of days of attendance at bridewells or houses of correction, &c.; during the

Leinster.		Connaught.		Total for Ireland.		Average. Per Union.	Average. Per Dispensary District.	Average. Per Medical Officer.
6.	7.	8.	9.	10.	11.	12.	13.	14.
. .	1,278,989	. .	621,067	. .	5,174,836	32,142	7,187	6,880
. .	4,876,918	. .	4,802,086	. .	20,819,928	129,316	28,917	—
. .	£4,768,440	. .	£1,365,840	. .	£18,006,235	£80,747	£19,898	—
. .	39	. .	28	. .	*101	—	—	—
. .	938	. .	515	. .	3,444	21	5	4
. .	202	. .	98	. .	720	4	—	—
. .	327	. .	140	. .	1,139	7	—	—
. .	239	. .	114	. .	816	5	—	—
. .	15	. .	3	. .	42	—	—	—
. .	144	. .	27	. .	925	—	—	—
£		£		£		£ s.	£ s.	£ s.
7,312	. .	4,058	. .	26,577	. .	104 10	37 7	33 4
2,725	. .	1,072	. .	8,528	. .	52 19	11 17	—
807	. .	80	. .	1,031	. .	6 8	1 0	—
20,730	. .	12,457	. .	80,722	. .	657 6	124 12	110 15
1,801	. .	161	. .	2,780	. .	—	—	66 7
2,870	. .	291	. .	5,274	. .	22 16	—	—
2,258	. .	1,878	. .	10,067	. .	62 11	14 0	—
8,000	. .	1,054	. .	18,075	. .	84 10	19 0	—
. .	£46,722	. .	£23,800	. .	£157,085	£981 2	£219 8	—
146,239	. .	52,877	. .	406,840	. .	2,521	564	501
52,571	. .	14,099	. .	164,396	. .	1,021	228	203
. .	198,810	. .	67,076	. .	570,236	3,542	792	704
. .	64	. .	21	. .	214	—	—	—
. .	20,522	. .	14,118	. .	88,996	—	—	—
. .	625	. .	186	. .	1,751	—	—	—
. .	128	. .	24	. .	808	—	—	—

* See note on page 190.

No. 4.—Vaccination:—Summary of the number of persons vaccinated in the workhouses and auxiliary establishments of the several unions in Ireland by the medical officers of those institutions; and of the number vaccinated in the several dispensary districts, by the medical officers thereof, in the year ended 30th September, 1889;—abstracted from returns made by the respective medical officers.

Provinces.	No. vaccinated in *workhouses* by medical officers thereof.			No. of cases vaccinated by medical officers of *dispensary districts.*	Total number returned in columns 4 and 5.	Provinces.
	Successful cases.	Unsuccessful cases.	Total.			
1.	2.	3.	4.	5.	6.	
Ulster, . . .	507	36	543	31,076	31,619	Ulster.
Munster, . . .	217	6	223	23,279	23,502	Munster.
Leinster, . . .	341	7	348	20,522	20,870	Leinster.
Connaught, . . .	79	1	80	14,118	14,198	Connaught.
Total, .	1,144	50	1,194	88,995	90,189	

No. 5.—Number of cases of Scarlatina, Smallpox, and Fever, reported by medical officers of dispensary districts in Ireland, as having been attended in the Quarters ended 31st December, 1888, 31st March, 30th June, and 30th September, 1889.

Provinces.	Quarters ended	Scarlatina.	Smallpox.	Fever.
Ulster, . .	December 31st, 1888, . .	99	–	306
	March 31st, 1889, . .	70	–	312
	June 30th, 1889, . .	53	–	293
	September 30th, 1889, . .	123	–	504
Munster, . .	December 31st, 1888, . .	267	–	361
	March 31st, 1889, . .	190	–	339
	June 30th, 1889, . .	120	–	256
	September 30th, 1889, . .	187	–	263
Leinster, . .	December 31st, 1888, . .	171	–	240
	March 31st, 1889, . .	110	–	257
	June 30th, 1889, . .	97	–	259
	September 30th, 1889, . .	78	1	260
Connaught, .	December 31st, 1888, . .	100	–	115
	March 31st, 1889, . .	79	–	218
	June 30th, 1889, . .	38	–	218
	September 30th, 1889, . .	48	–	186
Summary.				
Ireland, . .	December 31st, 1888, . .	637	–	1,022
	March 31st, 1889, . .	458	–	1,176
	June 30th, 1889, . .	307	–	1,026
	September 30th, 1889, . .	436	1	1,218
	Total, ...	1,838	1	4,441

No. 6.—Index list of Dispensary Districts; with names of unions in which they are situate, and references to pages in which the Districts are to be found in the Appendix.

[continued.

[continued.

[continued.

Dispensary Districts.	Unions in which situate.	References to		Dispensary Districts.	Unions in which situate.	References to	
		Dispensary Districts' Statistical table; App. E, No. 1.	Dispensaries' financial and relief table; App. E, No. 2.			Dispensary Districts' Statistical table; App. E, No. 1.	Dispensaries' financial and relief table; App. E, No. 2.
		Page	Page			Page	Page
Gort,	Gort,	-	184	Killygordon,	Stranorlar,	-	159
Gortin,*	Gortin,	-	163	Killyleagh,	Downpatrick,	-	159
Gowran,	Kilkenny,	-	176	Killyon,	Parsonstown,	-	177
Graigue,	Thomastown,	-	177	Kilmacthomas,	Kilmacthomas,	-	173
Granard,	Granard,	-	178	Kilmacrenan and Milford,	Milford,	-	159
Green,	Tipperary,	152	173	Kilmakevoge,	Waterford,	-	173
Grey Abbey,	Newtownards,	-	160				
Gurteen,	Boyle,	-	187	Kilmallock,	Kilmallock,	-	170
Headford,	Tuam,	-	185	Kilmeaden,	Waterford,	-	173
Hillsborough,	Lisburn	-	156	Kilmihil,	Kilrush,	-	165
				Kilmoganny,	Callan,	-	170
Hollymount,	Ballinrobe,	-	186	Kilmood,	Newtownards,	-	160
Holmpatrick,	Balrothery,	-	174	Kilmore,	Monaghan,	-	163
Holycross,	Thurles,	-	173	Kilnaleck,	Cavan,	-	157
Holywell,	Enniskillen,	-	160				
Hospital,	Kilmallock,	-	170	Kilpatrick,	Cashel,	-	171
				Kilrea,	Ballymoney,	-	156
Inchigeelagh,	Macroom,	-	167	Kilrush,	Kilrush,	-	165
Inishannon,	Bandon,	-	165	Kilsallaghan,	Balrothery,	-	174
Inistioge,	Thomastown,	-	177	Kilshannig,	Mallow,	-	167
Innfield,	Trim,	-	180	Kilsheelan,	Clonmel,	-	178
Irvinestown,	Irvinestown,	-	161				
Islandeady,	Westport,	-	187	Kilskeer,	Kells,	-	179
Jamestown,	Car-on-Shannon	-	185	Kiltamagh,	Swineford,	-	187
				Kiltegan,	Baltinglass,	-	178
Johnstown,	Edenderry,	-	177	Kiltinan,	Clonmel,	-	178
Johnstown,	Urlingford,	-	177	Kiltoom,	Athlone,	-	181
Kanturk,	Kanturk,	-	167	Kiltormer,	Ballinasloe,	-	183
Kealkill,	Bantry,	-	166				
Keadue,	Boyle,	-	187	Kilworth,	Fermoy,	-	167
Keady,	Armagh,	-	186	Kingscourt,	Bailieborough,	-	157
Kells,	Kells,	-	179	Kingstown,	Rathdown,	-	175
				Kinlough,	Ballyshannon,	-	157
Kenmare,	Kenmare,	-	169	Kinnitty,	Parsonstown,	-	177
Kilbeggan,	Tullamore,	-	177	Kinsale,	Kinsale,	-	167
Kilbrittain,	Bandon,	-	165	Kinvarra,	Gort,	-	184
Kilcatherine,	Castletown,	-	166				
Kilcock,	Celbridge,	-	175	Knocknadona,	Lisburn	-	158
Kilcooly,	Urlingford,	-	177	Knocknalower,	Belmullet	-	186
				Knocktopher,	Thomastown,	-	177
Kilcullen,	Naas,	-	176	Labasheeda,	Killadysert,	-	165
Kildare,	Naas,	-	176	Laghy,	Donegal,	-	156
Kilderry,	Londonderry,	-	161	Larne,	Larne,	-	156
Kildorrery,	Mitchelstown,	-	168	Laurencetown,	Ballinasloe,	-	183
Kilfinane,	Kilmallock,	-	170				
Kilgarvan,	Kenmare,	-	169	Leighlinbridge,	Carlow,	-	174
Kilgobban,	Tralee,	-	170	Leitrim,	Car-on-Shannon	-	185
				Letterkenny,	Letterkenny,	-	159
Kilkee,	Kilrush,	-	165	Lettermore,	Oughterard,	-	186
Kilkeel,	Kilkeel,	-	169	Limavady,	Limavady,	-	161
Kilkelly,	Swineford,	-	187	Limerick, City of,	Limerick,	-	171
Kilkenny,	Kilkenny,	-	177	Lisbellaw,	Enniskillen,	-	160
Kilkishen,	Tulla,	-	165	Lisburn,	Lisburn,	-	158
Killasn,	Ballinasloe,	-	183	Lismore,	Lismore,	-	173
				Lisnaskea,	Lisnaskea,	-	161
Killala,	Killala,	-	185	Listowel,	Listowel,	-	169
Killann,	Enniscorthy,	-	181	Littleton,	Thurles,	-	173
Killanniv,	Ennis,	-	165				
Killarney,	Killarney,	-	169	Londonderry, City of,	Londonderry,	-	161
Killashee,	Longford,	-	178	Longford,	Longford,	-	178
Killea,	Londonderry,	-	161	Loughbrickland,	Banbridge,	-	160
				Loughgall,	Armagh,	-	156
Killeagh,	Youghal,	-	169	Loughrea,	Loughrea,	-	184
Killeen,	Dunshaughlin,	-	179				
Killenagh & Wells	Gorey,	-	181	Louisburgh,	Westport,	-	187
Killenaule,	Cashel,	-	171	Louth,	Dundalk,	-	178
Killeroran,	Mount Bellew,	-	184	Lowpark,	Swineford,	-	187
Killeshandra,	Cavan,	-	157	Lucan,	Celbridge,	-	175
				Lurgan,	Lurgan,	-	156
Killiney,	Rathdown,	-	175				
Killorglin,	Killarney,	-	169	Lurganboy,	Manorhamilton,	-	185
Killough,	Downpatrick,	-	159	Lusk,	Balrothery,	-	174
Killoughy,	Tullamore,	-	177	Macroom,	Macroom,	-	167
Killucan,	Mullingar,	-	181	Maghera,	Magherafelt,	-	162
Killybegs,	Glenties,	-	158	Magherafelt,	Magherafelt,	-	162

* See also page 164.

[continued

* See also page 164.

[continued.

Dublin Castle,

2nd July, 1890.

Sir,

I have to acknowledge the receipt of your letter of the 30th ultimo, forwarding, for submission to His Excellency the Lord Lieutenant, the Report of the Local Government Board for Ireland for the year ending 31st March, 1890.

I am, Sir,

Your obedient servant,

West Ridgeway.

The Secretary,

Local Government Board,

Custom House.

No 1

DIAGRAM

SHOWING THE FLUCTUATIONS FROM WEEK TO WEEK IN THE

NUMBER OF WORKHOUSE INMATES IN IRELAND,

During the period from the Week ended the 9th of February, 1859, to the Week ended the 8th of February, 1860, as compared with the corresponding Weeks in SIX previous Years.

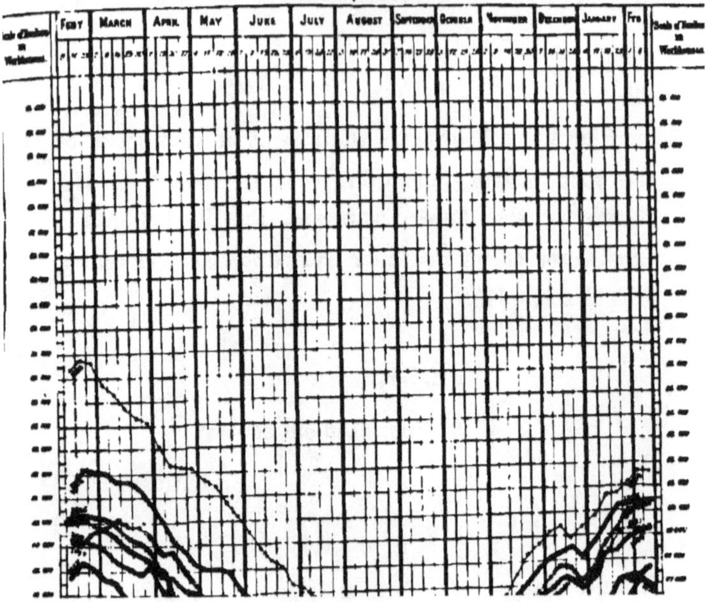

Scale of Numbers in Workhouses.

FEBY | MARCH | APRIL | MAY | JUNE | JULY | AUGUST | SEPTEMBER | OCTOBER | NOVEMBER | DECEMBER | JANUARY | FEB

Scale of Numbers in Workhouses.

DIAGRAM

SHOWING THE FLUCTUATIONS FROM WEEK TO WEEK IN THE

NUMBER OF PERSONS IN THE RECEIPT OF OUT-DOOR RELIEF IN IRELAND,

During the period from the Week ended the 9th of February, [illegible], to the Week ended the [illegible] of February, [illegible], as compared with the corresponding Weeks in SIX previous Years.

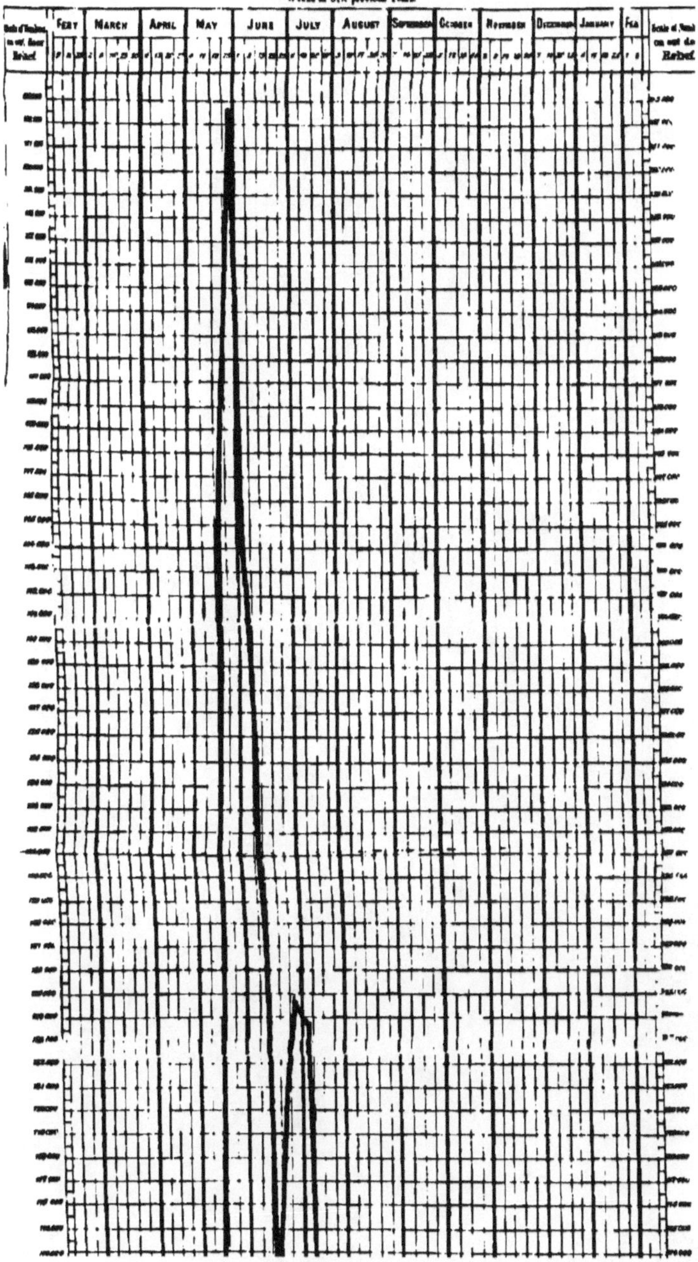

Scale of Numbers on out-door Relief | Feby | March | April | May | June | July | August | September | October | November | December | January | Feb | Scale of Numbers on out-door Relief

www.ingramcontent.com/pod-product-compliance
Lightning Source LLC
Chambersburg PA
CBHW020856230426
43666CB00008B/1208